THE OTHER GROCER'S DAUGHTER

THE OTHER GROCER'S DAUGHTER

JACQUELINE SMITH

*For Linda,
With my warmest wishes,
Jacqui Smith
x
4/10/11*

Copyright © 2011 Jacqui Smith

The moral right of the author has been asserted.

Apart from any fair dealing for the purposes of research or private study,
or criticism or review, as permitted under the Copyright, Designs and Patents
Act 1988, this publication may only be reproduced, stored or transmitted, in
any form or by any means, with the prior permission in writing of the
publishers, or in the case of reprographic reproduction in accordance with
the terms of licences issued by the Copyright Licensing Agency. Enquiries
concerning reproduction outside those terms should be sent to the publishers.

Matador
5 Weir Road
Kibworth Beauchamp
Leicester LE8 0LQ, UK
Tel: (+44) 116 279 2299
Fax: (+44) 116 279 2277
Email: books@troubador.co.uk
Web: www.troubador.co.uk/matador

ISBN 978 1848766 945

British Library Cataloguing in Publication Data.
A catalogue record for this book is available from the British Library.

Typeset in Book Antiqua by Troubador Publishing Ltd, Leicester, UK
Printed and boud in the UK by TJ International, Padstow, Cornwall

Matador is an imprint of Troubador Publishing Ltd

I DEDICATE THIS BOOK TO:

Ron, the love of my life

Especially for: Robert and Simon

For Linda and Alan

Very special thanks to John and Lynn, for their amazing support for this book and a precious new friendship in my life

To: All the people whom I love and to those that I have loved and lost.

FOREWORD

I do not think I would have started this book without the total encouragement over the years of friends and family who, every time I recounted an incident pertinent to our many conversations, came out with the age-old statement – "you know, you really should write a book".

This is my attempt and to all those people I owe a great vote of thanks for all their encouragement. I will, of course, be thrilled if I can find a publisher but, published or not, by writing all of this down, it will be out of my system and now a matter of record…

CHAPTER ONE

Discovering the moon

We all hope to achieve something special in our life.

I am told that the first words that I strung together in a sentence were, "I want de moon". My mum said that I was about two years old at the time, watching the big moon through the bedroom window. I will leave it up to you, the Reader, to decide.

My father, Alfred George Ashton, a stern, unapproachable product of a very Victorian upbringing, was born in Hinckley, Leicestershire on the 9th November 1906, one of four children; his eldest brother Harry, who was killed in the First World War, Auntie Grace and my Uncle Tom. Their mother, my grandmother, Alice Maud Ashton, was born on 8th September 1876 and died in 1954. I know that this may seem unusual, but I never met her. It was only after her death that my mother revealed that Daddy and his Mother had not got on because he was ashamed of her, so that was the reason we didn't know of her existence and, as a result, we never really thought it was strange that we did not all go to her funeral.

My mother Winifred Gladys Ashton, was a real Yorkshire lass, born in Castleford, Yorkshire on the 28th August 1907, one of seven surviving children to Samuel Llewellyn and Esther Hollows. Big families were not so unusual in those days. They moved to Hinckley around 1920 when there was no work available in the Castleford area, and because my Grandad, who had worked in the mines before the war, had, like so many other men at that time, returned shell-shocked from the 1914 -18 war and couldn't face going back down the pit. He decided that the family would move down to Leicestershire to find work. One by one the Hollows clan started to work in the hosiery factories in Hinckley, the brothers maintaining the machinery and the sisters doing welting and other such jobs. It was good, reliable work, although it didn't pay that well. They had had tremendously hard times back in the 1920s; nowadays people would find it hard to believe the way poor people lived then. I remember my grandmother telling me once that she had never, ever had her long hair cut in any way and could sit on her two long plaits. One day – short of food for the family, she took the scissors and lopped off both plaits and sold the hair, which was much sought after by the wig makers in those days. She said it fed the family well, but my grandad gave her a jolly good thrashing for it when he came home.

The paternal Gran whom I never knew had apparently been forced to sing in the local pubs for pocket money and for gin, whilst her boys from a very early age took whatever work they could get. I was told many years later that my father was deeply ashamed of his background and origins. Britain was much more class conscious in those days and his working class roots in the slums of Hinckley were a source of shame to an ambitious, upwardly mobile young man determined to better himself. Daddy once told me that when he was nine years old, to help fill the coffers for his mum and bring some money into the house, he had not only worked in the local slaughterhouse, but also for local undertakers, where he had helped look after the black horses and the hearse for the funerals. A child of nine should never see the inside of a mortuary or a slaughterhouse, never mind actually seeing animals being killed and butchered and laying out human corpses. But times were very hard in those days, and the use of child labour was common among the poor, although happily it would never happen nowadays. Inevitably it bred hard, even callous folk. But that's the way life was then.

Mum and Dad had met several times in Hinckley and I remember my mother telling me how dashing and handsome this young soldier was, he was very self confidant and was definitely pointing himself in the direction of becoming something better in his life, he was determined to leave the slum streets of his background firmly in the past and make something of himself. He had no trouble finding girl friends, all the girls were after him. Mum and her sisters really used to enjoy themselves, despite their hard working lives and went together to all the local dances – she said they were the "original good time girls", though extremely straight laced, as girls had to be in those days.

Daddy had joined the Leicestershire Regiment of the Territorial Army on 13th March 1924, when he was seventeen and transferred to the North Staffordshire Regiment on 26th January 1926, his ambition being to gain a full education and eventually to become an officer. In 1938 his regiment was back from a spell in Ballykinler in Northern Ireland, a place that was to haunt him for the rest of his life, and I used to wonder if this affection for this little place in Ireland was due to some kind of loving relationship there that had been extra special. However, that was as far as you could get Daddy to talk about it, it "had been a favourite posting". Daddy was now due to be posted out to India. His elder brother, Tom, also in the forces, had warned him of the dangers of arriving in India without a wife, as the half-caste girls out there were considered outcasts and needed husbands desperately,

Alfred George Ashton – Daddy

especially if the men were white-skinned. My father, who lived in awe of his elder brother and took to heart everything that he told him, was sufficiently worried by this to make a plan. He would go to the Hinckley town dance that Saturday evening with the distinct objective of seeking out a wife for himself. He would see them all there, all his many girlfriends, and pick out the one who would be the most likely to be able to support him through his future with his plans for his army career, and to achieve this he intended to propose that evening and secure an acceptance, if possible from the one of his first choice. Calculating and ruthless? My father could be just so if he was out to get something that he wanted badly. Mum just happened to be the one he singled out and he duly proposed there and then. Mum, who had worshipped Daddy from the time she had first gone out with him, accepted immediately – she was getting no younger, 31 by this time, and of course, she was not aware that there was a ruthless mission in place that evening. Mum, on her own admission was no stunning beauty as such and she knew it. She was very self conscious of her rather protruding teeth, and she had had few serious boyfriends, but she was what they would have called in those days 'a strong looking lass', dependable and extremely bright – Mum was nobody's fool. She was also very honest and straightforward and never in her wildest dreams did she believe that the most handsome and dashing man in Hinckley would choose her to be his wife. What she did know was that she deeply loved Dad, this would have been everything that she would have dreamed off but dare never assume, he had been her favourite for a long time.

They were married on the 5th November 1938 and, just five days later on the 10th November, he was shipped out to India with Mum to join him there as soon as the official arrangements could be made. I can only imagine the sort of time she would have had making all her arrangements, choosing her wardrobe for the trip of a lifetime for a Hinckley factory lass, sailing alone out to India then, married now to the man of her dreams. It would have been like a cruise, and being an officer's wife, she would have been treated very well indeed. Just to think of it: from stocking factory to an ocean liner to India and a new life with servants and all the rest of the privileges, and all in just five days.

The war in Europe broke out a year later and India must have seemed a completely different world from war-torn Britain. In 1940 my eldest brother Brian was born in Poona, which must have been quite an awesome experience for a woman of her age and away from friends and loving family, with Indian *'ayahs'* or maids there to do all the 'womanly' things. Giving birth naturally for the first time is a most frightening experience and I cannot imagine that she could talk to Daddy about those things at all, let alone feel that he was there for her. It must have been very much the same when, two years later, in Bangalore, brother Bobby came

Mum, Dad, Brian and Bob – 1943 India.

along. Mum was six months pregnant with me in 1943 when she was suddenly sent back to England. After the Japanese attack on Pearl Harbour, Singapore and Burma, the war had come to the gates of India. So, in the middle of the war, through shipping lanes ravaged by German U boats, the family went back to England along with hundreds of other dependants. Fortunately her convoy got through unscathed and they moved back to Leicestershire. I can only imagine that this would have been a huge lifestyle change for her to re-adjust to, to come back to the basic life of a manufacturing town from the opulence of regimental dinners, cocktail parties, servants and all that her recent lifestyle had embraced. Down to earth with a bump I would have thought.

She managed to rent a house, in Park Road, Hinckley and I was born on the 28th January 1944, Daddy coming home in the April of that year. My sister Gillian was born in 1946 to be followed in September 1948 by my youngest brother David. Mum was 41 when he was born and she always maintained that she was too old for babies by that

Jacqueline Ashton.

time, but there we were, all five of us. At least she was lucky enough to have one of her oldest and dearest friends in attendance at all three births; 'Mac' as she was affectionately known was one of the old fashioned school of midwives.

We had hardly settled down when, on the 2nd July 1949, Daddy was shipped off again, this time to Nairobi in Kenya for a tour of duty, because of The Mau Mau uprising that had broken out at that time. The Mau Mau were terrorists and the core of the rebellion against British colonial rule was formed mainly by members of the Kikuyu tribe, who had started killing the white settlers, because the whites owned most of the 'plum' land. Because of this the Mau Mau had taken to the Bush in an anti-British guerrilla war. This tour was to last five or so years and the plan was for Mummy to follow him out there, with all of us children at a later date. I do wonder now whether she would have looked forward to this dramatic life change yet again moving our family of five and readjusting to this new lifestyle and a new language to contend with.

At the ripe old age of five, I had no idea what life had in store for me, nor any inkling of the exciting times to come.

CHAPTER TWO

Bye-bye Bobby

The earliest memories of my childhood start at about the age of five. What must have been my very first day at school, Church School, Hinckley, stands out in my mind. I remember coming home through 'Church Walk' – beautiful natural gardens, with flowerbeds lining the walk and weeping willows trailing in the water. We fed the swans and ducks on the small ponds that were dotted right throughout the walk. It really was idyllic, even to a child's eye. I was to do that walk many times in my young life and I always loved it.

One of my first and dramatically vivid memories at this time was one afternoon, when I arrived home from school. Mummy was in a terrible state, she had obviously been weeping profusely, her eyes were swollen and red and her sisters, Rhoda and May were by her side, not really knowing what to do to help her. They had been crying too, but were trying desperately to make us three children feel as normal as possible. It was a very sad day in that little home that was usually so happy and welcoming to come back to from school.

I was only five years old but I knew my brother Bobby was terribly ill and in hospital in Nuneaton and Mum was travelling to and fro by bus to see him. Apparently he had picked up an illness called 'infantile paralysis' or poliomyalitis, he was being kept alive in something called an "iron lung", which was doing his breathing for him, and he was very poorly indeed. Of course, I didn't understand much of any of this at the time so I didn't know what all the sadness was about. I was only to find out much later that this outbreak of this cruel disease had been hard to bring under control and had left so many crippled and their families so helpless. Nothing was explained to us, I seem to remember, except maybe Brian had been told because he would have been nine years old by then, but my brother had died, as the poliomyelitis had gone to his brain and his body just shut down because the brain ceased to function completely. He died in the night, in his sleep, he was only seven years old. A few days later, I stood at the front railings and saw these two big black shiny cars pull up, the first one carrying a long box in the back, covered in pretty flowers. Mum, weeping helplessly, dressed all in black, got into the second car with her sisters, and away they drove. Daddy who had been posted to Kenya the month before, had been informed of course, and was on his way home. All I could understand was that I would never see Bobby again, as they were taking him away to be with Jesus in heaven. Daddy flew back from Nairobi on compassionate leave and spent a couple of weeks with Mum, taking us all to Blackpool to get away for a while. They did their best, but what a sad holiday that was.

When we came back I recall Daddy taking us on long walks beside the railway lines, presumably to help Mum by getting us out of this house of grief to give her some time on her own. He would take us over the courting stiles, as they were called, and we would watch in total awe as the locomotives thundered noisily by, seemingly alive with all their smoke and steam and flashing coupling rods. To a five year old those old steam engines were truly awe-inspiring in their size and might. We used to chase the steam from one side of the bridges to the other and Daddy used to make up verses about what the trains were saying in time to the clackety-clack of the wheels. He would make us walk all the way to Burbage – probably two miles or so from Hinckley and a long walk by a child's standards, but oh at the journey's end – we would arrive at the big pub on the hill with the special room for children where we drank Vimto from the bottle, through straws and ate crisps with the little blue bags of salt that you sprinkled on yourself. Absolute magic! But what joy if your packet had two salt bags. In my mind, Daddy did not seem at all loving to us at that time especially, and he was very, very strict. Of course, we didn't know what mourning meant at that age but the death of Bobby must have had an affect on both of my parents to an extent that, now I am a mother myself, I could only imagine when contemplating the loss of either of my lovely children and now, with life and experience under my belt, I now know that you never do come to terms with the loss of a child. Once my father's compassionate leave was over, he went back to his rebellion in Kenya and my mother was back to coping, and relentlessly grieving, on her own.

A few weeks later, still deeply in grief for the loss of one of her children, my mum lost her own mother. I had sat with Nan only a few days before while she lay in her bed and I can remember reciting my 'times tables' for her that we had learned at school. She kissed me and said that one day I would be such a clever girl! I never saw her after that, and mum was crying all over again. Looking back, it seems that there was so much sadness to take on board at such a young age, but it was all part of life in those days, and it seemed quite normal to have the coffin lying in state in the front parlour for all to say their goodbyes. Although we were shielded from the more gruesome aspects to some degree, we were made aware of death to a much greater extent than they do nowadays and there was some normality introduced by the acceptance of it.

However, having put all this behind, time did not stand still and suddenly we were travelling all over the place with Mum to Birmingham, Leicester and special visits to our doctor to have the most painful inoculations and vaccinations against tropical diseases. One of the injections, I recall, left us all with our arms out of action for several days and oh so painful to the touch. We were told all the pain would be worth it because we were to sail away on a big ship named "The Empire Ken" to join Daddy in a place very far away called Africa. We could all only wait and wonder with great excitement as we boasted to all of our friends that we were all sailing away to a new life.

It seemed like a dream as we arrived in Southampton where, at the dockside, we saw this huge white ship tied up and which we boarded up a long gangplank. Such a hustle and bustle of excitement everywhere, the big funnels, passengers and crew boarding, the blowing of the loud siren, the shout of "all ashore who's going ashore" and, eventually, slowly pulling away from the side as the band continued to play on the quay, which got further and further into the distance. We all stood at the rails waving goodbye to England, away to a new and exciting life and a new beginning for my Mum after the traumas of that last year.

I was five years old and we were sailing to start a new life in Kenya.

CHAPTER THREE

The Sailor in Me

Looking back, the sea voyage was, for me, something of a fairy tale, with all the hullabaloo and excitement of things never experienced before and new people to meet. When I think about it now, just imagine all the feelings of wonder and awe that a child of five would feel, even now in these days of unbelievable sciences and advanced technology, to be actually arriving at the docks at Southampton and about to sail away to a life which I couldn't even begin to imagine, never in my wildest dreams.

They looked after us extremely well on board. I think they were sympathetic to Mum's situation, a sad and quiet woman sailing alone with four children under the age of nine, to a strange country abroad, and no husband to make the journey lighter.

During dinner in the evenings, we had our own waiter who was kind and lovely and very, very handsome, and in the evenings he sang with the band. He would sometimes come over to our table, gently pick me up and sit me on his knee and sing – I believed – just to me. I don't know whether it is possible, but as far as I was concerned, I was in love at the ripe old age of five!

Exciting things happened when the ship docked at various ports en route, and I especially remember Port Said, where tradesmen got onto the ship, selling their wares. Mum bought a leather bag, the leather all embossed with camels and palm trees. Typical tourist memorabilia I suppose, but it and the people selling it, held a mystical quality for me. I remember too going through the Suez Canal – what an impact that had on me even at that early age, I clearly remember being enraptured by the sheer majesty of it and everything seemed to be happening in slow motion and so deathly quiet, you could almost hear a pin drop!

The day we had all been so looking forward to finally came when we docked in Mombasa – our destination. Daddy, resplendent in his starched khaki uniform, was on the quay to meet us, waving and smiling his handsome smile so broadly, I thought his face would crack. He was so overcome and we had a joyous reunion. Then came the moment Daddy had been waiting for. He swept us off in two big khaki-coloured army staff cars, called Standard Vanguards, to our new bungalow home in Nairobi. This was all so exciting, and standing outside the bungalow in line and awaiting our arrival were three black men, dressed in long white robes and wearing on their heads red fez hats with long black tassels. I had never met a black person before and Mum explained that they were to be our 'servants'. I don't know how, but I seemed to know exactly what this meant. We were introduced to them in turn, first to Laban, who was to be our cook who grinned from ear to ear and said "Jambo" (hello) to all of us in turn and "Jambo Memsahib" to my Mother, then Ruka the house man and waiter and a young man, whose name I cannot remember, who was to be our houseboy/gardener; they were all overjoyed to welcome us. We were told that we should not get too familiar or friendly with them, a rule that at the ripe old age of five I instantly ignored. All three of them were great characters in their own right, and set about making a wonderful happy house and home to come back to.

They called Mum "Memsahib" and Daddy "Bwana". We were "Toto Jacqueline" or "Toto Brian", 'toto' meaning child. They spoke this funny language amongst themselves and, little did I realise it then, but before long I was to become relatively fluent in Swahili. When you're a child you don't even realise it's another language: it's just new words, which you easily assimilate into your own little world. I can only remember a few words and phrases now, but I am still fascinated by their whole culture and languages, and especially I adore their music. I was captivated, even at that early age and continuing as I grew up, by everything to do with Kenya, from Kisumu on Lake Victoria, which is exactly on the equator line as are the Aberdare Mountain range and Mount Kenya itself, to the coral reefs and mangrove swamps of the coastal strip. Nairobi itself with its Sikh temple, Snake Park and the National Museum (including the largest collection of butterflies in the world), from Mombasa to Turkana in the north and Tsavo National Park in the south. All of this new world was absolute magic to the little girl from drab, post war- Leicestershire.

We used to have great fun with Laban and Ruka, they used to make us laugh so much that you felt sure your sides would split, and one such day started with my Mum in the kitchen trying to order some breakfast. Laban kept saying "my eye, my eye Memsahib" to Mum so many times that she, for want of a better word "plonked" him down on a chair and proceeded to check his eyes. Only after a great deal of hullubaloo did my Mum let him go, only to be informed that "my eye" in Swahili meant "eggs"! It was a bit like a Monty Python sketch. That night Laban made us some ice cream by freezing custard in ice cube trays, then proceeding to cavort around the dinner table with a pillow stuffed up his long white robe and reducing us all to fits of laughter while Mum and Dad entertained their guests to what she called "gin and its" or "Sundowners" on the verandah, served with little delicious nibbles such as home made crisps, cheese-stuffed dates, cheese straws and the like. This happened most evenings at "Sundowner" time and their nibbles always seemed infinitely more interesting to me than our meal, especially as Mum had let me help her make them. These "nibbles" would turn out to be something so big in my life, but at the time I was just a little girl helping her Mummy. However, the golden days of running and playing and getting under the servants' feet all the time couldn't last forever.

I was off to school…..

CHAPTER FOUR

Our Kenya Adventure

School in Nairobi was near Delamere Avenue and the one to which all the Army officers' children went. Mummy said that Delamere Avenue was famous and was named after Lord Delamere. His wife was Lady Delamere who was involved in the notorious scandal at the Happy Valley Country Club and was the subject of the film "White Mischief" about the death of Lord Errol and the ensuing court case. It caused a tremendous scandal at the time and, looking back, I supect that they were much more *risqué* times out there in the expatriate community than my parents would have had us believe.

I really enjoyed my lessons and school in general, was far more advanced than the little school in Hinckley that I had started at. Mental arithmetic came very easily to me and I loved reading and doing stories. More than most, I enjoyed school plays, reciting poems and reading out loud, I suppose because I was good at it and I love words, and this must have come from the 'actress' in me that my Mum always swore was naturally there. It was always a tremendous adventure and extremely dramatic to think of children of my age and older going to and from school because we travelled in Army trucks with soldiers carrying rifles. To us this became a normal part of daily life. In fact, our bungalow was inside a special army camp ringed around in high barbed wire. This was to keep us all safely in and the Mau-Mau definitely out.

One of the most frightening aspects of all this excitement and drama though was the experience of lying in bed at night hearing this regular monotonous beat of the thud of native feet being stamped on the ground in unison and the continuous chanting of the words "Kwenda, Kwenda, Kwenda…" which means "Go". As it was, as children, we did not really understand, but even so I was aware of being somewhat frightened by it all. When helping Mummy to make the beds and seeing her revolver under her pillow, I don't suppose we gave it much of a thought, other than were not all children brought up this way? Certainly all those around me, at school and elsewhere in Kenya at that time were. Years later, when watching the famous film "Zulu", which was the 'in' film of the time, it brought back tremendous memories for me of that sound, the monotonous 'thud, thud, thud' of the feet, threatening the impending doom that was surely to follow and I remember thinking at the time that it just terrified me. To think back now that I had lain in bed and heard those exact sounds and, in my innocence, I not had the slightest inkling of what those sounds actually meant to us all, but think of the imaginings of both of my parents with their little family tucked up in bed and what just could be! – terrifying.

My father's hobby was livestock and farming and we had chickens in the garden – hatched from eggs in one of his wooden army trunks, rigged with heating and kept in our dining room till they could be housed outside. We children would all sit round the dinner table, having our supper and all you could hear was this 'cheep, cheep' from the box next to the table. Daddy was fiercely proud of his "White Leghorns" and "Rhode Island Red" chickens and lovingly watched them develop from eggs hatching into fully grown birds. I was later told that most ex-servicemen had one of three ambitions after leaving the Armed Forces, it was either to farm, keep a shop or have a pub. He was to almost achieve all three, but, as everyone has to start somewhere, my father began with the rudiments of farming, which was his passion then.

Furthering this interest, most weekends we travelled out of Nairobi to stay on a farm belonging to a lady called Elsie Butcher. How my parents met and became fond of her I do not ever remember being told but we children called her "Aunt Elsie" and I am led to believe that a book was eventually written about her life story. Apparently, she went out to Africa as one of the "Kenya Settlers" with her new husband. They bought this large amount of acreage, as did so many 'whites' at that time, in the nineteen twenties and thirties, near to a place called Mitabiri, outside Nairobi, and built their dairy farm with a large herd of Friesian cattle. Her bungalow, the main building, was a large round building, and it had a thatched roof. The lounge had huge open beams above, and you could see right up into the pointed circular roof. It had a 'magical' quality, I had only ever lived or stayed in square buildings. She had an enormous oak desk in her office, with a big round cannon ball size paper weight on it (a hair ball from a cow's stomach she told me – ugh!) and fly switches made by the natives from the long hair at the end of the cow's tail, called a "chowrie" – these always fascinated me; the Mau Mau leader, Jomo Kenyatta always carried one to shoo away those aggravating Kenya flies.

Very quickly after their arrival and settlement on the farm, Aunt Elsie's husband had died tragically apparently, some kind of accident or incurable illness, but this was not going to beat Elsie Butcher, she was a lady of total commitment and self-determination. So she had lost a husband – that's life, she merely determined that she would stay on alone and farm her land and milk her herd of Friesians. This was her home, her land and her future, if a somewhat lonely prospect. To my child's eye, she really was a formidable sight. She had a very hard and weathered sort of face, no softness in it at all. Her mode of dress was very much in the same vein, and she wore long army-type socks up to the knee, covered in laced up khaki coloured puttees and long khaki shorts down to the knee, an open-necked shirt, a man's watch, a bush hat with an animal fur skin band and strapped around her waist, her leather holster and revolver. She was the picture of a woman that you simply did not 'mess' with and who was to prove several times that she did not need a man to do what she felt she had to do.

Aunt Elsie used to organise hunting parties with all her fellow settlers and to which Daddy was always invited. I once asked him why he went out shooting the lovely Thompson's gazelle, Impalas and other helpless animals, and he quickly reassured me by telling me that he always took careful aim, so as not to attract the eyes of the other hunting members, but then he always misfired at the last minute – hopefully still unseen – so he did not shoot the gazelle or whatever game they were going after. When the skins were divided after the hunt was over, Daddy used to keep his in a locked cupboard in his and Mum`s bedroom so that we children could not see the skins with the bullet holes in them. He was to prove totally incapable of killing animals, which was to become very apparent later on in my life, and now, analysing this, I think the roots for this abhorrence must go back to his early life as a nine year old, working in the local slaughterhouse, that must have made an unforgettable nightmare of killing, for a nine year old boy.

Aunt Elsie had a most wonderful and trusted farm

manager called Jamieson, I remember he was always smiling and so very willing to please. He and his family, whom he absolutely adored, were also Kikuyu tribe, but he was so unswervingly loyal to his "Memsahib" and did not follow the ways of the Mau Mau. He lived in a set of circular mud and thatched huts down by the cattle pens with his pregnant wife and nine children, the eldest of whom was a girl Dosa, the same age as I was. We were about the same height but she was more well built than I was, and she had that lovely African openness and innocence about her face and her demeanour and an unstoppable sense of fun and inquisitiveness. We were to become best friends and kindred spirits and to spend many happy hours together.

It was in 1953 when one of my greatest excitements took place. Princess Elizabeth and her husband Prince Philip came to visit Kenya. She was presented with "Treetops" – a house built up in a tree. I was very proud when she came to our school and, it was at this time that her father, the King, had tragically passed away and she was called back to England prematurely, to become Queen, of course. I was one of the children who were lucky enough to be presented with a blue plastic beaker with her head on the emblem and the date 1953. I still have it to this day, albeit very 'weathered', and I treasure it. I made scrapbooks of all the newspaper reports on her trip to Kenya. I was in total awe of this lovely princess – as most young people were with Lady Diana – Princess Elizabeth in her day created the same magic and received just same kind of following. After all to most children being a princess was as good as being in a fairy tale, and I had been standing next to her and received my memento. Wow!

Not long after this wonderful excitement, I became very ill. I was finding it hard to keep food down, even if I could eat it in the first place, and my weight dropped dramatically. The trouble was that no-one seemed to want to discuss what was wrong with me in front of me and there was a great amount of secrecy involved, even the doctor, who we called Uncle Glyn, the Army Medical Officer, just gently said "that I had to be taken great care of", so it was decided to send me out to Auntie Elsie for three months nursing and convalescense. Before I left for the farm, my mother called me into the bungalow and, wielding a large pair of scissors, proceeded to break my heart. My pride and joy, my lovely long ringletted hair was all lopped off, no previous discussion, no persuading me gently that what was about to be done was for my health, all I got from Mummy was a short, sharp: "Long hair weakens you, it saps your strength". Mummy, quite heartlessly it seemed to me, did the deed and gave me the most awful short cut that my sister and I always called "the pudding basin cut" – go on, use your imagination! We both hated that haircut and the only thing that was worse was the Saturday ritual of soaking the hair for the whole day in coconut oil, not to be shampooed off till bath time, and to this day, I cannot bear the smell of coconut in any form.

On the farm I was put on a rich diet with maize porridge called *posha*, (which I hated with a passion, and if I could get away with it, I tipped behind the big Welsh dresser in the breakfast room!), I never even considered how stupid this action was, because it could have attracted all kind of vermin, not the least rats. I was also forced to take supplements of malt and codliver oil, lots of fresh fruit and lashings of cream – as much cream as I could drink. I was encouraged to hold my mug under the cream separator in the milking parlour and drink the milk and cream straight from the cows. Luscious. My mother never, ever was to tell me what my illness was and it was to be many more years, forty five in fact, before I found out that it was tuberculosis (called 'consumption' in those days). I don't remember anyone querying whether the herd of Friesians was tuberculin tested or not. One did not admit to suffering from consumption, there was a definite stigma attached to it because it is contagious, it was treated I suppose as a sort of 'pauper's' disease, asociated with dirt and poverty. However, none of this could quell my excitement of spending days on and at the farm with Dosa as my constant companion. I suppose it was during this time that my knowledge of Swahili, or 'Ki Swahili' as the local form of it was called, was improved greatly, though it always picked up a little more after each visit to the farm. I was much happier with the native children or *totos*, than with my own kind and I loved the language, their culture and their whole demeanour. They led the most simple but very loving and close family life.

Dosa and I went out every day with the herd of calves to graze them and we wiled away the days making little model mud villages in the banks of the stream and her teaching me to speak her native tongue. At sunset, we would make our way back to the farm with the calves and we usually took the same safe route, because that way we could be found easily if the need arose. One such evening, going home, Dosa and I saw these two native men carrying long spears and shields made of animal skin. They just stood there in front of us and stared at us menacingly. Dosa was obviously petrified, I had never seen anyone as frightened as that before and so I was scared too, but of what I wasn't really aware. Dorsa told me we had to get straight back to the farm as quickly as possible, pretending everything was normal. I don't know why, because the murderous Mau Mau were everywhere and killed anyone, children included, but fortunately they did not try to stop us or harass us in any way, and thankfully, they did not pursue us. Dosa ran quickly up to Aunt Elsie, both of us trembling with utter fear tried to tell her that we had seen two dangerous men."Mau-Mau, Memsahib, Mau Mau", she said. Aunt Elsie became very short tempered and literally pooh-pooed the whole thing and flippantly said that because she had Kikuyu workers on the farm, they would never harm her and that we were just children talking typical nonsense and "making a mountain out of nothing, not even a molehill". She said we had over-vivid imaginations.

After about three months or so, my tuberculosis was miraculously brought under control and I recovered well. However, not only was this to be the end of that recuperation holiday for me, none of us were aware that it proved to be that we were never to visit the farm again. We had stopped going to the farm before it burnt down, because my parents said it had become too dangerous. I have no doubt that they must have tried so very hard to persuade Auntie Elsie to leave too but she would have stood absolute and rigid and would have flatly refused to leave.

Just a few months later, Aunt Elsie's farm was attacked by the Mau-Mau – some of her own workers amongst them. This could only have been one of the most frightening experiences that anyone could go through, a mass of Kikuyu warriors, all wielding spears and machete knives, screaming and chanting and absolutely hell bent on death at all cost to the whites and, although we didn't realise it at the time, on anyone who dared to help them – black or white. Jamieson was true to form and immediately left his own family and went first and foremost to make his 'Memsahib', his number one, safe, but he had to find her first. He did find her trying to hide herself in the back bedroom of the bungalow. He saved her life by bundling her out of the window of that bedroom, rolling her down the slope into the paw-paw grove below where he lay over her all night, shielding her till the last of the attackers went away. Next morning, having made sure that she was safe, he returned back to his family to find that they were all dead, his wife and all his children butchered and mutilated with *pangas* (a kind of machete knife) and the wife, who was pregnant again, had the child cut out of her stomach. They lay there dead where they had fallen all strewn around him, all his beloved, innocent children brutally, brutally murdered whilst he remained faithful to his beloved boss and made it his priority to save her life. I don't suppose he even considered that his own people would murder their own kind, especially the children, and what could this poor man do with his life after burying his dead and getting Aunty Elsie to safety. One can only wonder and pray that God took care of him and found him some kind of solace to face his future alone.

Mummy could not find the way to tell us till a long time after the incident, after she had received a long letter from Aunt Elsie from a nursing home on the south coast of England where she had come to live out the end of her days, broken-hearted till the end. There were photos of what little was left of the burnt out farm and farmhouse and her life's work. She was a totally broken woman. Mum would not show us the photographs, they were too upsetting. I was very saddened by this terrible, tragic loss of life and the thought that my best friend, Dosa, the same age as myself, had died such a tragicically horrible and frightening death and was no longer able to enjoy her life and look forward to the future as I was able to do. We had had some wonderful times when we went to Mitabiri, there were always picnics to places like the Fourteen Falls, and a stupendous day in the fabulous Rift Valley, not to mention the barbecues on the farm, and days out sitting astride the headlamps of Aunt Elsie's beautiful white Riley convertible, while she drove us home during the maize harvests, this beautiful vintage creamy white motor being used to bring home the maize! No-one can take away those memories and Dosa and Auntie Elsie do stay in my heart and will forever.

Very soon afterwards, still in 1953, we were told that we were returning to England. I was nine years old at this time, and my last vivid memories of my beloved Kenya were of the servants waving us goodbye, with tears streaming down their faces, as we drove away in those big green army Vanguard cars to the Airport. We flew back to England in an old Dakota, with a stop at Entebbe on the way and I remember Daddy telling us to watch the next plane landing, as it was part of history in the making, – the first commercial Comet flight came in to land.

I was not very comfortable flying, though too scared to say so, and when a little bald headed man in the seat in front told his lady friend, who was busy painting her long fingernails bright red, that our plane felt like it was held together with string and finished off with a few loose nuts and bolts, and that it would be a miracle if it stayed up there the whole way home! This completely freaked me out. I was petrified and I hated the way it kept dropping in the sky giving you the feeling that your stomach was coming up to meet your throat. I never forgot my first flying experience in that old piston engined, war time Dakota and even now, I have not lost that fear, I always have to take a sedative before I can fly, preferably with an accompanying medicinal shot of alcohol to wash the tablets down, for that little extra courage!

It had not occurred to me to think of our futures, once we landed back in England, but what I was sure of was that I didn't want to be there, I wanted to be back in Africa. I had only ever known Daddy in the Army and, remembering back now, I do not remember hearing my parents discussing the future and what it might or might not hold for everyone. I suppose they must have done, but I had not even thought about the possibility of the radical changes that were to come.

CHAPTER FIVE

A Grocer's Daughter

We all arrived back in Hinckley again and Mum and Dad rented a council house on Sketchley Hill estate – the area where my brother Bobby had picked up his polio virus – until they could decide what they wanted to do, and more importantly where. I found out through Mum that Daddy had opted for early retirement from the army and commuted (officially borrowed) part of his pension so that they could buy a property. They went on to purchase a house, set in one acre of orchard, in a village in Leicestershire called Congerstone. It was a dear little village, so olde England and is near Market Bosworth, where the battle of Bosworth Field was fought. Lovely rolling Leicestershire countryside with little villages and hamlets dotted here and there. Truly rural settings, and Congerstone was one of those villages. I remember it had a tiny little village shop cum post office and the air cloated with the aroma of the big round cheeses that sat on the counter with a cheese wire to cut them. The shop was run by two little old ladies, who were sisters and who both wore long frocks, frilly white aprons, their white hair in neat little buns in the napes of their necks. They would 'ritually' cut you off a little bit of the cheese to try, or told you to help yourself from the broken biscuit tin at the front of the sacks of sugar and potatoes, next to the scales. Magic!

The house was called "The Limes" and it was absolutely my dream home, a big detached property with a large plot of land surrounding it. The house had huge bay windows up and down and my father built a porch over the front door and walls all around it. He was very talented with his hands, he even went on to build brick buildings to house our pig "Cynthia" and her litters, and of course, the inevitable flocks of White Leghorn and Rhode Island Red chickens. It seemed to me that he was trying to "re-invent" Kenya all over again in this little corner of England.

There were double gates to the driveway and Gill, my sister, and I had a favourite game of throwing an old sack over the top of a gate each to form a saddle, and ropes for the bridles and stirrups and, "Hey presto", they became our horses. I would sew together, into a circle, the big shiny green laurel leaves from the hedgerow and garden flowers to make posh hats, and we would use the sealing rings from the jars of sandwich paste hung round our ears on cotton loops, to make tarty earrings. We were then kitted out to ride our horses like the wind, we used to feel so chic and grown up. It was to be the closest I ever got to having my own horse, always an ambition, never fulfilled to this day.

We had an upright piano in the front room and I was the only one of us who chose to take piano lessons. Sadly, these had to end when my parents could no longer afford anything but the necessities, which saddened me greatly as I loved playing and thought I was doing quite well, I had reached the Brahms and Chopin stage and had taken my first exam.

It was at this time that I was to learn how strict and rigid my father was and, indeed, would become. We were beginning to grow up of course, and every night when we came home from school, Brian then thirteen and myself then nine – but not Daddy's favourite Gilly, nor David who was too young, we had to go out into the orchard and clear the ground of stones and rubbish ready for ploughing and sewing. It was heavy work for children and Daddy was the hardest of taskmasters. He built a large garage in addition to the animal sheds where he housed his rotovator, and we had to help with the planting of fruit and vegatables and weeding etc. I suppose this lifestyle was the original concept for the television series "The Good Life", trying to be self sufficient.

Thinking back to the shooting parties in Kenya, Daddy proved true to form when it came time for Cynthia's piglets (who, of course, all had their own names) to go to market, he just couldn't do it, he couldn't bear to think of them as bacon! So they all duly went to good homes instead.

As a part time job, Daddy used to keep the accounts for an old folks home in Market Bosworth and sometimes, he would do a night shift to help them out. The owner of the home had bought his daughter a Welsh Corgi dog – the same breed that the Queen always has – called Roddy and he had bitten everyone in turn there, from the workers to the residents. They told Daddy that they were going to have to have the dog put to sleep. Daddy could not accept that, he was quite sure he "could do something with him" as he put it, so we inherited Roddy. Of course, despite the fact that we all loved the bright little dog, he bit all of us in turn. He did settle down eventually and lived his life out with us. This was just another typical example of my father, his abhorrence of killing, and his devotion to his beloved animals.

It would have been about this time, 1957 that my eldest brother Brian left home. He had a terrible row with Daddy over wearing "jeans" – Daddy said that they were typical 'Teddy Boy' clothes. Brian, instead of doing as he was told, had reached the age of answering back. He said they were sensible, hard-wearing work trousers. My father was so

Brother Brian

strict, we weren't allowed to play the radio or listen to records if they were pop music or any of that modern rubbish! Brian was a teenager and was, of course, growing up and beginning to hold his own views on life and styles, so it ended up after having had the dreadful row, with Brian walking out, his suitcase in his hand, never, ever, to return. He went to London where he joined the Metropolitan Police and he and Daddy were hardly, if ever, to speak again.

There was never any room for negotiation or compromise with my father – his word was law and final, and yours, or anyone else's, feelings and emotions never entered into the equation. I suppose you would call him a true martinet. He was not a big man, about five feet nine or ten inches tall, tanned by the years in the sun which left him with a natural dark skin, and he had brownish/black wavy hair and a typical military moustache. He was very good looking by any standards but through this attractive exterior beat a heart of solid rock. By this time Brian was over seventeen years of age and felt that his opinions counted and he decided that now was the time to challenge this man of rules, and that scenario did not come in for consideration even with Major Ashton. He was absolutely and resolutely rigid, and children should indeed be seen and not heard and somehow, enjoyment of life and growing up was never an issue. You did as you were told without argument and you obeyed his rules.

This incident was to prove too much for my mother and in the fullness of time, she managed ways of getting to see her beloved first born over the years that followed, usually through me, using various schemes and white lies, once I had also left home. Apart from my sister, who was definitely his favourite, we were all to follow in Brian's footsteps very rapidly and all under similar circumstances.

Gill, David and I attended the village school in Congerstone, Brian having passed his exams from there and gone on to Dixie Grammar School in Market Bosworth. I was very advanced for nine and it was recommended by

Sister Gill and her family

Brother David

my school in Nairobi when I left, that I sit my eleven plus exam immediately upon my return to Britain. The Headmaster refused, saying that the only child to pass the eleven plus exam before their time would be his own son first, then he would consider others and, despite great efforts on the part of my Mum, through the Education Authorities, she was denied and I was instead to help the teachers during classes till I was old enough to take the exam – almost two years. This set me back tremendously at the time, but fortunately I was bright enough to cope a great deal on my own and learned many more alternative skills in this 'idle' time than I might not have done, such as sewing, embroidery and the like and, not least, how to keep subordinates in order . . .

At this time, bearing in mind I was still only nine plus years old, I had been having trouble with my teeth, the aftermath of the tuberculosis, and Mum took me to a dentist in Hinckley and, without even talking the whole thing through with me first, she had my six top, front teeth removed. Mum asked what the alternatives were but the dentist maintained that this new procedure called "capping" would be far too painful for a child to bear. This was absolute rubbish, of course, and I then had to bear six weeks with no front teeth before a denture could be fitted and, as a result, I suffered a terrible time at school. I suppose in modern jargon I would have been called "a child traumatised by constant bullying and cruel taunts and jibes", but in those days I was just supposed to get on with it! The trouble was that I went through my school days until actually finally leaving at sixteen, with the same crowd of people, and so when it came down to doing the natural things like pairing off as 'girlfriends' and 'boyfriends', which had started when I was about fourteen, no-one wanted to know the girl with the false teeth – who would want to kiss her! It all left me with the feeling that I was some kind of freak and it has traumatised and haunted me all my life, and still does, right to the present day. When I used to smile, I used to cover my mouth with my hand in the hope that no-one would realise.

When I was thirty six I was awarded some money in the form of dental treatment (which I ended up never following through because of the red tape) and the action of the dentist in removing the teeth was formally declared as gross medical negligence, for which then in the seventies, and even more so now, she should have been struck off, and, what is much more important, I could have sued – would that I had known at the time. Not much consolation now I can tell you, but I do remember my father being absolutely horrified and furious when my mother brought me into the house, devoid of front teeth. He would have believed that all the pain in the world would have been worth keeping my teeth.

After sitting my eleven plus exam, I went on also to attend Dixie Grammar School and this was very traditionally high Church of England and very centred on the religious aspects. I loved it and I was in the choir and much enjoyed the services in Latin which we were learning as part of our corriculum. It followed on with my involvement with the Church at school that I got increasingly more attentive to our village church, St. Mary the Virgin. Initially, Daddy had made us go to Sunday School every Sunday, even though my parents did not attend and eventually, I found out that we were made to go because it was good for discipline, nothing at all to do with my parents' beliefs! But I did not mind, it was part of my life now. I willingly participated, even at that early age and I was even learning to become a bell-ringer. I joined the choir as a soprano and the culmination of the year's events was our "Sermons Day". We used to parade through the streets of the village, marching hand in hand to the Church for the service and back, singing hymns lustily, and all the mothers vied with each other for whose daughter had the most stylish, pretty and up-to-the-minute fashion. I have to say Mum made Gill and me some exquisite dresses and she went on to teach me how to use the sewing machine and interpret a dress pattern. This was to stand me in very good stead later on in my life, especially when money was short and the need to be smartly dressed was the order of the day.

When I told Mum that I wanted to be 'confirmed', she told me that I would have to make promises not to smoke or drink and there would be lots of other rules and regulations. I was only eleven at the time and could not see the significance in that! One of the rules was that I was not allowed to eat or drink anything before taking communion. I was too ashamed of appearing ignorant to ask my Confirmation teacher and these rules were never mentioned in class. My mother only went to church for the obligatory weddings and funerals, so she knew very little of religion proper. As a result of all this, on the morning of my confirmation, reaching my turn to kneel before the Bishop, I did no more than to pass out completely. I awoke on a grass verge in the graveyard outside, with the verger leaning over me to give me a small nip from his hip-flask (brandy I think) to bring me round. So much for the promise not to drink!

Life went on at "The Limes". We were very hard up and to help fill the coffers and feed the family, Mum used to catch the bus to Hinckley every morning to work in the stocking factory again – they paid the best money locally. Her two sisters and my cousin worked there too, so despite the work being tiresome – putting the tops onto stockings – welting they called it, it was all very much family and friendly.

Every night at seven o'clock I would help her off the bus to carry the shopping bags, having come home straight from school and done all the housework for her. Monday was washing, Tuesday ironing, Wednesday clean upstairs, Thursday downstairs and Friday was special jobs like cleaning the oven and windows and keeping the outside clean and tidy, and of course, Friday night is, by tradition, fish and chip night, which was always ready for when she came home. Every evening I had the supper cooked for us all so that Mum had as much help as possible. She used to get terribly tired as she had had anaemia and a bad kidney infection, resulting in about ten weeks in hospital. This took her a lot of getting over, but she went straight back to work. I was therefore the little mother in her place for all those weeks. Cooking Sunday roasts, breakfast for the whole family, packing up Daddy's daily lunch pack and the snacks for our 'tuck' boxes. I suppose now, when I look back, I honestly don't really remember being a child, I was always Mum's little helper – taking care of the family in her place till she came home. I am sure that I was not actually given any option in the matter, but I did it willingly for my Mum.

There were many times that she found her own ways of giving me something back for all of this. I know she felt often that Daddy was far too hard on us, more or less treating us as little workhorses. Of course, he had had to do it as a child himself, and one passes on always something of your upbringing to your own children, I know that I did. Mum would get round Daddy's rigidity when it came to any form of enjoyment. A good example of this was when I was about fourteen and just before we moved from Congerstone to Leicester, Mum saw a notice in the Bosworth newspaper. There was to be a Saturday night dance with a beauty competition to be judged by a television personality of that era – MacDonald Hobley. She induced the total wrath and anger of my father by entering me in the contest and fought bitterly till Daddy agreed, under protest, to take us there and bring us back.

I came second, the organiser's daughter won it – Mum was furious and protested "fixing" but to no avail. However, for me still being very self conscious about my denture, I was thrilled to come anywhere in the final, especially second. Daddy did not speak to Mum for about two weeks after that, and I noticed this happening more and more between them. He used to sit behind his paper and continually clear his throat and was totally unapproachable – and this trait was to continue for many years to come. I was not supposed to enjoy life and I am sure he dreaded me growing up and what was to come later.

I was becoming more and more aware about this time too, from the wolf whistling for me at the beauty contest, that I was not really as ugly as I believed, but of course it never occurred to me that other people did not know that I had this denture. I became very ultra – sensitive over the whole thing. Mum also let me go to the village dances and started to buy me much more grown up, feminine dresses for the Church Sermons Day, which cunningly doubled for dance frocks! I had to be home before Daddy came back from his late shift (and when my return was due, my big brother Brian was sent out to bring me back), as these jaunts were all arranged without Dad's knowledge and the secretiveness of it all seemed so wicked and exciting. Some of the lads at the dances were the sons of local farmers and the like, and I was suddenly being asked to dance by men at least seven or eight years older than myself. I remember one called David Grimmer, who, as soon as I entered the dance hall, came straight over and asked me for the first dance. He was very sun bronzed from working outdoors on the farm every day, and he was very 'muscled', which made him look handsome, I thought, with lovely blonde wavy hair. I was very aware that I liked him a lot and I did let him kiss me goodnight on a few occasions, which started those little flutterings in the tummy to begin – I seemed to have no control over this feeling and it felt very exciting, if very naughty. I had to be very discreet though, as all of this was my and my Mum's little secret. She made me feel special as a person – she used to tell me how beautiful and talented I was and that I would be discovered one day and become a famous film star!

Just after this, the bombshell came.

My parents decided to sell "The Limes" and bought a shop in Leicester, so that was the end of the farming side of every ex-soldier's alleged three dreams – now for the grocer's shop. It was a heartbreaking decision for everyone, we all loved the house and the village way of life, and I remember being absolutely gutted by the whole thing. I didn't want to live anywhere else. We had slotted very well into the Congerstone way of life and I was beginning to mature with people around me that I had come to get to know and whom I liked, but more importantly, they seemed to like me. At the end of the day though, my parents were really struggling to make ends meet and giving the livestock away didn't help. However, Gill and I were already travelling by bus every day to Dixie Grammar School, so to live the same distance away in another direction did not affect us when it came to time and inconvenience. So eventually a deal was struck and my parents were to purchase a corner shop, 67 Hopefield Road, Leicester from a Mr. Best. It was like the shop featured in the television series "Open all Hours", in the exact same type of "Coronation Street" set-up, and of course, back then there were no such things as supermarkets – not yet.

The day we went over to the shop for the last time before the completion of the transaction, which was at a delicate stage as my parents were struggling to find the purchase money, Mr. Best cornered me in the hallway of the living quarters and tried to "touch" me, reaching out to grope between my legs. For a fourteen year old girl this was a very frightening experience. I didn't know what he wanted and it all felt very menacing; but I knew that it was wrong and I was very, very scared. It horrified me and made me feel as if I wanted to be sick – I was literally trembling.

I screamed for my father and he duly came running. However, I was totally devastated by his reaction. Instead of rounding on this disgusting ageing groper, my own father made light of it. He didn't even stick up for me, let alone fight for his daughter's honour. Later, and somewhat embarrassed, he excused his failure to floor the randy old bastard by saying somewhat lamely that he could not afford to risk losing the shop at that stage and that one day I would come to understand, but that he was sure that old Mr. Best meant no real harm! "Come to understand" – the whole incident genuinely disgusted me. I knew nothing about men and sex at that time, but I knew that something very bad had happened. And not just from old Best either, I actually realised at that point that I hated my father's failure to stand up for me: there was something so totally missing from the whole scenario and, no, I didn't understand.

Up till that moment I had believed that my father's

strict moral code was absolute. Now I discovered that it was in fact negotiable and convenient. I realised, for the first time in my young life, that adults – even my own father – could be hypocrites: even for their own family. After that, nothing was ever the same. However, a few days after we moved in, the owner came round yet again with a bouquet of red roses and apologised. I was left with a distinct feeling of being let down by my father – he of the great principles, no boyfriends for you, my girl and certainly no "hanky-panky". Of course it did serve to bring home to him that I was fast growing up and capable of being pursued, but I still wondered what this older man wanted or could see in me!

At this time too, I made a best friend of a neighbour's daughter, Christine Hooper, whose father cleaned ours and everyone's windows and her mum, Beattie was a good friend of my mums and a regular customer in the shop. Mum used to tell Daddy that Beattie had "asked" if I could go with Christine to the cinema or out wherever in the early evenings and she would emphasize how good a customer Beattie was and it would not be wise to upset her as there was another shop on the next corner in both directions!

Dad used to let me go of course, not realising Mum and Beattie's scheming, or at least I never thought he did. Mum did this not only to help me to get a little normal enjoyment out of growing up, but to say 'thank you' for coming home from school, going straight into the shop and working every evening serving customers until we closed at 7pm and then either cleaning the ham and bacon slicing machines, (jobs which she loathed) and re-stocking the shelves or cooking supper for everyone and washing up before going up to my room to do my homework, (five subjects every night). At the weekends Daddy used to get me up at 6.00am and I had to scrub the shop floor from front to back with a bar of green soap and a scrubbing brush, stock up the shelves and then serve all day till we closed at 7.00pm. This was back-breaking work, even for a child of my age, but I did it for Mum and because I did not know that this was not the way all children were brought up. Nowadays I suppose I would have been able to sue my Father for child abuse or cruelty or even some other such nonsense. I have to say categorically at this point, that my upbringing, as strict as it was, never did me any harm, to the contrary, it gave me character and always stood me in good stead. It taught me never to 'whinge ', to get on with the task or life, whatever the situation and never, never to give in. You may be the judge of all this yourself, dear Reader.

My mental arithmetic was not taught in vain, as there were no adding machines or calculators in those days, so when I was serving a customer, I used to add it up all in my head, item by item and we were not decimal then so it could be 19s.11d 3/4d plus 14s.6d. and so on, packing the bags at the same time. It was not very often that any customer queried my addition, as they knew me, but it did happen one day and Dad unpacked the whole lot, re-packed them and did the addition on paper for the lady customer. I wasn't even out by so much as a farthing!

"There you are Mrs. Brown, that will be four pounds six shillings and eight pence halfpenny as Jacqueline so rightly said".

He was obviously quietly proud, though he never said so or gave praise for anything, and most certainly never any affection, but his reaction was praise enough for me.

Christine and I became firm friends and she told me about a boy she loved in Treorchy in Wales. I asked her endless questions about how she felt to be in love – she did try to explain to me on many occasions, and it all sounded very exciting and somehat naughty but these still remained feelings I did not yet understand. We went everywhere together when we could, and once we had slipped out of sight of Daddies' shop, we would hide in an alleyway to put on our make-up. On the way back we would stop, spit onto our hankerchiefs and rub it all off before we got home (no such thing as 'wet wipes' in those days!) I have to admit that I really was in envy of Christine, she was allowed to wear all the modern fashions like hooped skirts and starched petticoats which made the skirt billow out and pretty feminine fashions and shoes. Though my going out was tolerated, this fashion was not, nor the pointed, high heeled shoes of the day. I once saved all my pocket money to buy a pretty flat pair, but because there were butterfly bows on the front, Daddy burned them. He said that they were "tarty". I remember running up to my bedroom and sobbing for hours.

I came home from school one afternoon and the atmosphere was so gloomy, just like when my brother Bobby had died all those years before. Mummy told me that Mr. Hooper had died that day of a heart attack, it had been completely unexpected. I went round immediately to see Christine and of course, she, her sister and mother, Aunt Beattie, were sobbing heartbreakingly. Mr. Hooper was such a nice man, so gentle and kind. Before a month had gone by, Christine came home from school and found her mother kneeling on the floor in the kitchen with her head in the gas oven – she had committed suicide, and I remember not being able to understand why and how she could have done such a thing. The note said sorry to her children but she could not face life without her husband.

The next thing I knew, my best friend was shipped off with her young sister to live back in Wales and I never did see her again. I often wondered if she ever found her love again or not. I missed her greatly for a very long time,

Christine had let me in on little secrets that girls shared that helped me to understand this thing called "growing up", something which I thought I already was. I suppose it was Christine who made me realise that, in fact, my upbringing was not the 'norm', hers was far nearer the mark, but it was to take me a long time to reach any kind of understanding of just how much I was actually being used and 'abused'.

CHAPTER SIX

College Days

Time, of course, did not stand still and I busied myself at school with the annual school play. I gained the female lead role playing a Persian Princess "Zara" in a play called "Tobias and the Angel". This was a great coup for me, as the whole fifth and sixth forms auditioned for the various roles. I took the part well and truly to heart and gave the project every ounce of my ambition and acting ability that I could muster. It paid off in the end and after the first performance, my acting especially got great reviews in the Leicester Mercury newspaper. Throughout the whole performance, I could hear my Dad coughing loudly in dissapproval, especially when it got to the part where the leading man and I had to kiss. I was only fifteen at this time, and, come to think of it, it was my first kiss in public, (and I couldn't stand the boy playing the part, so it meant little at the time to me). I do remember though, that it caused arguments between Dad and my mother all the way home. Mum was very proud of me, another fine example of the film star quality she always believed her daughter had, and was equally proud that her daughter, out of the whole of Dixie Grammar school female acting 'wannabees', got the part.

This pride was to be even greater enhanced when I also won a French verse-speaking competition, reciting the poem

"Le Cigalle et la Formie", beating some of the senior sixth-formers to achieve that one. If that actress quality is really in me, then it has come in extremely useful over the years, believe me!

After this brief exciting respite, came the time to sit, what was then known as the 'O' Level examinations. My subjects were English language and literature, French both written and oral, Biology, and Art (at which I was naturally talented). During the art examination, we were left with time to spare at the end and so the Art Mistress, Miss Jones, gave all of us who had finished, some spare paper and told us to amuse ourselves till the time was up. I doodled quite a few dress designs – I loved fashion magazines and stylish clothes. When all the papers were collected in at the end of the exam, Miss Jones looked through them and then came over to me and asked me to stay behind. I was somewhat intrigued.

When the room had cleared of students, she asked me what I intended doing when I left school. Knowing that I was not going to stay on and sit more advanced exams, I really had not given the matter much thought. She said that she was much impressed with my designs, so much so that she would like to contact my parents with an idea for the use of my art. I was of course very flattered and excited, that someone should actually take a personal interest in me, appreciate me and praise me and also felt that I could make something of myself.

Miss Jones duly made an appointment to see my parents and told them I should be encouraged to take my art further. Then came the best surprise of all, she asked their permission for her to go ahead, on their behalf, and make enquiries for me to enter Leicester College of Art and Dress Design – to include a basic art course as well. My head was spinning and my parents were most impressed. They said 'yes' immediately. I went for my interview, and joy of joys, I was accepted.

Thus, began my time at Art College. It was wonderful and I was fully enjoying every minute of it, because, at last, I had found something that really appealed to me and somewhere where I immediately fitted in. As part of the basic course, I took fabric design, dress design, lettering, still life and even life drawing. I just loved it all and very soon had a large collection of drawings and designs in my portfolio. My father thought that some of the life drawings were disgusting because, of course, they were nude. He made his feelings exceedingly clear and so, I kept the offending drawings well out of the way, up on top of a wardrobe on the landing.

To get round my father's rigid rules of what I could and could not do or wear, I kept my duffle coat and thick black tights (the definite requisites for every female student of the "arty" type in order to feel one of the gang!), in my locker at College and I changed into them when I got there, and before I came home. I made friends very quickly and soon had a real, though not at all serious, boyfriend called Graham. It was, at this stage, all very innocent, and to be honest now, I cannot even remember what he looked like – it was a teenage 'girlie boyie' thing. We just used to walk in the Castle gardens, hand in hand, during the lunch breaks and the odd 'peck' on the cheek. It was on one of these occasions, I saw my father coming in the opposite direction. I looked at him and smiled and it was obvious that he was going to completely ignore me, which he did, and just walked on right past me without a word. Oh my God, the look on my father's face as he passed us. I knew at that point that I was in big trouble. Holding hands with a young man in public!

I dreaded going home that night, but I was in no way

prepared for what came on my arrival. The tirade started immediately. Daddy was white with temper and told me that in no uncertain terms, as far as he was concerned, my art college days were over. To my horror he produced my priceless portfolio of work and seized the the whole file, including the offending life drawings. Before my own eyes, he burned all the contents, calling them filth, and if this was the kind of thing that College put into my mind, then that was the end. What he found so offensive, I shall never understand, but we never saw eachother in the nude in our home and risque items on the television could not be watched. I came to the rapid realisation that Art College was completely out, as far as he was concerned, and I knew that he meant it, that was definitely the end.

"You get yourself a proper job tomorrow, my girl!" he shouted.

I was dumbstruck, completely poleaxed, and I was furious, very very furious. What the hell did he know about art? A rebellious streak began to stir within me, I realised that I was well and truly angry with my father, he had no right to do what he did, and I was never to forgive him for it either. But there was no arguing with my dictatorial father. He insisted that I had to find myself a job and earn my keep.

I was totally devastated and heartbroken, but, at the end of the day, it was my fault, I knew what he was like and I should have known better but more than that, I had brought on his wrath by openly disobeying and defying him with this boy. I mean, walking in the park holding hands – how disgusting! I was clearly totally devious and devious people always got found out. I paid dearly for my misdemeanour and my world was shattered. I had no close friends, my male peers at Dixie were all classed as "teddy boys" by my father, without exception, sight unseen, and were strictly not tolerated, I was not close to any girlfriend since Christine and I had lost my chances for the career I dreamed about (and was good at), and of course every night and weekend was the work in the shop. However, throughout all of this and previous years, I never considered this unkind treatment, to me it was normal, at least in my world and I had brought this on my own head by breaking the rules – his rules.

However, life has it's own way of surprising you and I had no idea of the changes that were soon to be in store for me, nor the lasting impact they would have.

A year later, I discovered men for real: or, to be precise, one special man.

CHAPTER SEVEN

Courting Days

Early one evening, I stood in the shop on my own waiting for customers, and I saw a young man standing on the opposite corner of the street. He appeared to be staring in at me, which rather un-nerved me. I did nothing except I kept my eye on him and then, after what seemed like ages, he eventually crossed the road and came into the shop. I felt my heart beginning to pound for no reason, and again, I felt those butterflies in my tummy. What was all this about? He asked me for a packet of cigarettes, paid me for them and generally chatted to me just passing the time of day. I noticed

Nigel Christopher Brown – circa 1959.

that he was smartly dressed in a pin stripe suit and crisp shirt with gold cufflinks. He was tall, dark, very handsome, oh so suave and beautifully spoken with the most wonderful smile. He made some small-talk for a while and then left with his purchase and I watched him until he had walked out of sight. Oh well! I sighed and thought of what an impression one chance, brief meeting with this young gentleman had made on me, and I pondered as to what kind of man I would end up meeting one day and spending the rest of my life with. Wouldn't it be wonderful if it could be someone like that young man? Hey-ho, it was just a young girl's daydreams, but something had been stirred.

The next day I had an interview with a firm of Solicitors called Chapman and Goddard, based in Leicester High Street, as a junior receptionist, switchboard operator, trainee secretary and general *factotem*. I needed this job badly, my father was expecting it of me, and I chose my outfit for the interview extremely carefully. I decided I had to be dressed smartly, so I opted for a nice pencil slim skirt, with my cardigan on back to front with the buttons going down the back, (all the fashion at that time), and with a single string of pearls and matching earrings, and I carried my forbidden high heeled court shoes in my bag to change into when I got to my destination. I was trying to look sophisticated and older than my sixteen years.

Mr. Goddard himself interviewed me, he was a man in his fifties, with a lovely round smiley face and the demeanour to go with it. On first impressions, he seemed extremely impressed with me and gave me the feeling that he liked the way I looked and carried myself. It was a very good interview for my first time and he gave me the job on the spot – he was so kind – telling me that I would go to shorthand and typing lessons twice a week on afternoon relief. This was to be my very first job, with a ridiculous salary by the standards of today, but then on three pounds per week, and on that first payday, I felt I had really grown up. I was a real working woman now.

With my first salary burning a hole in my hand, my first thought was for my hard working Mum and all she had done to get my teenage years here to this point with some enjoyment in them, so I came to an immediate decision. I went straight into the jewellers below our offices and bought Mum a string of 'real' pearls and travelled excitedly home on the bus. I felt so proud when I gave them to her, I loved and admired my Mum so much. Then the 'proverbial' hit the fan – Daddy came in and demanded my wage packet. He had apparently expected it intact, unopened and from which he would take my board and lodging and give me back the rest for my bus fares and just a little for me for saving, for clothes, shoes and so on. Someone had omitted to warn me. What a terrible argument that caused. From that day on, I came home with my wage packet pristine and untouched and handed it over like the good little girl that I was. When would he come to realise that I was not only growing up and needed schooling in the art of being an adult. After all I was expected to perform adult tasks in the home and in the shop and had been since a small child. Now more than ever, I needed to be treated like one.

The era of the sixties was now coming into it's own and big changes were taking place in the structure of society as we had known it post-war. After secretarial school, I used to call into a new establishment that was to become one of the "in" places for young people to meet in the city town centre. It was the first 'coffee bar' and they served this fabulous up-to-the-minute fad, gorgeous frothy coffee and glorious fritter rolls (long, soft bread rolls filled with hot sliced, fried potatoes, or mushroom stalks – scrummy!) This became my stop-off place every week, twice a week and I began to start making new friends, friends slightly older than me. It didn`t dawn on me at the time, but in my own way I was developing my own options and decisions in my choice of setting out to meet new people, and expand my horizons, but even so, I felt somewhat guilty and very risque, that in some way, I was doing wrong, I was defying my father – he always made me feel this way, as though for thinking normal thoughts, I was somehow devious, I had fits of conscience about absolutely everything.

I was having to work especially hard at college because the policy was that when a secretary left and her post became vacant, every one of the typists moved up the ladder in order of seniority and the trainee secretary became secretary to the man with the junior post in the office, the litigation clerk. This situation occurred within a few months, so I was promoted very quickly with the relevant raise in salary, and a new trainee receptionist etc. was recruited. This man also turned out to be a 'groper' like Mr. Best and would pinch or stroke my bottom as I bent down to do the filing in his office, or lurk in doorways for me after work. I handled it my own way this time and plucked up the courage, after one grope too many, to point out to him that the next time he did it, I would report him directly to Mr. Goddard. He was a family man, and to lose his job for this type of misdemeanour would have been disastrous, it would have gone around all the other solicitor's offices in the town immediately, and no-one else would have touched him. It stopped immediately, fortunately for me without recriminations, he wouldn't dare. However, this quick promotion meant that I had to work doubly hard to finish my secretarial college as quickly as possible, as litigation was a very busy department of the practice and one which I was not particularly fond of, it could be extremely boring and I was anxious to move out of as soon as possible.

One afternoon after lessons, as usual, I called into the coffee bar for my welcome frothy coffee and fritter roll. As I sat down, I noticed that the lovely young man who had called into the shop for his cigarettes was sitting on the opposite side of the room, looking as sartorially elegant as I remembered him. I sheepishly looked over at him and he smiled back at me. My heart just went thump, thump, thump, I felt as if it was in my throat. My stomach suddenly did somersaults and filled with fluttering butterflies as I saw him get to his feet, pick up his coffee and roll and come towards me. Oh God, he's coming over. What shall I say, what shall I do? Will I make a complete idiot of myself? My mind was racing in all directions, emotions I had abolutely no control over. Suddenly he was there, he got to my table and said:

"May I?", gesturing to sit down.

"Of course" I said, as I sat there trembling, and he sat down opposite to me. I am sure that I must have been blushing, something I never normally do, but I felt very hot and exceedingly nervous all of a sudden, and my heart continued to pound in my chest. He said how pleased he was to see me again since our meeting in the shop, and we chatted on generally for some time. He said his name was Nigel Christopher Brown, but he preferred to be called Chris (his parents called him Kit, but he was not very keen on that).

Thank God he was doing all the talking because I genuinely was dumbstruck at this point. He went on to explain to me that he had been in Hopefield Road, where he and his parents had once lived, selling vacuum cleaners as a part-time job whilst looking for a career. He was just twenty years old and seemed so mature to me, a real man. He said that he had seen me in the shop from the opposite side of the road, and found the excuse of purchasing the cigarettes just so that he could talk to me, he said, because he thought that I was extremely beautiful. I was so flattered it all went straight to my head; this was a complete first for me. No boy had ever shown this kind of interest before, let alone this hansome, mature young man. He asked me if he could take me out and I explained how strict my father was, and the loss of my alibi, Christine, made it difficult for me to get permission for the evenings. The good news was that we could at least meet in the coffee bar and have lunches and Daddy would not be any the wiser. He happily agreed and said he would meet me the next day.

I skipped all the way home from the bus stop that night, my heart so full of joy and happiness, it was fit for bursting. My Mum knew me so well, and she was very used to seeing me normal, but not particularly happy. She could see that something had obviously happened to change my usual demeanour so she asked me why I was looking and acting so 'full of bliss'. My answer was immediate and without hesitation. I told her that on that very day, I had met the man that I was going to marry. Where that statement came from, I had no idea, but I firmly believed it. She laughed and asked me to tell her all about him. I told her as much as I knew and she was intrigued, she wanted to meet him, so we had to devise one of our 'shopping expeditions' for an hour or two so we could accomplish this. This was arranged and we met in our coffee bar. Mum thought he was gorgeous and became my strongest ally over the weeks and months that followed. My "courtship", as they called it then, had well and truly begun.

Chris was to tell me that he was sent away to school when he was just eight years old, to Westholme School, Arnside, in the Lake District. His parents were great lovers of this part of the country, especially his Mother who had been a serious walker and rambler in her time. This was naturally in-bred into Chris, influencing him for a great deal of his formative years. His mother proved to be the type of woman who would only ever have one child and then not be the 'mothering' type, hence the upbringing until his late teens in scholarly institutions and character forming activities in an effort to persuade him into 'wholesome' manhood. After his eleven plus examination, he attended Wyggeston Boys School in Leicester where he stayed till passing his A level exams. During his main holidays, he attended the Outward Bound Mountaineering School in Eskdale and this culminated in an expedition with them to Labrador on a reconaissance and mapping trip for eight weeks, July to September 1958. He also told me that he had been to Germany once on a walking holiday where he met his pen-friend Monica. On returning from Labrador, he had met Sir Vivian Fuchs and they had exchanged reminiscences. He was very proud of that and being prompted to follow Sir Vivian's example – he took up guest lecturing on the expedition, illustrated by the many wonderful slides he had taken. He was a very talented photographer. He had also met Sir Edmund Hillary, who had climbed Everest, one of Chris' own ambitions and yet another of his great heroes, and both meetings were recorded in the local press.

Eventually, one of those 'inevitable' days arrived. Chris and I met as usual on a Sunday, and he told me that he was taking me home to tea to meet his parents, George and Margaret Brown. This I had been dreading, he obviously respected his parents very much, but calling them 'Mother' and 'Father', I had to wonder what kind of formal ogres they would turn out to be. I had never met a boy's parents before, and Chris was twenty and a man, this was going to be a far more serious situation than two young teenagers in their 'puppy love' days.

Their house was in Hamilton Street in Leicester, not a 'posh' area, but an imposing and very large three storey

"Mother in law from hell" Margaret Brown as a young woman...

terraced Victorian home. It was full of gorgeous antiques and wonderful oil paintings and fine furniture and bric-a-brac. We waited for them to come into the "Drawing Room", a 'best' lounge to my peers, and I sat nervously looking around the room, waiting to meet them. We were introduced. Margaret Brown stood before me, she was a slim, fairly tall lady. She had what I would have described as a "pointy" face, her cheek bones and chin had a chiselled look and she had a very beaky nose. When she smiled, it was always one of those smiles that are very put on and not in the least sincere, and she was openly and deliberately very cold and withdrawn – she looked to me positively witchlike. Mr. Brown was much warmer and nicer, he was not as tall as I thought he would be, with Christopher being six feet two, but he had a jolly face and demeanour and a very bald head. He was warm and welcoming and immediately shook my hand and said how pleased he was to meet me. Mrs. Brown insisted on taking me around the house and boasting about all of expensive and valuable possessions and the inheritance that would one day be Christopher's. Making nervous small talk, I admired one picture his mother showed to me called "The Choirboy". She went on to tell me that that picture and

...and just before she died, 1980's.

one other, purported to be attributed to the artist Van Meer, and a set of decanters called a "Tantalus" had been presented to Chris's grandfather, George William Brown of Leicester, (1840 – 1924) who had been custodian of the Royal Collection at Hampton Court from 1895 to 1905 and these were gifts from Queen Victoria on his retirement. "These will all belong to Christopher one day" she said, coldly and rather morbidly. She gave me shudders down my spine, it was like something out of Charles Dickens, or even Wuthering Heights or the like. It became quickly obvious, she had a positively threatening and immediately protective attitude towards any liaison between myself and her son.

It was quite obvious from the first instant that we met that Mrs. Brown disliked me intensely and made no attempt to hide her feelings. She was to treat me with this same contempt for the whole of the time that I knew her, I have no doubt until the day she died. 'The grocer's daughter' was definitely and absolutely not at all the kind of person she wanted for her son to be involved with, let alone contemplate a future together. From that moment on, she was to make every attempt that she could not only to put a stop to the relationship, but to deliberately invite girls of her choice to lunches, teas and dinners in an attempt to force her son's alliances elsewhere and this tactic was never to end.

After Chris settled into his first proper employment after leaving school, and the vacuum cleaners, (I do not know with whom), he received a serious bang on the head whilst jumping up onto a loading bay. This seemed to affect him badly with terrible headaches and serious mood swings, and so his mother consulted a phrenologist – a procedure of which I had never heard before – and she had the bumps on his head read. The phrenologist predicted that he would recover and would follow a profession of some kind with the use of words and the arty side of his character – obviously alluding towards journalism and its off-shoots. A fairly broad spectrum but nevertheless it proved to be somewhat near the mark.

Chris and I had been seeing each other for some six months and knew, by this time, that we loved each other, and we had told each other so. One day he met me from work at lunchtime and said he wanted to take me to the cinema that evening, there was a film he wanted me to see which had just been released. I said that my Daddy would not even contemplate a boyfriend, let alone for me to go out till late at night. He said this was absolutely ridiculous and I was to phone home that afternoon and tell my father that I was bringing a friend home from work for him to meet. I remember so vividly, to this day, the other secretaries (who were like big sisters to me) urging me to make the call and trying to reassure me that all would work out fine in the end. So I took the bull by the horns and asked my boss Dennis if I could use the phone. I phoned home and Mum answered. I told her Chris was insisting on coming home with me that night to meet my ogre of a father!

Mum went into a total flap and said Daddy would never agree. I told her she had better put him on the phone as Chris was going to turn up come hell or high water as they say. So I spoke to Daddy and he told me that if it was a male friend that I wanted to bring, then not to bother – he would not agree to even meet him. I said it was a gentleman friend and he was insistent and would come anyway. My father slammed the phone down on me.

At six o'clock, Chris met me from work and we boarded the bus for home. I told him Daddy would be furious and I was so, so frightened – every inch of me was trembling.
He told me to let him do the worrying and handling of the whole thing. He was very self assured and confidant and I could only but trust him in this situation that I didn't want to be in. When we got home to the shop – Daddy had left Mum to close up and gone off in a huff saying nothing. We helped Mum finish off and got supper ready. Eight pm came and we ate and left the food for Dad in the oven. Mum kept protesting that it was futile and that if Chris insisted on staying and facing this thing out, then she and I would be very deeply in the 'you-know-what'!

"He will take forever to get over this Chris, he probably won't forgive me or speak to me for weeks, you don't know what you are dealing with" Mum told him – sometimes he makes my life pure hell".

"Mrs. Ashton, I will wait, no matter how long it takes, to get over this ridiculous situation with Jacqui's father, we simply cannot continue in this fashion. I am here because I care for Jacqui, I will do nothing, ever, to harm her in any way and Mr. Ashton mut be made aware of this" Chris said very forcefully.

Well, it took till pub closing time and we heard Daddy come in through the back door, doing his throat clearing ritual to show his disapproval. Oh dear, my heart sank; now

I really was scared. Chris firmly and with dignity, stood up to his full six feet two inches and faced my father with his hand outstretched to shake hands:

"Good evening Major Ashton; my name is Nigel Christopher Brown, Sir" he said in his lovely deep, velvety, refined voice – "I have been waiting some four and a half hours to meet you".

My father looked up into his face and, I swear that if a huge hole could have appeared and swallowed him up, I think he would have done and been glad to do so. He was so taken aback by this tall, elegantly dressed and smartly groomed young man – not a teddy boy suit, chain, jeans or leather jacket in sight – just a picture of pure confident male sartorial elegance standing there. Immediately, with his confidence and wonderful manners, Chris had completely de-fused the situation and taken the wind out of my father's sails. I had never seen my father so dumbstruck ever before – he, always the one in charge. They shook hands very firmly, sat down next to each other and proceeded to talk non-stop, with intercessions of the odd peach brandy, the only drink Daddy had in the house, until the early hours of the morning, two or three a.m. I remember.

When Chris came to leave he said "Major Ashton, I came tonight not only with the intention of meeting you, and removing these ridiculous rules and regulations, but also determined to ask your permission for Jacqui and I to become engaged".

I stood there in total amazement, I was floating in seventh heaven, Chris had given me no idea at all of his intentions. My parents were delighted and gladly gave their consent, but on the understanding that I was only allowed out for one late night a week on a Saturday and I was to be home no later than ten thirty, the house rules still applied, irrespective. Try that today! We agreed, it was a start, and

Chris and his 'friend' Monica.

Chris said the next day in our lunch break we would go and buy a ring. This we did, a beautiful small Mexican Fire Opal surrounded by diamonds, like a precious little flower, and we became officially engaged on 1st May 1960 – I was just sixteen years and four months old. I didn't believe there would ever, could ever be another day or situation in my life where I could be happier than I was on this day.

Chris's mother, very predictably, was absolutely furious at the engagement and continued to try and belittle me and to make me feel even more unwelcome. More dinner parties for this girl and that took place. She then took the huge step of inviting his pen-friend, Monica, over from Germany to stay for two weeks. Chris had been to Germany and stayed with her previously. Monica was absolutely stunning – she had the most beautiful face and smile, she had long thick blonde hair which she piled high on her head, and of course, she had a perfect figure. She made me feel totally inadequate and inferior which was, of course, the whole intention. Chris tried to reassure me that they had been only pen friends, but something was niggling. I, of course, was not invited to the lunches, teas and suppers during Monica's visit. It was very difficult and most hurtful, but where his Mother was concerned, Chris was obviously either a complete coward, or desperate just to keep the peace, or was he maybe contented to have the best of both worlds on the pretence of making his mother happy? I tried to believe it was to keep the peace and desperately praying that it was not the latter, though I found it all very difficult to understand. Monica went back to Germany and we too became pen friends but 'Mother' never ceased to take every opportunity of reminiscing and extolling Monica's virtues in my hearing.

Despite all of this, our courtship continued. Of course back then in the sixties, holding hands, kissing and cuddling were the norm, but nothing more. All very proper and above board, sitting in the front parlour, with Chris maybe playing the piano, an Etude or something or just sitting together on the carpet, Chris with his arms tightly around me and listening to classical records, usually Beethoven's Emperor Concerto or Bruch's Violin Concerto. Wonderful! And Mother's head popping round the door from time to time 'just to check'.

On the 21st November 1961, it was Chris's 21st birthday and his father went out and bought him a new Morris Minor motor car. We were so thrilled because his father, had not even considered consulting Mother on the matter, and I knew that he had taken quite a 'shine' to me and he knew it would please us. He was desperately trying some of Mother's tactics, though in reverse, to try and hold us together. I often wondered what he thought of her meddling and interfering and how he felt it would affect their son in the long run. I must say, George Henry Brown was a man of few words when it came to his wife! We christened the new car "Aggie" (I don't know why, it should have been 'Doris the Morris' I suppose!). However, Aggie changed our lives considerably. We could actually stay at the cinema and watch the end of the film, instead of having to leave early to catch that dreaded last bus to get me home for 10.30pm. and of course, that gave us the precious time for kissing and cuddling in the car before saying "goodnight". Life was beginning to open up, not only for me, but for us as a couple and I was feeling the strangest of sensations that I had never felt before, but, as so often in my early life, there was no-one to whom I could turn, not only what all these feelings meant and to where they were leading, but, more importantly to me, how I was supposed to respond to them. Maybe I was just going to have to learn things for myself and trust myself enough not to let me down.

CHAPTER EIGHT

From Grocer's Daughter to Mountaineer…

Chris and I were invited to a pre-wedding party for two quite close friends we had made through our coffee shop crowd. We asked the couple, Fiona and Stuart, how late the party would last and they felt until about 1.00am, it was to be on the Saturday night. By this time I had turned seventeen, Chris and I had been engaged for some twelve months, and so I went home and told Daddy about the party. I was completely honest and up-front with him, and said that Chris and I would be going. He told me that, whatever the circumstances, the rules remained the same and we would have to be home by 10.30pm.

I tried to explain that it was a special party for an engaged couple, who were really special friends, and could he make an exception. I pointed out politely, quite justified in my mind that if we were going to do anything wrong, we could do it just as easily before 10.30pm as afterwards. At that remark, he became totally enraged and flatly refused to discuss the matter further and so I then committed what were to be the cardinal sins, not only did I answer my father back, but I shouted in temper. I shouted that if he was thinking all these things, it must have been because it was what he had already done himself! I screamed at him that I was not that kind of girl, his alluding to my behaviour hurt me and made me feel dirty and untrustworthy. He flew into a violent rage, stamped all the way up the stairs and took a suitcase down from on top of the wardrobe. He threw it on my bed and told me to pack, to get out and never to come back. He never wanted to see me or hear from me again.

My heart was thumping, I was shaking from head to foot both in temper and with fear, and I could hardly breathe, as I duly packed and left the shop. I got on a bus and went, without thinking that I might be intruding, to the home of one of the secretaries that I worked with and she, Jenny, and her husband kindly put me up that night. Despite having cried myself to sleep and being in a complete state of devastation and disbelief, I went into work with her the next day, complete with suitcase, determined to make it on my own. I asked for a couple of hours off and went up to the Y.W.C.A. Hostel at the top of London Road, in Leicester not far from Chris's home. I got myself a room, albeit shared, and moved in that evening. They all made me feel so welcome and my room-mate Anne, turned out to be about thirteen years older than me, and she sort of took me under her wing. She was really very kind to me. I was shaken, very frightened and lonely, but determined and resolute that this was the point where my life would truly begin anew, I was alone and ready to make my own decisions about me, no-one doing it for me. I was definitely on my way.

Next morning I went back to work and during my lunch hour, I went out and bought myself the highest pair of pointed toed shoes that I could walk in, black mascara, eye shadow and a black hair dye! I really went to town that evening when I got home. When I met Chris that night, he flew into a hell of a rage, said I looked a complete tart and if I wanted to go out with him I should go right back and wash all the make up and hair dye off. He said that he loved me especially because I was *not* like that, and I suddenly felt very silly for my temporary streak of defiance, and I washed it all off. We then went out for our first unrestricted date, although there was a curfew at the Hostel of midnight, but oh, what freedom in the knowledge that from now on I was totally responsible for myself. My Mother, on the other hand, was beside herself with worry, but she phoned when Daddy was out and we arranged for a regular meeting time and place on her afternoons off and, of course, I assured her that I could perfectly well look after myself.

Chris had taken employment with the East Midlands Gas Board as assistant editor and photographer for their "in house" magazine. This was the start in journalism that he had been waiting for. He covered items of interest all over the East Midlands area, from cookery demonstrations using state of the art gas ovens to a night shift at one of the gas plants. He seemed very well settled and our future looked more secure, but the job was necessitating him being away for a week-end here and a few days there. He told me of the assignments and I was very happy for him, but I never stopped to give it a thought that during this time away, he might just get involved with other women. 'Mother' was very happy, of course, because he stood the chance of meeting other ladies who might be more suitable than a mere grocer's daughter.

It was at this time that Chris was to re-kindle his love for the mountains and introduce me to his first love! He took me to a specialist sports shop in town and bought me a pair of lightweight climbing and walking boots called Klettershoes, and some out-door wear and a new climbing rope and we took off in our beloved Morris Minor, Aggie. We set off down the A5 to Wales where I was taught how to climb and experience the joys of camping, the mountains and of course, the culmination, the 'apres climb' and my first pint of beer! We camped just below Snowdon in our small tent and Chris gave me my first lesson in cooking on a primus stove. We each had our own sleeping bags – in those days no discussions on the subject ever took place. Until you married, nice girls just didn't, you kept your chastity intact for your wedding day – hence the virginal white wedding dress.

It rained most of the weekend but that did nothing to affect my joy of sitting on the top of Tryfan, after completing my first long climb, and looking down on the world. Not having our climbing guide book with us, we did not know the classification of the climb Chris chose to teach me on, but when we reached the end of the climb at the summit, two other experienced climbers were there to tell us that it was what they call a 'v.s.' or very severe. What an induction, but what pride I felt when we did find out. Wales was very quickly to become a favourite destination at the weekends, because it was a relatively short journey, and we made lots of friends. I loved every minute of it and my climbing, though still in its infancy, became quite proficient. What I didn't realise too was that I was going through the stages of maturing and learning how to deal with other people on a more grown up plane.

Life seemed so exciting at the moment and there was just so much to do and see and so much to learn, and so much more to come I was sure, although what was to come was not necessarily what I would have expected.

Quite the reverse in fact...

CHAPTER NINE

Broken Hearted

Though the rift with my father really troubled me, life went along normally for some time and I now, at the age of seventeen, felt very grown up and in complete charge of my own destiny. I was me, Jacqueline Ashton; I lived away from home; I dressed as I wanted to; I went out as I pleased but all still very much within the bounds of my upbringing. Why could my father have not trusted me to be the girl that he had raised? I had great expectations for myself and had the most high moral standards – Chris, I believed knew exactly the way things were, and was happy with that situation.

One evening, Chris invited me round to his parent's home for supper – a rare occasion as his mother was just about tolerating me at this point, and she was still extremely unpleasant. After the meal, we went into the front parlour as usual to listen to our beloved Beethoven and The Emperor Concerto, still a special favourite of both of us. We listened to the slow movement, me sitting on the carpet at his feet, but this time he did not sit with his arms around me, he did seem somewhat preoccupied. I loved him so much, I felt so completely safe with him, but could something be wrong? When the music had stopped, Chris suddenly said that he needed to talk to me seriously about things, his voice sounded strange. I had wondered what was going on.

He said that he felt that he had reached a point in his life where he had to make some serious decisions. I asked him if it had anything to do with the fact that he had been away on assignments most weekends recently and I was beginning to feel that he had become sort of distant from me. He said it had, he was so sorry, but he had met a girl at a cookery demonstration a few weeks before and that some of his trips away had not been business at all, but to see and spend time with her.

In that split second, I realised that my mistrust of some of those weekends and assignments had been well and truly deserved and my whole world just fell apart, the thing I had dreaded for some time now, was suddenly here. He said he wanted to break off the engagement, though he would still see me from time to time to make sure that I was alright. So that was why 'Mother' had deigned to cook dinner for us! The old bat must have been rubbing her hands together with sheer delight as he walked me back to the Hostel. I just sobbed all the way, my heart was breaking, I felt completely unloved, unwanted and already, so absolutely lonely. At the door, I gave him back his ring, and, trying to hold on to what little dignity I had left inside, I just said 'goodnight', closed the front door and ran up to my room. I poured out my heart to Anne, my room-mate; I was just seventeen and I had lost my beloved Daddy, my home and now my first and only love. What ever was to become of me now, what could I do?

Once the crying subsided, I tried to pull myself together, I took a deep breath and attempted to think things through logically and without histrionics. I made my mind up firmly on where I was going from here – What were those last words from him, "see me from time to time, and make sure I was o.k." No thanks – not this girl, not Jacqui Ashton – No way. I would put myself in a position which showed him that I did not need him to make sure I was alright. It was now none of his business, that was his choice, and the last thing I needed from him was his pity. He had made himself a part of my young girl's dreams and plans for mine and our futures and then simply, when the mood took him, dashed them like a piece of crystal on the rocks; I felt like the crystal, so easy to see into and then in a split second, shattered into a thousand tiny pieces

The next day I did something that I would not normally ever do, I lied. It was out of character for me and difficult to do, but I rang in sick to work. I got myself dressed in my best outfit and took a bus to Hinckley. My Mum's elder sister Aunt Lil (I called her Tetty) and her husband Uncle Jack lived there – as did most of our extended family still. They had an apartment on the estate where we lived after coming back from Kenya, I used to visit them often, so I was on familiar territory. Not being able to have children of their own and having always envied my parents for their five, they had always begged to have me as their own, and of course, Mum had always refused. I knew I was wanted there and so I was delighted when Tetty and Jack agreed to have me live with them and to do a special bedroom all of my own just for me. A sense of great relief came over me and suddenly I felt as if I was at home.

Now I needed to work. I then immediately walked down into the town to the only firm of Solicitors at that time, and point blank, asked them for a job. I told them my experience in Leicester as a junior legal secretary and, to my surprise and utter relief; they gave me the position of secretary to the conveyancing clerk, Sam Barratt. I was to start as soon as possible, so I went back, packed my bags, told my boss and thanked him and my kind friends at Chapman and Goddard and at the YWCA and set off for a new start in Hinckley – I didn't attempt to contact Chris to say goodbye or let him know where I was going and I decided to put him firmly out of my life and move on. No-one was going to pick me up and drop me and discard me like a piece of old rag. I told my Mother what had happened and what I was doing and gave her strict instructions that, under no circumstances whatsoever, was she ever to let Chris, or anyone else, know where I had gone. Rejection was not an option with me, nor would it ever be. I discovered an ability within myself to be able to shut the hurt away, despite grieving dreadfully, and to move on to the next stage in my life – I had to for my own sanity's sake and more importantly, for my dignity. Good heavens, I was only seventeen and a half years old, but felt well used, and abused but I was able, and would prove always to be, able to make use of this worldly wisdom.

I was headed for a new start in my young life and a new future, I was headed for unknown territory, but I felt that I was growing up very fast, I was on my own and there was only me to take care of me. That was OK.

Maybe I was only very young, but I was about to prove to myself and, more importantly the rest of the world, that I could well and truly look after myself. Yes, I was on my way, I could handle anything from now on- just watch me.

CHAPTER TEN

Womanhood Gained

I cheered up more and more as the days went on, Tetty and Jack treated me just as their own daughter. I really loved my work, Sam was a great boss, and all my bosses, throughout my life, were to make me feel valued and that I was good at what I did and made a real contribution. This did wonders for my self esteem and at the same time, my cousins Richard (who has been always very special to me and a true friend) and Roy were to take me under their wings like big brothers and they took me swimming, to the cinema, to dances etc. They were actually quite strict with me and truly acted as chaperons. Life was lovely with Tetty and Jack, he taught me the joys of betting! Sitting in front of the television on

Tetty and Jack – my stand-in parents – circa 1930.

Saturday afternoon watching the horseracing – he having placed the bets in the morning. I remember my first winner at 33 to 1 was an outsider called 'Prima Ballerina' and he had placed for me a sixpenny bet. He howled with laughter when I had picked it and said it would never win, but it did. He insisted I bought him a pint at the pub and we took a 'snowball cocktail' back for Tetty.

I was in regular touch with my mother through fair means and foul, and I saw her every week, on her afternoon off and, despite my heartbreak at hearing that my name could never be mentioned in front of my Dad, apparently Chris had been contacting her more and more and was beside himself at not being able to find me. He had kept on ringing and pleading with my Mum to tell him any news that would help him to find me. As I said before, I had told my Mum and my friends and employers in Leicester that they were, under no circumstances, to let him know where I had gone. I was still grieving my loss of him and still feeling totally rejected, he had been my first love, but he had chosen someone else over me. I was resolute, I did not want him to know where I was and this gave me my greatest strength, which was that he may have temporarily taken my self esteem away from me, leaving me feeling totally inadequate, but the most precious thing of mine, my honour, was still in tact. I had my life before me and something in my head kept telling me I had to take advantage of this situation, leave him where he belonged, in the past and to just get on and do things for myself, and that was how I was determined to go about my life.

A year sped by and I was quite firmly embedded in a comfortable feeling of familiarity with my home, my work and my new friends and I don't remember at that time where, or if I had any inner thoughts as to where next I was going to go – if anywhere – from there, nor what I intended doing with my life when, one Saturday afternoon, bets placed and television on, there was a firm knock on the door. Jack got up and went to the front door to answer it and called me. He didn't say who was at the door, he merely shouted out:

"It is for you, Shonner" (his pet name for me).

When I reached the hall, there stood Chris. I was absolutely shocked and surprised to see him standing there. He asked me if I would go out for a drive, he needed to talk to me. Tetty and Jack looked worried and disappointed and my heart was beating so hard I almost felt sick. He begged and pleaded with me:

"Just go for a short ride with me, I beg you, I have important things to say to you".

I'll never know why I simply caved in, I had made my mind up if this situation ever arose, I would stand my ground and say "no" emphatically and tell him to 'sling his hook'. Of course, it proved itself, I had the determination of a jelly fish!

We set of in Aggie for a drive into the countryside and Chris told me that he had been round to see my parents, and told them that he had been utterly wrong and had made the worst and most terrible mistake of his life. He needed to find me. My father didn't know where I was and abruptly told him so, but Mum liked Chris so much and she just started to buckle. Chris pleaded and said he wanted their permission to ask me to marry him. He said he truly loved me. I could see my mother on hearing this just completely 'melting' and giving in to the pleadings and 'so called' confessions of stupidity from Chris – he was very plausible when he wanted to be; he had managed to convince me for one and a half years that he truly loved me and there could never be anyone else for him. Of course she was going to buckle.

Daddy, also, apparently changed tack completely at this

statement and gave his immediate consent, but, he said that there was a condition. I had to come back and be married properly from home, full church wedding, reception, in fact, "the whole works" as they say. There is no sense in trying to put into perspective what I felt at that moment, and in true Jacqui fashion, of course I said 'yes' immediately, with all my heart and Chris put my ring back onto my finger. We kissed tenderly for quite some time and he told me what a fool he had been, I was the only girl for him and he hoped against all odds that I could truly forgive him, it would never, could never happen again he assured me. I was in seventh heaven and, of course, I totally, utterly believed him. He had seen the error of his ways, but I had shown him that I could stand my ground and be absolutely resolute, I could survive on my own and could be totally independent. I was also speaking out for myself. His antics had changed me considerably and I had grown up even more as a result. I had become a woman.

When we arrived back at the apartment, Tetty and Jack said of course they were happy for me, but just the looks on their faces said it all, I knew full well that they were completely devastated. Their role as surrogate parents and best pals lasted so short a time, though I always truly loved them and they me, and I would always be grateful for the support they had given me in helping me over what had been, without exception, one of the worst experiences and episodes of my short life.

So I returned home to Hopefield Road and the shop, and my father seemed overjoyed. We made up and proceeded to make plans for the wedding. Chris had told his parents of his decision before coming to see me, and although 'Mother' was bitterly disappointed and totally against it, they reluctantly accepted the situation, and said that I could now officially call them Mother and Father. Of course, given this *fait accompli*, Mother then had to take over the whole situation, she just had to be in control. They therefore chose a small terraced house for us as our starter home in Lyme Road, about one quarter of a mile from them. They paid the deposit and re-carpeted the house as their wedding present to us. Chris took a mortgage out for us of one thousand pounds, it seemed to me at the time like the national debt. There was no consultation on the purchase of the house, 'Mother' would have us where she could keep an eye on us easily. The house was purchased from the estate of an elderly lady who had died and so the whole house came completely furnished right down to the gas copper boiler and aged gas cooker in the kitchen! The double bed had a 'knitted' metal base and feather flock mattress. Out of the ark or what? However, it was a complete home and ready to go. We had a good start off to our married life with this little investment. It had three bedrooms and a lovely up to the minute bathroom. A typical Leicester terrace house, but very substantial.

Mother said that she would not be buying a new outfit for the wedding (almost as if she did not expect it to last five minutes.) She had a perfectly good suit and a hat that would complement it too and they would do. Father was much kinder and insisted we went away for a honeymoon and paid for us to go to a hotel in Bognor Regis for two weeks. Chris's artful mother, of course, invited Monica over from Germany to stay at their home in Hamilton Street for the duration of the wedding. My heart truly sank at this news. I knew what was in the back of her mind, she would have been hoping against hope that Chris would change his mind at the last minute, when he saw his beautiful penpal and call the whole thing off. Not so however, and so, the date for the wedding was fixed, 14th August 1962 and the Church was booked. I borrowed a wedding dress and veil from my cousin Margaret, my sister was to be bridesmaid and Mum made her dress for her. The reception was booked at a fine local hotel by Daddy himself. This grocer's daughter was to be seen having the very best that the grocer could provide.

It was now one week before the wedding and whilst we were quietly chatting, Chris suggested that we go away to the Lake District for the weekend to another of our favourite haunts, Derwentwater, to celebrate our reunion. I thought that was such a romantic thought and I really looked forward to it. I was again so full of love, excitement and expectations.

We drove leisurely up to the Lake District at the beginning of that weekend. On our arrival at Derwentwater, Chris immediately set up camp, raised the tent, made the fire and then we settled down to gaze out at the wonders of this glorious place and here I was in it with the man I wanted to be with for the rest of my life. Chris took out a bottle of Madeira and poured us a celebratory drink each. We gazed into each other's eyes, sitting by the peaceful lake, the water lapping on the pebbles, the wood fire flickering in the clear night air and drank to our future together. Everything looked sort of misty to me, when Chris tenderly kissed me and then said:

"Darling, I thought it would be a romantic idea for us to come away this weekend before the wedding and share a sleeping bag. You know, I want our wedding night to be perfect, especially for you, I want us to make love tonight".

My heart was racing, partly with anticipation, partly with excitement and partly with a natural trepidation – trepidation because I had been taught that this was wrong and should not happen until you had been 'churched', as my mother quaintly put it, and you were truly married. I really did not have time to think out any clever answer, if I were to truly confess it, I suppose that this little plan of his came as no great surprise. My mind was racing in split seconds as to how I would react to his statement, and I instantly decided that there was nothing that was going to spoil or get in the way of this perfect weekend, he was to be all mine this night, and so, for the first time in my life, I had made one of the most important decisions that a girl can make, I gave the man I loved my chastity, and as a result I found out what all those strange, deep feelings had been and what they finally led up to. Wow!!!

He was such an incredible and amazing lover, so patient and tender, and we made wonderful, wonderful love. I had never experienced anything quite so unbelievably pleasurable and I loved him even more, if that were possible, because I now felt complete and he seemed so proud of me. He held me in his arms, our bodies all wrapped around each other and fell into a perfect sleep. I awoke the next morning wondering how I would deal with the situation of facing my Mum and looking her straight in the eyes, but somehow I did. After all, to me it felt all so completely natural. Looking back, it never occurred to me to wonder how he had learned to make a woman so happy . . .

However, I was to experience a most unexpected situation which I could never have anticipated, and which was to hold a huge surprise for me on the day before the wedding. Monica having arrived at Hamilton Street, she, Chris and I went out for lunch and we had a really lovely time. It was the first time that I had met her properly and she seemed extremely nice. In fact, she was stunningly beautiful as I had noticed from the endless photos 'Mother' had kept on showing me. 'No wonder she preferred Monica to me as a wife for her only son', I remember thinking to myself. In fact, Monica made me feel totally inadequate, and I could admit it to myself.

I realised that this was unwelcome uncertainty on my

part and felt the best way forward was to gain her support. While Chris was away from the table paying the bill, the opportunity presented itself beautifully. I told Monica of the circumstances of the break in our engagement and my fears of the resurrection of other women after we were married. She told me not to worry and tried to reassure me, telling me she believed that Chris really did love me very much. She was very reassuring and credible and I felt a lot more confident as they escorted me to catch my bus home.

They saw me off to spend my afternoon and evening in the final preparations for the big day tomorrow. Chris said he would be taking Monica out for dinner that evening if I had no objections, after all she was one of his oldest friends. Even after all that had happened, I was expected to, and I did, accept this at face value. How could I even stop to consider anything ominous? After all, we were to be married tomorrow and we had had that wonderful time the weekend before. Silly me!

On that evening, the night before my big day, there was a knock on my bedroom door. Mum came into my room and sat on the bed. I had been dreading this moment because I thought I knew how the conversation would go, but I had a shock coming to me. Mum pointed up to my wedding dress, shrouded in its sheet and she asked me, point blank, if I was entitled to wear the white dress. I took a big swallow and a deep breath because I knew that she was actually asking me whether Chris and I had made love and I did not want to lie, but my heart sank with shame as I said:

"Yes, of course I am, Mum", the previous weekend still fresh and blissful in my mind.

"Then, my dear" she said, "we must have a talk".

My mother had told me nothing of life, except small confidences when Daddy and she had had problems over their relationship, now of course I know the reason for his moods, she had refused him sexual relations since David had been born – what an awful, frustrating and unloved life he must have endured. My mother never told me what to expect from men when it came to approaches etc., nothing of the menstrual cycle till the morning I woke up screaming in my bed, thinking I was going to die from loss of blood, nothing of men in general or sexual relations, I don't think she would ever have been able to say the word 'penetration' and certainly nothing about the way babies were made. So, she proceeded to tell me that, on the following night when we went to our honeymoon bed, Chris would want to do 'things' to me, as she put it. I listened intently and innocently as she fumbled her way through her description of love making.

"However darling, it is something men have to do – sometimes a lot – Chris will climb on top of you and push his 'thing' inside yours and it goes on for some time. You will have to tell yourself that it will soon be over and once he has given a sort of groan, he will just roll over and go to sleep afterwards".

Nothing was mentioned about love, tenderness or, indeed, the fact that it should ultimately end in the production of a baby. And of course, there was no question of whether or not I would enjoy it. To do so, I expect that she thought would make you one of 'those loose women'. My heart went out to her, she obviously hated sex even though she adored and worshipped my father. How could I tell her that it had been the most wonderful experience for me and I couldn't wait for the next night; but in those prim and proper days, women were not expected to enjoy 'it'; it was just one of those things in life women were expected to endure.

We turned the matter round to more enjoyable topics and on a jocular note she said to me:

"You know, with a surname like Ashton, you could have chosen a new one nicer than Brown. If there were to ever be someone else, remember to always go one better". We laughed but I could not contemplate even thinking that there would ever be anyone else.

Even at this point, looking back, things about my parents and the ups and downs of their life together still did not click into place. I was not yet experienced enough in worldly matters, nor did I have the remotest idea as to just how much adjusting one has to do to being married and sharing a life together. I put all thoughts of everything else out of my mind, creamed my face and got into bed to sleep, my last night as a single person, and a complete new future for me with the man I loved so deeply. Tomorrow I will be Mrs. Brown at last, and for always.

I couldn't wait.

CHAPTER ELEVEN

Wedding Bells

Tuesday the 14th August 1962 was the most perfect day of my life. On my father's arm, he gave my hand a tight squeeze in the in the foyer as we entered the church in Imperial Avenue, and he proudly walked me to the alter, to the man I loved so much waiting there for me, looking so handsome. I was simply floating with joy and the wonders of love and happiness as we became joined as 'man and wife'.

After the ceremony, we all arrived at the reception, which Daddy had insisted be at a proper Hotel and with all the trimmings. That is exactly what he arranged. We were to have a continental style seated reception, with small tables of four all encircling the top table. However, the Hotel had not allowed for the presence of Mrs. Brown Senior! 'Mother', of course, true to character, took over everything. She parked herself on the top table and surrounded herself with all of her cronies and left Chris and I and the rest of the top table entourage "seatless" as it were. She flatly refused to be moved, even when the Restaurant Manager objected and got very hot under the collar with her. It didn't matter to her. It was her Christopher getting married and even if she did not agree with it, she would make it her day and make her mark on

Wedding day 14th August 1962

it in no uncertain terms. Looking back I now realise that I came to see her as the 'wicked witch of the west' from the cartoon films of the time. She was absolutely determined to keep on influencing Chris and she definitely thought that I was not, nor would ever be, the woman for her son, even though we were now legally 'man and wife', a state which she should have respected, being the bible-thumper that she was.

We could not bear to have anything mar our day, so Chris and I moved and the staff laid us up a special smaller table at the side and we were joined by the rest of the original top table.

Reception over, we set off for our honeymoon in Bognor Regis, but by this time it was late, as we had married at 4.00pm in the afternoon and the heavens had opened. It was pouring and blowing a gale, so bad that it was hard to see. Father came up to us as we were about to leave, saying that he was worried about our safety and the wisdom of driving through the night, and he simply pushed some extra money into Chris's hand and told us to stop the night half way to Bognor, as he felt the driving conditions were too bad to do the whole journey in one go and that we were to telephone and say we had done so and arrived safely.

And so, the new Mr. and Mrs. Brown set off on honeymoon in Aggie, our beloved Morris Minor. We got as far as Oxford and the weather was not improving. We stopped at the first hotel we came to, a small olde worlde Inn, telephoned Father to say where we were, and booked ourselves into the honeymoon suite.

Whilst Chris went to the Bar to order us something bubbly to celebrate with, the receptionist rang the bell for someone to take us up to our room. There suddenly appeared this elderly, stooping lady with white hair scraped back in a little tight bun at the nape of her neck, and wearing a long black dress almost down to her ankles. Spooky! I thought that bellboys and concierges were the order of the day in a hotel, not a little old crone.

"Come this way my dear" she croaked at me and proceeded to climb the very shallow, narrow and uneven wooden staircase. We climbed three flights right to the top, the old lady puffing and panting loudly. When we finally reached our room she opened the door and there were two double beds in the room. Take your pick! I mused. She turned to me and croaked breathlessly:

"Just married eh? Hope you have more luck than I did my dear, I was widowed after five years".

She left me open-mouthed and went off mumbling to herself. It was just like a scene from an old black and white film. Chris came in with the bubbly and we laughed as I recounted the incident. He took my champagne glass from my hand, held me in a tight embrace and tenderly kissed me.

My first honeymoon night was as perfect as I had hoped, he was the most amazingly wonderful, charming and tender lover that a girl could have, it was Derwentwater all over again only much better, because it all seemed so natural. We made love for what seemed a never ending blissful eternity. I was so much in love and my heart was overflowing. At that point in time, I had everything I had ever dreamed of, and now, more importantly, the little girl had disappeared and I felt like a woman. Remember, it was 1962, and how many girls of eighteen were married to a successful young businessman, had their own home, a car – everything it seemed. Not many, I can assure you and I was very aware of just how lucky I really was.

The next morning we went down to breakfast. "Good morning Mr. and Mrs. Brown", ringing in our ears. I felt a lovely warm glow and I have to admit, a slight embarrassment because everyone in the breakfast room seemed to know that we were in the bridal suite and I felt that they all knew what we had been doing. It was all so new and so strange but an amazing experience all the same. We tried to enjoy our time in Bognor, but by the end of the first week, it had rained every day. We were unable to really see any sights or to travel too far afield, we even ended up spending one afternoon at the cinema and so, after a long discussion, we opted to secretly drive home to our little house, hide 'Aggie' away in one of the side streets where Mother would not see her, and spend the following week away from everyone, settling into and enjoying the beginning of our married life together. I now truly felt that my world was complete.

Chris returned to work and I settled into being a

homemaker – Lord knows, I had had enough experience. His mother used to call in regularly, obviously to check up on the little trollop who had 'stolen' her son. She would do annoying and hurtful things like rubbing her fingers into the corners of window panes (which I used to scrub with a toothbrush) and lift mats and the like in the hope of catching me out and finding something on which she could pull me up for being a bad housewife. I remember one day her lifting the door mat outside the front door and accusing me of not scrubbing my step that week. (In those days, scrubbing the front step was seen as a sign of a clean house and respectability). She said;

"What kind of a home were you dragged up in?"

Why did everyone treat me as some kind of skivvy, I thought to myself? I just exploded in sheer temper.

"I was brought up in a home with servants, Mother – more than you will ever have". She looked at me with such hate and loathing and gave one of her sarcastic laughs and said:

"You are and will always be just a grocer's daughter." Then she left. She was to treat me like this always.

Despite Chris's awful mother, the next few months went dreamily by. Chris spent some weekends away on business, but I was living in my own perfect little world, keeping the home – our home. Then, in the December, I was queueing up in the post office for stamps for Christmas cards. As I got to the counter to be served I told the teller I felt very unwell and dizzy. I came back to consciousness in the back room of the shop with my head between my knees and feeling very nauseous. I had fainted out cold. I must have eaten something, surely?

The next day I went to see the doctor. I came out of the surgery and I skipped, singing all the way home. I was going to have a baby in June. I was so ecstatic. Chris came home and when I told him he was so excited. However in those days, it was not like it is now and I took on the role of expectant Mum on my own. I sat and lovingly hand sewed all my layette for the baby, lace trimmed and embroidered night gowns, little rompers, hand knitted jackets, bonnets, bootees and the shawl. The whole family seemed to be knitting from my Mum, sister, Chris's favourite maiden aunts Gert and Daisy (they really were called that!) who lived together four streets away from us, and of course, to Mother, whose contributions were always anything second hand she could pick up at the Red Cross sales where she helped – never anything new from her.

Actually this was probably because she was absolutely disgusted when we told her and Father about the baby and of the joy we felt at being expectant parents:

"Disgusting! You simply do not do 'it', unless you want children" she said to us. Poor old Father, I thought, just the same as my Dad!

By the 22nd June, the baby was overdue by two weeks and as I was of small stature, it was decided that I would go into hospital, in order to have the baby induced. My Mum came in with me; fathers were not welcome, nor indeed even considered being there, until after the birth in those days.

Simon Nicholas Brown was born on the 23rd of June, 1963. Chris came into the ward at visiting time, beaming proudly and carrying a single long-stemmed red rose. He picked up his son and lovingly gave him a kiss and came over to me, gave me my rose and kissed me on the forehead. He seemed very happy. The birth had no complications, so I was discharged the next day and Chris collected us and brought us home with our new son.

I loved our little home in Lyme Road, our baby boy, and I was a natural mother. We had our lovely little car; 'Aggie' and it just seemed to me that now we had everything as life settled down to domesticity and perfect bliss for the next six months or so.

What is it they say – just how wrong can you be?

CHAPTER TWELVE

Devastation

Chris had had assignments away from home during this time, his job seemed to keep him extremely busy, and everything to me seemed perfectly normal. So when he suddenly came home one day and out of the blue and in a very 'matter of fact way' said that he had been for an interview in Birmingham for a job with the British Motor Corporation, I didn't believe what I was hearing, I was absolutely totally gutted... I listened completely dumbfounded and open mouthed as he went on to explain that BMC as it was known, were offering him the job of editor of two of their magazines, and what was more and without giving me even a chance of speaking, he went on to say that he intended to take the post. He told me as bluntly as that.

"Will you be able to come home at night?" I stupidly asked him.

It was in the days before commuting, motorways and sophisticated cars. We only had our Aggie, and Birmingham to Leicester twice a day, plus Chris travelling miles for his job, he said that could not possibly have worked.

Then came the next shot from the blunderbuss –

"No" he said, "Mother and Father took me over and helped me to find a lovely flat in Northfield, a suburb of Birmingham, not far from the BMC factory in Longbridge".

"Mother and Father took me over and helped me to find a lovely flat..." I couldn't believe what I was hearing. Where did baby Simon and I come in all this? They had helped him to do all this behind my back, not a single hint of a word from all three of them. I was completely poleaxed, devastated, numb inside and heartbroken. I just couldn't take it in. They, all three of them, were all effectively splitting up our family of only about a year, deliberately. Chris just burbled on and said that of course it meant a prestigious promotion from assistant editor at the Gas Board, and that it was a step further up the ladder to becoming an editor and further up into higher management, but all of this was going in one ear and out of the other, I could only sit there and fume, all the time knowing in my heart of hearts that it was Mother who had pushed for all this and encouraged him.

I could hear her saying it to him when she got him on his own, "You get yourself away from her and leave her to fend for herself. You can do so much better for yourself. Her type will only hold you back." I can hear her saying it. But why I wondered had *he* not even told me about the job when he spotted it and especially the interview? He hadn't discussed it at all with me, let alone getting to the point of actually choosing and finding accommodation with his parents. Little Simon and I had not even been considered or included. I just couldn't believe it; how could all this be happening again, after all the promises the last time?

My mind was in a total and absolute turmoil of disbelief. Could Chris be that deceitful and, moreover, he must have been lying to me all along, I thought to myself.

"Chris, we have a home here and a baby, I don't understand." I said pathetically, hoping that he would take a step back and think things through in a logical way. He just didn't or wouldn't understand, he just wimpishly said that he would be home at the week-ends to be with us, and he tried to comfort me and get me to go along with what was, in any event, a *'fait accompli'*. He was going, Mother wanted him to, and so he did. He packed up Aggie and drove away, just like that, leaving me weeping and sobbing uncontrollably till I thought my sad little heart was going to burst. I got to the point where I thought that I couldn't breathe. Then Simon awoke and cried for his feed and I was brought back to earth and to face the reality of what I was going to do, but putting the wellbeing of my baby firmly in the forefront of my mind.

I should really have been able to predict the next events, as so many of these weekends that should have been spent coming home never happened, without explanation, he just did not come. I cried endlessly, I worried, I imagined all sorts of scenarios, I felt a failure, I started to feel ugly all over again and above all, I did not know what to do and I felt alone, oh so very alone and unloved. Did he not love me anymore? He wasn't sending me any money, was the mortgage being paid? I was completely at my wit's end, I just simply didn't know which way to turn, nor to whom.

As the weeks went on and he did not come, and in those days we had no phone, in sheer and utter desperation, never wanting to get to this point, I went to see Mum and Dad. I told them everything. They sympathised as much as they could and tried to console me, but my heart was breaking. They advised me to go and see his parents and try to find out what was happening, but to remember that I could always come home at any time. Is this what we had come to after only just under two years of marriage, was there someone else yet again?

By this time, my imagination having run wild, I became very angry. Our baby was only nine months old, I was twenty years of age and left alone, high and dry, not knowing what was happening, having been told absolutely nothing. He could have been dead for all I knew, I hadn't even seen the flat that he was living in, so I could not even imagine him there. I had the utter conviction, at that moment, that there must be another woman. This flat business could not be considered as normal behaviour, surely? So I stopped off at Hamilton Street and stumped up all the courage that I could muster and confronted my parents-in-law.

Father shuffled his feet and coughed and spluttered, looked embarrassed mumbled that it was nothing to do with him, it was Christopher's decision. Mother's response was different and totally expected on my behalf. She said that I was trying to stand in the way of his future – she believed he had a great career ahead of him and I would only "drag him down" and she felt that I should let him go. The fact that their son – my husband – had helped produce a new life in Simon and we had a marriage blessed before God, was obviously neither here nor there and they, or more correctly she, was simply not interested, and all this from a self-professed Christian. I left there so completely desolate and devastated and took Simon home to ponder our future together. I suddenly felt again so, so alone. I bathed him in front of the fire and put him to bed and cried myself to sleep by the side of his cot.

The next day was another day. I went back to the shop and told Mum and Dad that, I had heard nothing from Chris for so long now and I did not even know if the mortgage was being paid. I felt that I had been abandoned in every way. So there was nothing for it but for me to take legal advice, possibly sell 13 Lyme Road if I could and find myself a job to support myself and Simon, but of course, I would need a home and a child-minder. Mum spoke to one of her customers just yards away from the shop and she agreed to be my baby-minder. I set about looking at the "situations vacant" section in the local newspaper, and there was one advertisement for a legal assistant and secretary/receptionist at a firm of Solicitors in the town centre. I rang and made an appointment for the very next day.

The job was for a partnership of newly qualified Solicitors and friends, Malcolm Gardner and David Millhouse. They had one girl already called Jenny, and very charming she was too, and they needed another legally experienced secretary to complete the office. Malcolm always used to say:

"Jacks (as he affectionately called me), we didn't so much interview you, as it was you who interviewed us!"

I was offered the job immediately, despite the baby – not done in those days for married new mums to work. My time spent with them was gloriously funny, loving and enjoyable – we were like family. They were very good to both Jenny and myself. Jenny and I did everything in running the office and thought nothing of the hours or great effort, gladly given, and we did work exceptionally hard.

Malcolm and David wrote to Chris and, to my alarm, he only too-readily agreed to the sale of Lyme Road and the division equally of the proceeds of sale. In my heart I knew that it was all over but in my mind, it would not accept my marriage was completely shattered, and me still not knowing for sure what went wrong. I hadn't even been given the chance to fight for it.

I confess to not having given divorce even a thought at this stage, and I was back with Mum and Dad. They were wonderfully supportive and I just tried as hard as I could to get on with my and my precious baby Simon's life, work was most enjoyable, Malcolm, David and Jenny were unbelievably kind and considerate and at the end of the day, I had my health, strength of will and my wonderful baby boy made me want to make plans for our unknown future.. There is always an up-side to everything I suppose, and of course, the old adage is true, time is a great healer, but all of these trite sayings were of little or no comfort to me at this time.

I heard nothing from Chris until Simon's first birthday, 23rd June 1964. He just turned up in the evening, completely unannounced, carrying the biggest teddy bear I had ever seen and driving an expensive MGA sports car. Obviously 'Aggie' had gone to the big car graveyard in the sky; one thing for sure; the image that he gave off was quite a different one, no longer the loving husband and father, but a new 'bachelor about town'. What happened to the man who had said his vows before God and swore to love honour and cherish me till one of us died?

He was obviously not worried about the situation he had caused. He was completely *blasé* about the whole thing. It said it all to me – the biggest toy, the flashiest car yes, but no maintenance for Simon and I, we were so obviously not intended to be a part of his new life. Who was this monster? He played with Simon for a very short time and then asked if we could talk. I said:

"If we have to, though I can't imagine that there can be too much to talk about as you've made your position utterly and completely clear to me. As for mine, that is now for me to decide and definitely not for you to know". So he then proceeded, embarrassingly, to ask me to join him and live with him in Birmingham, just like that. I simply declined, no explanation of the last six months, where he had been, who with, and no reason why.

"Chris, I am not a complete idiot. You have absolutely no concept of what your actions have done to me, and I thank God that Simon is not old enough to know. Nevertheless, I have absolutely and positively no intention of jumping back in quite so readily".

We argued, very bitterly on my part for a short time, him telling me absolutely nothing about what had gone on – apparently he was "trying to sort his life out", whatever that meant. I told him that that was not a sufficient explanation or reason for his actions and I needed time. I was so deeply hurt, to my mind a non-repairable situation at this point and, moreover, I was not ready to forget, not ready to take all this deceit, hurt, and total desolation and destruction of my very being, all over again and I would have to consider things very deeply before I could give any kind of decision. I wanted him to go away and think over the consequences of his actions and try to get some idea of what he had put us through and I asked him to leave – so he simply just left. Every inch of my being longed for him, yearned for him, but I felt that I had to make a stand, my feelings were so hurt and my confidence at absolute rock bottom.

In the months just before all this happened and with no word at all from Chris, I had struck up a friendship with a lovely guy I met at the office called Stuart. He worked with the design team on the suspension for the new Lotus Cortina car. We became great friends, he collected and took me out regularly with Mum's help and Stuart helped me tremendously through all these bad times and restored something of my self-esteem, which had taken a considerable knock. Daddy didn't approve of the friendship because I was still married, but despite the fact that we made love on one occasion, we both decided that it had been a mistake and preferred to be just close soul-mates, which indeed we were. We could discuss just about anything and everything and we used to laugh a lot. It was the right decision.

Chris pestered me continually till I felt my parents were fed up with the whole situation and they really thought, and came to tell me often, that I should give it another try. I spoke to David and Malcolm, told them of my problem and that if I went, it would mean going to Birmingham and leaving them and they were very saddened, but pleased for me if it was what I really wanted. However they decided to let me leave with an opening which I never expected – but so typical of these two lovely friends. Malcolm went out and bought me a "Stag" suitcase.

"There you are, Jacks", he said, "just throw it in through the door when you want to come back, and please remember, you can come back any time. You are so good at what you do, but more especially, we love you".

I talked it through at great length with Stuart and he simply said:

 "You know, you are still so much in love with Chris in truth – go where your heart takes you". That was so typical of him, and if I did go with my heart, I would miss our friendship greatly, he had come to have great meaning in my life. Stuart was always there when I needed him – he would always tell me honestly what he felt, unlike Chris. It was not such an easy decision to make.

Simon was by this time eighteen months old and now I had to make this decision. Chris said he wanted us to try for another baby, he felt that this would help pull everything back together, at that point I was not at all sure that that was the way forward. If it all happened again, I would be left to fend for two children and myself – that was double jeopardy in my book.

We had copious conversations about what had been going on, and eventually he was to come clean. Of course, there had been another woman. He tried hard to avoid the subject and told me that things for him had been difficult, adjusting to married life and parenthood, but that he always felt guilty at the way he treated me and, of course, he admitted that his Mother had been a great influence on him and his marriage and pushed and pushed for his decision to

Simon and Robert Brown – 1968

move away. She had openly and with regularity, encouraged him. He had become even more involved with this woman in the full knowledge that we were still married and we had such a lovely young son. I had a lot to weigh up in my mind, Simon needed a father and, of course, I still loved my husband, the worshipping part was somewhat tarnished, but I found myself not giving in too much and standing my ground much more than I would normally have done. However, I did feel totally sick and abused. What in the hell should I do? Would it happen again if I give in now? I was in turmoil.

At the end of the day, my decision was to let myself succumb to his pleadings and, of course I laid out all my conditions for this second start to our married life and ultimately, we moved to Birmingham. Mum reminded me, knowing that things between Chris and I were fragile to say the least, and that I could always come home again if it went wrong. This made me feel more secure, as my self-esteem had taken a tremendous blow, I was not sure that it would ever completely recover. Above all, I still did not understand one thing – Why, why, why?

The flat was large; it was the complete ground floor of an old house, including the garden that had been a convent for years previously. To the left of the house was a walkway through to the little church and graveyard. Up above us lived a local couple with their baby Natalie – about the same age as Simon. It was all nice enough with the garden for the children to play in during the day, but it was never to feel quite like home.

I got myself a job immediately with a firm of solicitors in Birmingham town centre and I travelled in by train every day. The girl upstairs was glad of the extra money to baby-mind Simon and all seemed well. I did have a little trouble with my boss who obviously fancied me, but nothing I could not handle and, to be honest, after such a tremendous confidence knock, I was really quite flattered, even though he wasn't very good looking, grossly overweight and I didn't particularly like him.

However, I still could not rid myself of the belief that there was another woman still in the picture, Chris continued to go off frequently and cover features for the magazine and it always involved staying overnight or at weekends. He came home after one such weekend and left his suit hanging up in the bedroom. He had gone to the pub and I tidied up the flat and bathed and put Simon to bed. He was suffering from a heavy cold, and was quite miserable, so I gave him two of the raspberry flavoured baby aspirins that I had bought on the way home.

As I hung Chris's jacket in the wardrobe, I could see something in the top pocket. It sat there saying to me "Go on, take me out, read me". Of course, quite naturally I took it out and to my horror, though not disbelief I might add, it was a letter from a girl in London talking about their time spent together in the countryside and the scratches on her back from the bracken when they made love, and about a piece of music in the charts by Jim Reeves, "I love you because you understand dear", which meant a lot to them apparently – but Chris hated pop music with a vengeance, so what the hell was going on? How could he have blatantly lied to me, persuaded me to completely change my life all over again, give up my independence and home, move to this town which I didn't particularly like and all the time there was still another woman? Moreover, if they were so much in love and making love, why did he even want me around – he must have known that I would get to realise that something was still going on.

I was beside myself, and in a fit of sheer grief, I made a poor attempt at slashing my wrists, which of course I knew I should not do, it was a choice of being selfish for myself or abandoning my baby whom I loved so much. I ran the hot water, took the razor blade out of it's wrapper, plunged my hands into the water and attempted to make a cut, I merely scratched the surface and as the small trickle of blood swirled in the hot water, I dropped the razor blade and pulled the plug. We were both worth more than that and so I sobbed and sobbed till I cried myself to sleep in the chair from sheer exhaustion and utter grief.

Whilst I slept, unbeknown to me, Simon had climbed out of his cot and crawled out of his room into the lounge to the coffee table where I had left his baby aspirin – and of course, being raspberry flavoured, they were like sweets to him. I woke up with a start as I heard Chris's key in the door, to find Simon sitting on the carpet with an empty aspirin bottle and no tablets in sight. This was the kind of event that under normal circumstances, I was overly protective about. How could I have been so stupid and leave the tablets on baby sized furniture and not on a high level? Now was not the time to argue these or other things and so we rushed him straight round to the hospital, which thankfully was not too far, and they had to pump his stomach – they treated me as if I were a criminal and called me negligent. I truly felt at the time that I deserved that remark, I felt totally responsible and imagined all the possible consequences – I shuddered as I tried to get it out of my mind, I had greater issues to face at this time.

How much more would I have to bear? A lot more as it turned out. When we returned from the hospital and had put Simon safely to bed, I told Chris that that was it. I had had enough and just knew that I could not carry on like this any more. Chris broke down and admitted everything – yet again – and he said that it had all got out of hand, that they had become officially engaged and that he had taken her the previous weekend to buy a wedding dress! A wedding dress? I could hardly take it all in. He asked me if I would write to her and end things between them, he pleaded and begged me saying that he had tried so hard to break it off himself but she had threatened to kill herself if he did. Why, on that same evening of all evenings, did that sound so ironic?

Eventually, though only God knows why, I agreed to write to the girl. Her name was Valerie. She wrote back to me and she could not have been more concerned for myself and Simon. In its own way, the letter was very sweet and mine to her must have been very hard to take in. Chris had apparently completely fabricated his life for her during the weeks that they were apart, so my letter had come as somewhat of a thunderbolt for the poor woman. In truth of course, we had both been decieved and cheated. She assured me that none of us would ever hear from her again, nor to my knowledge, did we. I have to confess to having felt so deeply sorry for her, she was not so much the other woman as the other abused woman, like myself. Chris was always so plausible. It now seemed to me that everything was falling apart for me, for us – yet again.

The following day, feeling very unwell and finding it hard to breathe, I went to the doctor. He gave me a thorough examination. "I cannot prescribe anything for you to help calm you down Mrs. Brown, because you are pregnant". Now this I had not even contemplated, it could not be in the equation. How can you be elated and completely destroyed inside at one and the same moment? But I was. With all this going through my mind, I set off home. By the time I arrived I had thought it through and just prayed that God had meant for this to happen and maybe, just maybe, this new baby would help to repair the damage and, if we were to stay together then maybe it would bring us back together.

Chris did not come straight home, he had apparently gone to the pub first. When he did come home, he was covered in sweat and was an awful grey-green colour. He was trembling from head to foot. After calming him down, he told me he had gone to the pub to have a quiet drink and to sort his mind out after all the misery that he had brought upon us. After a few shots of 'Dutch courage' he decided to return and talk everything over with me. He set off the usual way, through the graveyard walk next to the flat. As he was passing, he saw a new grave covered in flowers, but he could hear the sound of someone screaming to be let out and something or somebody trying to touch him on the shoulder from behind. I decided now was not the time to discuss the baby, obviously, and, having thought it over for a few moments, I told him that I thought he should go round and speak to the vicar the next day and tell him, word for word, what had occurred. He agreed but refused to go through the graveyard to the Rectory.

After telling the vicar his tale, the vicar said:

"But Mr. Brown, there are no new graves in the graveyard, there haven't been any burials there for years".

They went together at the instigation of the vicar, to see the spot where Chris had seen the grave. There was no new grave, no flowers. The vicar did not know us personally, and suggested that maybe Chris needed some sort of help, maybe psychiatric.

That was a new word for me. 'Psychiatry' had never touched my life and I knew nothing about it. Something about this whole incident began to un-nerve me – I cannot describe exactly how, but my personal experiences had never included anything like this. However, when Chris got home he felt better for having talked to the vicar but in his mind, somebody had been buried alive years before. I told him at this point that we were expecting another baby and that we must try to re-build our lives and think to the future. He smiled at me and said "I am pleased, truly I am and we will be a proper family again, I promise you" .

Chris's words obviously meant absolutely nothing to him, he must have been trotting them out like the lines he used to speak when he was in the school play. His words and his promises were totally meaningless. Why did I believe this? – because the very next weekend, despite all the talking things through, becoming excited about the new baby, loving, kissing and making me all the promises in the world, and even more important, despite knowing that as I was pregnant, and that any shock or upset could be dangerous for me, he made no excuses, he simply left the flat and went back down to London. It was totally unbelievable – he said that he could not get Valerie out of his mind and he had to see her. My reaction was an utter surprise to me, I simply said nothing, I stood there and let him go. Then my mind simply clicked straight into gear and I proceeded to pack for

Simon and myself. The following day I was back in Leicester with Mum and Dad and threw my suitcase through the doors at Gardner & Millhouse. I told them everything and of course I could stay till I had the baby. I found a furnished house for rent near to the town centre, the same type as our first home and I took it.

That was it with Chris. It was a pattern that would not go away and I had to move on with my life, get my priorities right and keep happy for Simon and for this new baby. I knew that I really had got to pull myself out of this web of lies and deceit and make a secure and normal home and full life for my two children, my sanity depended upon this kind of normality.

I remember one day extremely clearly, on my way to work and feeling like the side of a house, a guy on the back of a lorry parked in our street gave a loud wolf whistle. I looked round to see who he was whistling at and he took me completely by surprise when he said:

"Yes darlin', that was for you – I wish I had been the fella that did that to you! You are lovely." gesturing at my bump. I have often wondered if I should have been insulted but I have to confess to having been utterly flattered. A little feeling inside of me started to tell me it was not possible for me to be that ugly and undesirable as Chris was making me feel, especially if other men could still fancy me when I was very pregnant and feeling at my worst.

CHAPTER THIRTEEN

A new life is born

It was now 1965 and some form of normality had returned to my life. I felt quite safe and secure in the little house, and although the loneliness at night when Simon had been put to bed was intolerable. I was managing to keep my feelings in check and be a happy Mum to the new baby now growing rapidly inside of me. As I sat there one evening, knitting away for the new layette for the baby, there came a knock at the door. I was not used to having evening callers and wondered who it could be. There he stood, the man himself – Chris – why was I not surprised? Despite making my mother promise me faithfully that she would not part with my address to anyone, she must have just given in yet again. Mum was really as bad as me when it came to resisting Chris's lies and pleadings, how could I blame her? Oh God. Have I really to go through all this scenario all over again?

Chris persuaded me that he had to come in. The baby was now almost due and his conscience would not leave him in peace where I was concerned. He told me that he had left BMC and wanted desperately for us to begin yet again. He pestered me incessantly and kept on talking and talking, saying that he had come to terms with how badly he had treated us and come to the conclusion that we had to have a fresh start before the baby came. Why did I let it happen? Across the years, I can't truly answer that question but eventually I let him persuade me to take him back one more time. He had become pathetic – simpering, whimpering, a broken man. He didn't know what to do next.

I had listened to all of the diatribe and rapidly came to the conclusion that Public Relations threw too many temptations at him, which he obviously could not walk away from, (at this point I was to learn that the 'other woman' had in fact been several, not just one or two) and taking into account his love of all things in the great outdoors, I insisted that we all not only needed, but it was imperative, that we have a complete change in direction if we were going to be together for the arrival of this baby and completion of our family – if it was worth saving. He applied for, and got, a job with a farmer in Northamptonshire outside a little village called West Haddon. It involved helping to run the farm and a lovely little tied, thatched, cottage went with the job. We both fell in love with the place, so very much and instantly. We met and found that we had got the greatest of neighbours, Chrissie and Eric. They were a lovely 'homely' local couple, true country folk. He was the game warden for the farmer and Chrissie stayed home baking all day. Some lovely delicacies came over the wall each day including gorgeous fresh quails' eggs. This all helped, because as a farm labourer, Chris earned very little compared with his previous career.

Although nothing could remove the hurt and pain and degradation of the last months, nothing could take away from me the joy I felt with the impending birth of our new baby. I was so hopeful that it was a girl that I had decided on the names Zoe Elizabeth, but not given thought to the names for boys. Everyone said it would be a girl because of the way the bump laid and all the rest of those old wives tales.

Nevertheless, I just wanted the baby to be perfect, as we had gone through the Thalidomide scare during my pregnancy with Simon. I was very conscious of health during my pregnancies and ate and drank all the right things and – no tablets.

Up to now, two and half year old Simon had been virtually ignored by his paternal grandmother except for one weekend when she came over to the cottage with Father and asked if they could to take little Simon back with them for a holiday at the seaside. Of course I let him go. He deserved to be with both sets of his grandparents, but it took ages to get him back and finally we had to go over to Leicester and physically take him away and bring him back. She maintained that she wanted to keep him; she had decided that she would have been a much fitter person to bring him up; after all I was only a grocer's daughter – she could never stop rubbing that in, time after time.

We brought him back home and heard little from them until one weekend, not long before the birth of the second baby was due, she completely took my breath away. She had gone out and bought the baby a Victorian hooded wicker cradle on a stand and she had lined it beautifully in quilted satin and lace – I could barely contain myself, it was the most beautiful thing you have ever seen. I began to think that maybe she was not all bad. Maybe her thoughts of me were mellowing. Only time would tell.

The birth was now coming closer and I was getting larger and larger. Chris had spent some of his evenings watching the World Cup. I hated football and the baby seemed to sense this and every time, it seemed to me, that someone scored a goal, the baby would give me an almighty kick. The final of the Cup was now on the next evening, and Chris settled down and watched it. During the game at a particularly noisy part of the match, when the final goal was about to be scored, the baby decided to do a complete turn, one hundred and ninety degrees and I felt the head engage. Then I heard those immortal words "They think it's all over, well it is now". It was not yet over for me though, was it? I had places to go and things still to do and a baby to produce.

My date to have the baby came and again I was over my time by about two weeks. Simon and I walked the two miles into the village and back again, hoping that this would move something – to no avail. I called the Doctor from the payphone and begged to be induced again. He agreed and I was then admitted into the Barratt Maternity Home in Northampton for the birth to be brought on. As before, Chris did not come in with me when the baby was born, and once more I was totally alone. In fact, seeing the funny side of it, if I remember correctly, Chris was milking the cows at the time the baby was born. Robert Julian Brown, not Zoe Elizabeth, arrived at 12.20pm in the afternoon of July 14th 1966. I telephoned the farm when I got back to the ward and the farmer answered the phone. I asked for Chris to come to the hospital as the baby had arrived.

"Were it a bull or a heifer, lass?" the farmer asked me. I smiled to myself and told him that that news was privileged and it would have to wait till my husband knew first.

Chris arrived at visiting time and strode down the ward with a long stemmed rose, as before. The midwife thought that it was the most romantic gesture she had ever seen, I felt cheated out of my bouquet, one like all the other new mums had received. The nurse said that my rose was better. On thinking back now, I suppose it was, because I can't, even to this day, look at a red rose and not think of Chris.

We lived in the cottage for a few months and then the farmer approached Chris and said that he thought the little cottage was too small for four of us. My heart sank at this point, thinking that we were to be without a home again, but no – he went on to say that his second farm at Long Buckby was empty and he needed Chris to go and run it for him. Whilst being at the same time sad at leaving our dear little cottage, we were absolutely overjoyed with the gloriously large, detached farmhouse that went with this job. We went to see it and I fell in love with the farm straight away. The house was wonderful and it had an Aga type cooker just like the one at Congerstone, and the view was stunning in Northamptonshire. The house was set in the fields, away from the village and memories of country life came flooding back. What a perfect environment in which to bring up the children. We had sheep, cows, chickens and of course, a sheep dog called Fan. Chris seemed very happy out on the tractor and we were almost totally self-sufficient. The best of all was that we were away from any other women! Suddenly I realised that that was my idea of bliss, remove the temptation, remove the problem. I hoped that it would last forever. We had a lovely year in Long Buckby, and the children were both christened at the local church.

I suddenly became worried all over again because, during this time, I had gradually begun to notice little things about Chris that gave me cause for concern. He was quite a good artist, among his many talents, and after doing one drawing, he complained that his hands had "set" and he couldn't release them. He went to the Doctor who said that it must have been psychosomatic. Alarm bells started to ring again and I began to realise that Chris was quite a complicated and somewhat unstable character and was still not always ready to conform to the norm. I began to wonder whether this was another symptom of some undiagnosed illness or other, never mind the bump on the head and, if so, in just how many more forms could it manifest itself. I have to confess that these alarm bells would be slow to go away and I seemed to be held 'in suspension' in my mind. Looking back, I realise that I was mentally always looking over my shoulder all the time, wondering what life had in store next and dreading the outcome.

I did not have to wait for long. Chris came in from the fields one day. I suppose we had been at the farm just over one year by this time, and he told me that he had decided then that if it really were some kind of mental pressure being put on him, it must have been the lifestyle. So, to my astonishment, he decided that he would find a job back in Public Relations. My heart sank and I looked at him in total disbelief and with eyes pleading with his not to do this to us. Oh dear God, please No, not again, I prayed to myself. I cannot go through all this again.

Although we had been getting on really well, I would, from that time, begin to wonder when the next female was going to invade our marriage and family life. I can't say I was at all at peace about this suggestion of change yet again, in fact totally to the contrary, I desperately wanted for us to stay exactly as we were and for as long as we possibly could. It had been the only stable period in the whole of our short and fiery married life together. However, I was also aware that it was the man in those days who was considered the breadwinner and I always believed that he should be happy at whatever job he was doing to earn those pennies, so it was up to you to support your man, whatever the consequences. This feeling still kept coming back and back – here we go again!

At this same time that Chris was scanning the PR magazines for alternative jobs, my parents too began to look for a farm to buy, our property and lifestyle in Long Buckby re-kindling Daddies' passion for animals. I cannot say that Mum was keen, after all she was sixty years old now and the shop had taken its toll. Supermarkets had arrived big time and life was a struggle again. Daddy plumped for a small hill farm – no luxuries just back to basics – called Pen Cawr Mill in a place called Blaen-y-Coed, just outside Carmarthen and the shop was put up for sale. Mum knew it was going to be really hard. Their farm house, when I say it was less than basic, it was a dump, and extremely cold and damp.

To get over her forebodings, Daddy promised her a Rayburn cooker – her favourite form of cooking and heating, and of course if Daddy wanted something and he felt that he could do it, then he didn't so much expect her to come up to scratch and go along with him, he more or less demanded it. Mum, despite being tired and ready for a normal life and some peace and quiet, did as was expected of her as his wife, and went along with it. She would do anything to make Daddy happy and keep the peace. I really wondered how all these changes would affect our lives in the future, my Dad had shattered Mum's life so often and now mine was about to change and be shattered yet again too. It was only with the passing of a lot of years that I came to realise that, in fact, mine and my Mum's married lives were inextricably linked and so similar, but neither of us saw it at the time. No wonder they both understood Chris so well.

My Mum might have had to deal with the foibles of a man with the 'Good Life' syndrome, but my husband and the life that we led held something much more sinister than that. Although I had serious misgivings about everything at this point, I had no idea of the situation that was about to unfold.

I could not have anticipated the future, nor the enormous and life-shattering experiences that would definitely change my life, yet again, once and for all.

And all because of Chris.

CHAPTER FOURTEEN

From Welwyn to Wales

After applying for several positions which gained us nothing, Chris was offered, and went for an interview, as a Public Relations Executive with a drug company called Smith, Kline and French in a new town called Welwyn Garden City in Hertfordshire, just outside London. He was offered the position there and then at the interview, and he had accepted it, not bothering to chat to me about it first, no discussions about the children, about moving and changing our lifestyle yet again. These things were important and should have been decided together, especially when it involved turning our lives upside down all over again. He always did this and it was hurtful not to have any input before the big family decisions were finally made. He came back to the farm very excited about the whole project, especially as there was a lovely brand new house for rent with the job, he had been to see it and said that it was perfect for us all and ready for us to move into. All totally decided by his goodself.

My children were lovely, they were my life and we had all had some semblance of normality for a short time, but I knew I had to move on with him. He had completely lost interest in our way of life down on the farm and without him, there was no farm, no money and no home. It had served its purpose and been very theraputic but now life was dull and his brain needed more taxing, or so he said! Chris was an extremely creative and talented man and he needed the accolades. However, I had a three and a half year old and a nine month old baby, and here we were and moving our family yet again, despite the plus side of the situation which he found so positive.

And so we moved to Welwyn Garden City and it soon became obvious that we needed extra money to live in that area and so, reluctantly, I went back to work. I found a local baby minder who was really nice, but I seemed to have had no time at all to spend with this new baby of mine and his elder brother who I had not seen growing up at all, as a mother I felt very cheated. I read an advert in the local evening paper and there it was, made for me, a local firm of Solicitors were looking for a secretary/ p.a to one of the Senior Partners. I was offered the position on the spot and accepted.

We began making lots of new friends and got to know the neighbours quite quickly but as life settled into a new routine for all of us, so I began to sense things just were not quite right with Chris – yet again! You couldn't actually put your finger on anything specific but he seemed almost a stranger to me, he didn't want to talk about work, he didn't want to discuss anything; he sort of went into himself and, what was even more difficult to bear, despite this supposed wonderful new and promising start, there was still no real family life. What road were we now about to go down, I wondered?

I waved him off to work one morning wishing him luck as he had to deliver an important presentation that afternoon. I took the children to the baby minder and walked on to work as usual. Just after lunch time, I received a call at my office from Chris's Company, asking me if I had seen him. They did not want to worry me unnecessarily but, apparently, he got up to give his presentation and then suddenly ran out of the room and they could not find him. I tried to ring home, but there was no reply. I left work and ran all the way home, my mind racing and darting to and fro in a complete frenzy, What was wrong, what could have happened to him to make him act in the way he had, and why?

When I got home, I hammered and hammered at the front and then the back door. There was just complete silence, no response at all. I was frantic. Thank God for my rock climbing experience because I had to climb the side of the house to get in through the bathroom window, I couldn't unlock the front or back doors. All the curtains were drawn. I found Chris in our bedroom, crouched on the floor in the corner. I couldn't get him to talk or respond in any way, he was quaking and staring ahead, sucking his fingers like a dummy. I called the doctor and he was taken by ambulance to the local hospital. I saw my own husband restrained on a trolley and sedated. They admitted him for psychiatric analysis. After about two weeks of test after test, I was to learn that his condition was serious, he was diagnosed as being an extreme 'Social Psychopath'. This sounded very frightening and the doctors did their best to explain it to me, but the realms of psychiatry and mental illness were still in their infancy, but, apparently, part of the condition was related to his mother and part to the fact that he could not accept 'a normal' lifestyle and the way things should be. This news devastated me. Apparently there was no known cure for his condition and the psychiatrists treating him said that he was so devious, he would find out what drugs they were trying out on him and go up to the hospital library, read up on it, and then show the relevant symptoms. He was very sly and clever, he had an uncanny sense of what would hurt me most and, without any thoughts of his actions, he would make his moves, leaving me weeping and at a loss to know what to do next – apparently, I was and had been his 'target' and this would continue to be so. It would have happened to any of the women that Mother preferred he be with, it was not down to a matter of choosing me, or someone else as a victim, it was just him and the way he was.

Unlike a raving mad murderer – which is usually what being a psychopath means, Chris's type, who seem to be apparently normal people, have a profound personality disorder that makes them a serious *psychological* threat to anyone with whom they come into contact, never mind those with whom they form close relationships. Chris was not 'mad' in the sense of the word that we normally understand it, of being detached from what is reality. Instead, he tended to concentrate on what made me vulnerable and how he could fit this in with the way he wanted to act, if that makes sense. His apparent lack of depth of love, his eccentric ways and total deceitfulness ate at everything that Chris touched or was ever to touch in the end, but most especially me and inevitably, his children.

This included his career except that his inexplicable charm overrode everything else and he was always very successful at what he did. He was very unpredictable and sly. I remembered the wedding dress and engagement incident whilst we were still married. He was always so utterly charming and showed absolutely no genuine remorse for anything he did, firmly believing that having another try at it, all would turn out well in the end. The truth was that all he succeeded in doing was destroying the status quo and painfully damaging us – his family that loved him, time after time, after time. In my thinking at that time it seemed to me that he did not seem able to take on board that he was responsible for this family unit, or if he did, then, in reality, he did not want that responsibility, but now I know that he, in fact, did not know.

With hindsight, I realise that Chris had a personality disorder from way back long before I met him and borne out by his Mother's action in taking him to a phrenologist. Whilst he was under treatment at Welwyn Garden City Hospital there was a strict order in place forbidding her to be allowed anywhere near him. She was considered a serious and dangerous threat to his mental stability.

She always maintained that everything that went wrong for Chris was due to the bump to his head, and the fact that he had married the wrong girl. But I came to see much deeper than that. Her urges to find him a suitable marriage partner, for which I did not fit the bill, was her last ditch hope that it would settle him down and make him face life more realistically. I now believe that he insisted on marrying me simply to go against her wishes, another symptom of the illness – non-conformity to the norm. The truth was that he had used me, because he knew that it would anger and thwart his mother. To him I was only just a weapon to be used against her. Sadly, it only ended up with me, and of course ultimately, the children, left to suffer the consequences. To other people he was outwardly the epitome of charm itself and highly successful. To us, his family, he showed total disregard, no real husbandly or fatherly affection and no interest in what we did, nor whether we suffered as a result of his actions, nor a realisation of the way he used us and the resultant suffering. One thing I noticed was that Chris seemed proud of the fact that he had now been "labelled" with a medical condition. He rose to the expectations of the diagnosis splendidly and, of course, it justified all his actions, especially when things went wrong.

However, they treated him as best they could and he

was allowed home. He would not go back to Smith Kline and French, he simply could not face them after his breakdown. Instead, he went into London for the day to look around. He strolled off the street into the offices of J. Walter Thompson, a famous advertising company, and simply asked them for a job. He was interviewed and they took him on there and then, gave him his own office and secretary. As for me? Well I just prayed!

During his time not working, I got a job in London, (the pay was much higher than in Welwyn). I took a job in Cavendish Square with a firm of Solicitors. My role was to prepare the Briefs to Counsel for all the shoplifting cases for John Lewis of Oxford Street. It was enormously interesting and responsible work, but I found life very hard. Simon had started to school and Robbie was growing. Like Simon, I missed his first teeth, first steps, and I came home every evening to be given all his progress by the baby minder and it hurt, by God how it hurt. It was just the way the lady who had minded Simon had charted his progress to me. I adored my children, they were my life and despite his somewhat lack of fatherly emotions, I still idolised, worshipped and adored my handsome husband. What woman, it seemed, didn't, wouldn't or hadn't and what was it about him that lured me back to him time and time again? I had a total inability to say no to this man, even though in my heart of hearts, I always knew that his promises meant nothing and it would always end in tragedy, one way or the other.

Of course, once back in public relations, the business trips raised their heads again with assignments, here, there and everywhere. He came home at erratic times, quite frequently ringing home to say that he was bringing someone to dinner whom he had to entertain and I had to come up with something 'special'. By this time, I had become an interested, inquisitive and increasingly accomplished cook and hostess.

Christmas came and apparently, so Chris said, wives of the Executives were not invited to the staff Christmas Party – an evening event in formal dress he told me. He would stay in London overnight he said. I was hurt, disappointed and suspicious for every good reason. I had even thought of casually ringing his secretary and asking her if the dress was formal or informal as an excuse to find out if wives were really not welcome but I was desperately trying to trust him and felt that I could not do that to him. It would have caused problems at his company and for him, but he made it so difficult.

A few weeks later, we were invited to the Hogs Back Hotel to his secretary's twenty first birthday dinner and party. I wondered how he had not been able to get out of taking me to this one, but apparently all other partners were invited. I decided that I would make a really extra special effort for him and for my self esteem, after all I had not met most of these people yet and he mixed with them every day. I felt I needed to make some kind of statement. I sat at my sewing machine and made myself a long, black, watered taffeta evening skirt and Victorian style lace-trimmed blouse with high neck and 'leg of mutton' sleeves. I had started to have my hair done with blonde highlights at this time and hairpieces were the fashion. I piled my hair up on top with my hairpiece and did a twirl for the children and babysitters – our good friends Kathy and Doug. They said I looked like someone off the movie set, and I must say I did feel glamorous.

We had a wonderful dinner, and it was the first time that I had seen a chef present the grouse dressed with the tail feathers and beautifully served. We also had raspberry sorbet, another first for me, and I was so thrilled when I asked to meet the chef, who kindly gave me his recipes and explained some of the techniques to me.

During the course of the evening, Chris had introduced me to all the people he worked with, including his secretary whose birthday it was, and she was a very pretty blonde girl who seemed obviously very comfortable in Chris' presence. Later on, I was sitting with a group of his associates and one of the female guests asked me why I had not been at the previous function. Of course, I made an excuse, but that was like an arrow to the heart, which one was he interested in? I wondered. I decided to keep this one to myself, I couldn't face going through all the traumas and excuses and lies all over again. However, I did notice that Chris seemed to dance an awful lot with his secretary, but I tried not to dwell too much on that and I was certainly not devoid of partners, including Chris himself. Later on in the evening Chris actually asked me to dance with him and at one point we were dancing a slow number. He pressed his body closely to mine as we swayed to the time of the music, and I knew instinctively as he kissed the side of my neck gently and tenderly that we would be making love that night. I was right. It was a wonderful night, too – why, oh why, couldn't we be like this all the time? He was still the man I had first fallen in love with and married, and surely this was how truly loving married people should always be, bound together with this love that endures. Obviously not for me though.

This all made me try to take a double take at everything, so I tried to shrug off the feelings of foreboding. Everything was fine, I tried to convince myself. But, try as I might however, I still felt there was some kind of an atmosphere amongst everyone from J. Walter Thompson, all present at breakfast as we came into the dining room. It was as if all of their hackles rose in the backs of their necks at one and the same time and they seemed to be shuffling their feet and feeling uncomfortable. Did all these people know something that I didn't?

Of course, before long I was to discover that everyone at JWT knew that he was having an affair with his secretary and the whole scenario started all over again. It wasn't that he didn't love me, he told me. I became very nervous and unhappy all over again. Chris was also drinking very heavily and even taking money from my purse for drinks and denying it when confronted. Friends, Kathy and Doug were great comforts during this time, and Doug was sure it was only a passing phase – if only he knew! He admired Chris so much as he had helped Doug to get into public relations, so there was a bond of loyalty there.

Things began to slide. I discovered that there were bills not paid, they were going to cut off our electricity also. In utter desperation I phoned Father and he tried to talk to Chris, but to no avail. Eventually, they did cut off the electricity and I was heating up food for the children over a candle! In the end, without telling my Dad, my mother sold her beautiful opal pendant which he had bought her in India – I wore it on our wedding day – and she sent me the money to pay the bill.

The drinking was now a complete nightmare and just to make matters worse, yet again, Chris just walked out and left his job in London without a word to me. We were comparatively happy in this house in Welwyn, I thought he was doing his job very successfully, and then the same old pattern set in all over again. He had been at J. Walter Thompson for what seemed no time and suddenly he decided that he was going to work from home. I had set him up an office in our spare bedroom for his birthday, desk, leather chair, typewriter, telephone etc., and he was getting freelance work, which appeared to be going quite well, but not well enough to justify his last actions or to support us entirely. At this time also, my parents had bought the farm in Wales and my brother David, was living in it till my parents could sell the shop and move down. Everything around me seemed to be moving so fast, but all so much in turmoil. I began to get nervous all over again and seemed to be lying in wait for the next disaster to leak out of the woodwork. I didn't have to wait long.

I came home from my job in London one evening and as I turned the corner to go to our home, I could see vans and cars parked outside. To my horror, all our belongings were going out of the front door, my treasured sewing cabinet, sewing machine, his new office chair and desk. When I reached home, it was all gone – everything but one mattress in the dining room for all four of us to sleep that night, and our clothes, packed into suitcases, on top of the car. Chris just matter of factly told me that he was taking me and the children back to my parents in Leicester and he was going to the farm in Wales to live till he could find us a home, and he would be setting up a farm holiday scheme he had dreamt up. Just like that! Our wonderful home in Welwyn, all gone, all our wedding presents, things other people had given to us as presents over time, all our familiar furniture and furnishings which made up the home, all gone and our future again in jeopardy. I was devastated, heartbroken, destroyed, all wiped out on the whim of an afternoon and a so-called bright idea. Words, and it seemed to me God too, just failed me.

We arrived at the shop the next day, to my parents' utter disbelief, where we were deposited and Chris managed to persuade my parents that it was for the best and that he should live on the farm and help David for a while. I am sure, by this time, my mother certainly could see some of the reasons why I was so completely shattered and dismayed by these latest actions, but Daddy just seemed to go along with everything. Chris then got into the car and set off for Wales and said he would send for me when he had found us a home.

Of course, I immediately set about finding myself a job, which I did the same day. I just threw my suitcase through the door at good old Gardiner and Millhouse – they knew the situation so well by this time, nothing was even said. Chris had given me the money from the sale of the belongings and said that he would sign on the dole when he got to Carmarthen and he could manage on that money, not taking into account the children and my share of it and, like a fool, I opened a joint account in our local Building Society, with the proceeds of sale of our home, and into which I was trying to put a little each week out of my wages. It was obvious to everyone that I was beginning to be chipped away at bit by bit and big time. It all became so much harder and trying to hide it from the children was a nightmare when my heart inside and self esteem were completely shattered.

I went to the Building Society to put some money in and found the balance had been going steadily down, through their branch in Carmarthen. I phoned the farm. I was so furious, it could only have gone on booze. David said that he had thrown Chris out – he was having an affair with the landlady of their local pub. I said that it was a pity he wasn't worth even his booze bill on the side!

My parents and I had a long talk. They had sold the shop and were getting ready to move to the farm. We could not go too, their farm house had only two bedrooms and David had one of those. Chris had found a small cottage outside Carmarthen right on the edge of the river Towy. He wanted me with him. My turmoil was unbelievable. Why did he want me back? Where could I go, I had no idea? Why did I go? I am not sure I can answer that, except to say that Simon was seven and Rob nearly four and I was so, so tired of it all, the constant moving, unsettling, changing schools and always at the back of it all, I still so desperately loved Chris, and maybe this time would be different, maybe it would be the last. What is it that keeps one trying again and again? Certainly, not how Chris felt about me, he obviously had little concern for either me, or the children.

And so, Chris came to fetch me, excuses about the landlady at the ready, and down to Carmarthen we travelled. Thinking back now, with all the turmoil in our lives at this time, I never took the time to look at the setting of this little cottage on the banks of the River Towy, the little coracles and the local fishermen fishing for wonderful sea trout and taking their catches back to sell to the restaurants, or to take home to their families, all the idyllic things that should have appealed to my romantic and earthly love of the countryside and nature itself. Everything here should have been perfect, back to nature, but it was all so far removed from that. It was a positive nightmare.

Chris had already signed on the dole, he had used up all the money in the Building Society and I managed to find myself a job, though only part-time, as secretary to the local Solicitor/Coroner. I typed everything from petitions to post mortems! Chris was pursuing his ideas for a farm holiday scheme, to buy up hill farms and turn them into leisure centres, with pony trekking, walking, rambling, climbing and each unit teaching self-sufficiency. Now when I think about it, it was brilliant and he was way ahead of his time – these places are there now. He went to see all the banks and got outline funding from one of them for £250,000 – an absolute fortune in those days. The problem was that it was conditional upon us doing it as a team – me doing the cooking and helping run the whole set up. The same day he got the offer of the loan, I found out that he was having an affair with a woman who lived about a mile from us; her husband was away serving with Trinity House on the lighthouse ships. I was devastated and very, very angry. I had reached the absolute end of my tether, I was turning into a completely broken woman – I had no self esteem, no heart to continue so, I flatly refused to have anything to do with his farm holiday scheme. This annoyed Chris greatly. He didn't see that I should take this attitude – after all it was only a dalliance on the side with this woman, – he was married to me; what was I worried about! This man was unbelievable in every sense of the word.

When I got home from work that day, I went into the children's bedroom to put them to bed. The house was so damp that there was mould growing on their blankets! My babies were sleeping in dank and mouldy surroundings. What had I brought my children to, and look at what I had ended up as. That was it, I could not take any more. I phoned Kath and Doug and asked them if they could lend me the money to get back to Leicester. Mum and Dad were still waiting for the final move, I could go to them for a couple of days till I got sorted – yes that was it. My mind was racing.

When the money arrived, having warned my boss what was happening, I packed up all I could carry and took the children to the railway station and we caught the train to Leicester. As I sat by the window watching the hedgerows fly by, the children playing excitedly on their very first train journey, I couldn't get the visions out of my mind of the long, white, hairy mould growing on the damp beds. What manner of father was it that could reduce his family to those conditions and seem totally oblivious to it all. Brought up by loving parents, pony trekking, rambling, rowing and climbing with his father, a very expensive and caring school life and everything so secure, all this for Chris so why was this not all there for *his* sons? We were in Wales, for God's sake; why on earth did my children not have small walking boots and learning the rudiments of climbing with their father, going on long walks, taking in the beauty that is so much Wales, doing map reading and plotting their routes together, all the things that Chris had been given as a boy and which were so solid and character building. My sons had nothing from their father, not even his time.

Where was he when they needed school uniforms, on the day before Christmas where was he when we were all decorating the tree, buying their little presents, on school parent days – all the things, despite my own Dad's strictness and frigidity, but who was always there for me. Nice homes, warm blankets, roaring fires and loving care. It was obvious that these things had never entered Chris's head – no man should have put his family through all that we had suffered and continued to suffer. We had no real home, no savings, no belongings and what seemed worst of all, nothing bright in the future to look forward to. We just seemed to go on and on, trudging from one place and job and home to another, but going further and further down in every respect. My heart was breaking, how much more could I possibly take? I sobbed inside, I couldn't let the children see and feel my heartbreak.

Within two days of reaching Mum and Dad, I found a job with a firm of Solicitors quite near the YWCA where this all seemed to begin. I found a ground floor flat near to Mum and Dad, and although they would soon be leaving for Wales, I knew my hometown so well and relatives and friends were not far. The flat was grotty, but it was going to be mine and in a complete state of mind of *deja vu*, I set about trying to start again. My first child minder stepped into the breach again. This was all so unsettling for the children – both had attended school in Carmarthen, Robbie having started when he was four and I was moving them yet again – but what else could I do?

It was also our 8th wedding anniversary at this time, something which Chris never ever remembered after the first one. As I looked out of my office window, across the road was a photographer's studio and shop and he specialised in portraits. I don't know what made me do it, but I wanted to have for myself a photograph which would be some kind of proof that, at a mere twenty six years of age, I maybe was not as ugly as Chris was making me feel inside right now. I needed something to document that all this pain and hurt were not getting the better of me, were not showing in my face and my demeanour. This image for other people was always so important to me, vanity maybe, I don't really know. So, in my lunch hour I went over and asked for a portrait to be done and the little old man in the shop was wonderful. He set up one of these old fashioned tripod cameras with the flash gun that was sparked off and left smoke trailing everywhere. He told me to look at the camera and think of something in my life which had given me the most pleasure or love. I looked into the lens and remembered our night at Derwentwater the week before our wedding. What a wonderful lover I was married to – as several other women could confirm – but that was not the thought on my mind as the gun went off.

The photographer put a huge copy of the photograph in his front window and it remained there for weeks staring at me and, as I looked deep into my own eyes, I still could not see beauty, just the grocer's daughter!

Father phoned me that night and said that Chris had told him what had happened – yet again (omitting the other woman, of course) and he asked me what I intended to do. I said that I had found myself a job and a flat and that I intended moving in as soon as possible. He asked me if he could come the next day and see the flat with me, he said he was very concerned for both me and the boys and I believe he knew that a lot of this had been caused by his wife's scheming and interfering in the past and especially with the way Chris was.

When he saw the flat, toilet blocked and stinking, very little furniture, old dirty net curtains, carpets and furniture, he became very upset.

"Jacqui, I want to move you into a house" he said.

I protested that I wanted to stand on my own feet this time and move on without his son, but thankfully he insisted. He just went out there and then and bought us a house on the Loughborough Road, just outside Leicester, and he furnished it for us. When he took me in, I was overjoyed. It was lovely and I suddenly felt a little more safe. I could not lose this home, it was in Chris's father's name and would remain so, it was for the grandchildren, I convinced myself. Then came the crunch – to keep the house, I had to give Chris one more chance, take it or leave it. How could Father be so cold and calculating? I thought he was trying to give me and his grandchildren a new and safely secure start without all the traumas of the past, but no,he was making a last ditch attempt to help his son whom he adored back to normality and he thought that by holding the house over our heads, this would make Chris suddenly come to some kind of normality. Father obviously was totally unaware of the severity or even the nature of his own son's illness, to him all Chris had to do was pull himself together and stop playing around. It was not as simple as that was it? So, with a great deal of reluctance and reservation but most of all, with the children at the forefront of my mind, I agreed.

And so, Chris was summoned by his father and came back from Wales with just his clothes and the car, nothing else to show for all that we had been put through. I cannot pretend that I was overjoyed, but at least the boys were safe, I convinced myself. We began the search for a new job for him and I heard of one with a PR Company with a branch office in Loughborough. He went for the interview, and of course, he got the job – Mr. Charm! He was to handle the Watney Mann account – a major company of brewers based in Northampton with a chain of public houses.

If God or someone else could have predicted for me where this latest adventure was going to lead, I think that I would have ended everything there and then, in one way or another....

CHAPTER FIFTEEN

'The Rose and Castle'

Chris had only been with the new job for a few weeks, when he went to a formal dinner after he had handled the launch of a new public house. At the dinner, the General Manager, a Mr. Ashton, said he he was very impressed with Chris' performance, not only with the launch, but his whole demeanour and the way he 'handled' himself. He went on to say that he thought Chris would make an ideal landlord and had he ever considered the licensed trade for a career – silly question! He suggested that Chris bring me to dinner the next evening. Chris had managed to do it yet again, his

"The Rose and Castle Inn", Braunston, Northamptonshire 1972

great charm and smooth sophisticated air obviously appealed to Mr. Ashton greatly, and now I was to be vetted by the great man. Of course, Chris knew that I would not let him down and would be a credit to him – the way that I was brought up to be.

We were – unusually – formally offered a pub there and then. Before I knew where we were, we were on our way again, despite the protestations of Father, who thought it was time that Chris settled down. This was the first time I ever remember him voicing his opinion and trying to influence his son to make the right decision. He had just bought us this lovely home, which was safe and ours as long as Chris behaved and here we were again – off on Chris' next jaunt. I cannot pretend that I wanted it to happen, it was the last thing I wanted for my children, and of course, with hindsight I should have stood my ground and refused to go, as I knew I had the backing of Father, but the job was offered to us. Chris accepted it without any discussion with me, and we were then off for one week basic training in a pub called The Wyken Pippin in Coventry. A Mr. and Mrs. Taylor were to train us and my very first time behind the bar – shaking with fear – I was asked for a Bloody Mary with all the trimmings. I was so proud to serve it until I realised that I had put angostura bitters in instead of Worcester sauce! Fortunately it was spotted by Mr. Taylor before the customer drank it.

I was terrified of this change in my career. I had never even dreamed of this kind of life. I was a trained legal secretary and proud of it. However, we moved into the Rose and Castle as it was then, in the little village of Braunston, right beside the Grand Union Canal in Northamptonshire. This was to be one of the first pubs for Watneys with food and it sported a beautiful restaurant with cocktail bar, which was built as a replica of a narrow boat (the old canal barges) and it ran parallel to the canal. The two barges 'The Rose' and 'The Castle' were moored up outside for the grand opening. I got to 'launch' the new venture with the High Sheriff of Northamptonshire, and we smashed the bottle of champagne over the bow in true nautical fashion!

We had about thirty staff, including waitresses, bar staff, cleaners, chefs, cooks, and ancillary workers. I have to say, it was a wonderful pub. People not in the know thought I just swanned about being decorative – little did they know. Chris left everything to me like staff duties, rotas, training, menus, etc., and I had to make these people believe that I knew not only what I was doing, knew their jobs better than themselves and, at the same time, was also completely competent and adept at running every aspect of this establishment. With exceptional help from the Chefs, I learned exceedingly quickly, and took in everything that I was told. I took care of food supplies etc., and ran the cocktail bar and restaurant whilst Chris took care of the main bars and the books, the money and wages.

Chris began to drink exceedingly heavily from the word go, because of course, it was there literally "on tap"! and most nights, our local farm workers, nice young guys, would slip round the back of the pub and carry Chris up to bed for me, he would be completely out of it. I had been learning to drive for years, since the time of our engagement, but had never taken a test. We had a vehicle allocated to the pub and I used to have to cash up, close the pub, leave someone with the children and then drive the staff home at night because my husband was incapable of driving in that state. The only job I did not even touch was the book-keeping and banking. The ironic thing about the whole set-up was that here I was covering for a husband who became completely incapable and, at this time, women could not hold a liquor licence in their own right but, with the help of very loyal staff who picked up very quickly on what had been happening, I was able to cover for Chris to a great extent and, for all this mayhem, the pub seemed to be running smoothly. I had to keep our personal problems private and act my way through each desperate day – our home depended on it.

He and I rowed a lot due to his drinking at this time and through suspicions and rumours, I heard that he stopped from time to time when out at a small hotel in Daventry which was run by a very nice lady and her two glamorous daughters – both unmarried, young and regularly very available. They did not seem to mind that the men were married. These stop-offs became more and more frequent but I tried hard, not only from the point of view of running the business, including keeping problems away from the staff, but mainly for the sake of the boys, to hide my feelings and pray that everything would be alright. I told you there was some actress in me!

One day, during a usually busy lunch-time, a very distinguished man came through the main doors and up to the bar. He asked for the Landlord, and Chris being out yet again, I introduced myself. He was tall, with a white moustache and shoulder length grey hair, with a lovely soft American accent, and sporting an elegant Yves St. Laurent shirt. He made an immediate deep impression on me and said that his name was Bill McCrow and he was the Art Director on a film that was to be made in our village, and did we have any rental accommodation. We had several rooms, and I took him upstairs to show him around. Apart from the letting rooms, we had a disused ballroom, a huge room with bar, high ceiling and a raised skylight structure in the central roof. He said it would make a perfect studio and could he have it. I said yes and so Bill and several of the crew moved in there and then and stayed at the pub.

The first thing to arrive in Bill's luggage was a whole case each of Tequila and Talisker Malt Whisky! The film was called "Running Scared" and the stars were Gayle Hunnicutt, Robert Powell and Barry Morse, and David Hemmings – husband of Gayle Hunnicutt – was the producer. They were a great bunch of people and it was wonderful because they spoiled us and arranged all sorts of surprises as special treats for helping them, such as a punt in the middle of the canal for myself and the boys to watch a yellow sports car catapulted over a bridge and into the canal, and trips with all the stars and crew up the canal on narrowboats with picnics and Bucks Fizz to help the journey along. When they left at the end of filming, the unit treated Simon and Rob to a new bicycle each with shiny bells. We had never been anywhere long enough nor had the funds to buy them cycles before. What an absolutely great gesture and the boys were so thrilled. The wardrobe mistress also gave me a beautiful long Edwardian style dress which she designed herself and made for me. I treasured it for years.

Bill McCrow became a very close friend and confidante of mine. He had a shoulder and a Tequila ready most nights when Chris was either drunk or not yet home by midnight. I wonder where he could have been? I also stayed with Bill and his wife in London and was introduced to the great delights of Biba – the great 'in' shop of the time – where I treated myself to an extremely elegant, beautifully tailored jersey dress in a delicate shade of smoky aubergine, and thigh length, high heeled, suede boots in the same shade. Suddenly I felt very sexy somehow. It was not a feeling I had had much of previously. Bill made me feel as if I were someone of worth and he liked me very much as a person. It was a very good friendship. There were no sexual overtones, I just felt very comfortable with him and I knew that he was fond of me, as I was of him.

I began to notice that other men too were becoming regular customers and I found myself very much in demand. One particular regular, a German gentleman called Klaus came in every night and lingered as long as he could. He was a very desirable and exceedingly good looking guy, who never took his eyes off me from the time he came in to the time he left and he was always trying to make conversation with me. Under other circumstances... but he was also heavily and obviously very married, and everyone knew it. He started to put the juke box on as soon as he came in and always played my favourite song – Harry Neilson singing "Without You" – it did what those songs are supposed to do, hit me right where it hurt. You can always make the words fit the occasion I suppose. He also bought me a copy of the disc and gave it to me and said whenever I played it, I should always think of him. I never did, it would always be Chris that I would remember, and still do.

I don't recall responding much to this new found attention from the men around me at the time, as I felt so utterly miserable and degraded inside. But it obviously embedded itself quietly somewhere, as I started to feel less "dowdy" than I had for a long time. I was always, and still am, very conscious of my appearance and, for myself, have always tried to be smart and well groomed – that hadn't changed, yet suddenly I had this feeling of elegance and stature creeping into my life. Strange.

Just because I was well groomed, make-up, hair and dress always perfect, this did not affect the many and varied things I had to face each day in this new career of mine. I was always the one who was called to see to awkward or potentially threatening customers – drink can be evil. So I had to know how to handle myself. One such incident involved a regular, a local villager, who was a little simple and needed regular medication to stop him being violent.

Overdue for treatment and over the top on beer, he tried one night to attack me from behind, in the public bar. I bent forward, pulled his trouser bottoms through my legs, and this totally took his feet from under him and floored him, hitting his head with quite a bump on the way down. The bar boys did a double take, I felt quite self-satisfied, it had had the effect I wanted. He never approached me again and always drank up and left promptly when I called time. That situation, I had not been trained for, it was pure instinct, but I went up a considerable number of notches in the eyes of the public bar boys – mostly strapping farmer's lads!

I was sad when the time came for the film crew to leave as it had been a very pleasant and interesting period in our lives, but leave they did. Life went on, but somehow I was now holding my head a little higher and quietly enjoying the responsibility and power, if that is the right word, of being in charge. All the staff needed me and let me know it. Chris was either not around or drunk, and I needed to give them confidence and hold on to our jobs to keep our home and money coming in, so cope I had to, and cope I damned well did.

The last Saturday before Christmas that year, Chris's Aunt Daisy had booked a Christmas dinner for her Company, Olivetti Typewriter Company, and they were to come by coach from Leicester. We also had *á la carte* reservations besides and this filled the restaurant to capacity, about one hundred covers. On the Friday evening, Chris came in as the restaurant was closing down for the night. He had been out all evening and he had been drinking heavily. He went into the kitchen and without a word to me or anyone, he stood there and sacked all the kitchen staff on the spot – the whole lot: chefs, commis-chefs, the cook, girls who made the starters – all fired. The long and short of it was we had to honour the reservations. It was far too late to cancel and, in any event I couldn't get in touch with all who had reserved, as we had no phone numbers to reach them. There was nothing I could do to unravel this disaster in the time available.

The following morning, Chris still asleep from his drunken stupor, and certainly not the time for recriminations, though it did cross my mind that he may have noticed that the pub was running exceedingly efficiently under my care and it could have been jealousy on his part and the only way to get back at me would be to watch me fail. With this thought firmly embedded in my mind and now working as a sort of catalyst, spurring me on to go ahead, I vowed that I would stand firm and get through this day and evening as best I could and with total determination. I went to the kitchens, sent for Vi, one of my sensible bar ladies from the village, two of my children's nannies and anyone I could rope in and asked them all for their help. They were all great, they all rallied round. I had never cooked on catering equipment before, but I made myself get on with it and not let the staff know, I knew my menu, I did all my preparations, and just kept telling myself that it was like having ten members of the family in for dinner, only ten times over – just multiply everything by ten girl! My common sense prevailed and I set about my first session as Chef.

We did it. One hundred meals went out that night and glasses of wine just kept on coming into the kitchen for the Chef! (Shame, I didn't really drink in those days, apart from a shot or two of Bill's Tequilas). When it was all over, I changed and went out through the back of the kitchens to the cocktail bar. A regular took one look at me and ordered a large scotch and lemonade for me. Down it went and I just burst into tears and sobbed with relief. It was nearly over. I took a deep breath and entered the restaurant. Aunt Daisy stood up and raised a glass to myself, and the bar staff and the rest of the restaurant stood up too, and they all clapped. I felt so proud – wow, what a moment!

When I went through the restaurant orders the next day, I had done fifty Christmas meals, plus T bone steaks, sirloins and fillets in sauces, trout, gammons, dover sole, mixed grills and not one complaint – it was all perfect. I have never discovered where this talent came from, but sheer guts and determination had a great deal to do with it that night, I can tell you. I have never been able to bear 'losing face', something for which I have to thank my father.

I never confronted Chris over his actions with the chefs and other staff, as he could never remember the next day what he had done the night before. By this time, my relationship with our Managers at the Brewery had become quite special. Rather than risk any trouble from "Head Office", to cover Chris's actions, I had to fabricate a tale about the Chef and his immediate team stealing stock. Because I was the one so involved with the restaurant, the Brewery seemed to buy the story that I had gone to Chris with the problem, and only then he had taken the initiative to fire them on the spot as an example to the other staff. I was trying so damned hard to keep our home and our jobs and not let the Brewery realise what I was fighting. It was becoming more and more obvious that Chris was well on the way to no return and I was trying desperately in my mind to lead us through this and come out safe at the end, one way or the other and by fair means or foul – this worm was actually now beginning to turn, and not before time.

The Christmas hurdle out of the way, we engaged new staff, which also developed into a potentially dangerous situation. We took on a chef, who was living in with us, only to discover that he had knifed someone in his past. I cannot now remember how this came to light, because we did all the usual professional checks, but we had to have the brewery and police there whilst he was dismissed, because he carried his bag of knives with him wherever he went. He left reluctantly, but thankfully, that was the last we saw of him.

All of these recent events resulted in the inevitable. Things between Chris and I became steadily worse, he was doing less and less work and drinking more and more, and when he said that he needed to get away for a weekend back to the Lake District, to try and sort himself out, I agreed, because life was much easier without the tension and overhanging cloud of his brooding drunken presence. Everyone breathed a sigh of relief when he had gone. It was like living with a time bomb! However, on his return Chris did another of his 'tricks', he left a piece of paper sticking out of the breast pocket on his jacket as always, where it would obviously be seen and, just for good measure, he left the jacket hanging outside the wardrobe. Of course, I took it out and took a look. Oh, please God, no! not again, I remember saying to myself. Of course, it was a receipt for a double room in the name of Mr. and Mrs. Brown for that weekend in the Lake District. Our favourite courting place! How could he take anyone else there?"

I went down to the restaurant kitchen, and was unpacking trout, when Chris came in. I was so totally devastated and heartbroken and I could hold myself no longer and asked him what the hell was the meaning of all this, yet again. He admitted that he had taken the younger of the two daughters from the Hotel in Daventry and yes, he had slept with her. The words burnt into my very soul, I just couldn't take any more, the feeling of utter degredation, I felt ugly, inadequate, but most of all hurt – hurt in a way that I no longer wanted to bear. For the first time, I really let fly and the most awful row broke out. He suddenly picked up his fist and in a gesture of total anger that said 'I have no real excuse for myself yet again, I have let you down and I feel guilty', he hit me from one side of the kitchen to the other. I caught my head on the trolley as I crashed to the floor.

He tried to help me up and apologise, totally shocked with himself at what he had been capable of but I just staggered to my feet, faced him coldly and said:

"That is definitely *it*, that is the end – you and your antics have finally succeeded in wrecking our marriage. It really is the end and I just can't take and won't take any more. I shall be at a Solicitor's office in the morning".

He tried to make all kinds of excuses, he had messed up the books, hundreds of pounds were missing and the stocks were all wrong, we had a huge deficit (naturally, from his drinking binges), and his way of dealing with all of this was to go away for a dirty weekend and desert his wife and children? What a devastating reaction. I didn't want to hear any more. I'd had enough.

I phoned a solicitor the following morning and a friend ran me to Coventry to set the wheels in motion for a divorce. There was no turning back now in my mind, I was fighting for my sanity and for the welfare, and now the safety, of my two sons. They deserved a better father than this and they most certainly deserved a life. So I then took the step of phoning our District Manager at the Brewery and telling him what was happening. He couldn't believe what he was hearing. The pub had achieved such a great reputation. He was very concerned and told me to hold tight and he would be in touch.

An emergency meeting was called and it was decided that Chris would receive instant dismissal. What I had not bargained for was when our Manager and District Manager came the next day to do the deed, I was told that we *all* had to go, there and then, and that relief managers were on the way. At this point, Chris was working in the cellar, cleaning the beer pipes and for the moment, I had the Brewery to myself to discuss the situation. I stood my ground and flatly refused to go and told them that if they ejected me and my children, I would expose them in every newspaper in the land. They were very taken aback by my attitude, but they said they understood my position, I was certainly going nowhere with my husband from this moment on. They decided that they would firstly speak to all the staff in turn, explained the situation, and they all backed me one hundred per cent and told the brewery how things had really been, how I had run the business and kept things going, doing my best to cover for Chris and his misdemeanours. And so, it was decided that we could stay till a permanent couple could be found, but I could not hold the license and would have to have a male licensee responsible for the business and he would come from Coventry every night and cash up and do the books and take the banking. Chris was dismissed by the Managers and ordered to leave the premises with his belongings there and then and, under no circumstances, ever to enter the premises ever again. He looked at me and tried to plead with me to help him, but I turned my back and refused to speak to him and the Managers escorted him from the premises. Where he went to on that day I never knew, nor did I want to know. I had made my decision.

I was now happy with my situation and the Managers quickly telephoned another publican from Coventry. Later that day, this lovely man called "Toddy" arrived at the Rose and Castle and the Managers left me in his tender care. He was a lovely man and told me that he was going to make sure that I was alright and would come over every evening and cash up and do the books. This he duly did, but not before he had pressed a sizeable 'bonus' in my hand for a good day's work and told me:

"It's for the children, luv" and he would wink and put his finger to his closed lips to encourage me to keep it between ourselves. Over the few months that I ran the pub, Toddy was extremely generous and kind and I shall always be grateful to him.

From that day on I kept the pressure on Daventry Council until, three months later, they gave me the keys to a brand new council house opposite the Ford Motor Company Parts Centre. That proved to be exceedingly convenient for me, because I now needed a job to go with our new home and as the boss there had been a regular at the Rose and Castle for business lunches and the like, and it made sense to try there first and so I made an appointment and went over to see him. He was very surprised to see me, but gave me a great welcome. When I told him that I was looking for a job because I had given up the pub, he said that my timing could not have been more perfect. He needed a new P.A. and Customer Liaison Officer for emergencies when vehicles were off the road due to the lack of the relevant spare parts. This was an extremely important position and he immediately offered me the job. I was extremely flattered and obviously accepted there and then. I liked this man and I knew we could work together well.

Life therefore started to have some semblance of normality about it, but I have to confess to being exceedingly sorry to leave the Rose and Castle. I really had quite taken to this new career and I liked the constant contact with the public, producing services for them which, ultimately gave them pleasure; but more than that, I loved being the *chef*. I enjoyed creating in the kitchen. We arranged for the boys to go to my Mum and Dad in Carmarthen whilst I sorted a new home and this new career out and new schools for them. They ended up being away for a full sixteen weeks, but better with the grandparents they adored and away from all the hurt and trauma of those terrible weeks.

The divorce was made final on the 19th November 1973. All this had happened in just eleven years of marriage. The "Swinging Sixties" had certainly not been swinging for me! The only mementos of all of this were my two lovely boys and a record of Nillson singing "Without you" which Chris gave me before he left the pub for the last time, so now I had two copies!. It still makes me cry every time I hear it – but as time has gone by, I wonder why and what for – for what could and should have been at that time maybe...

Chris' parents were to make several visits over the next few months in an effort to try and persuade me to change my mind and take him back. However, this time I was resolute, there was to be no turning back, no way of returning to that life any more, I had truly come to the bitter end of my tether. Being placed at the bottom of Chris`s list of priorities was something I could no longer bear for myself nor tolerate for my sons.

So, a new house to go to, yet another new beginning and what did the hands of fate have in store for me now?

Much, much better luck was what I was praying for.

CHAPTER SIXTEEN

Mrs. Brown goes it alone

I moved into my new house, 33 Nene Walk, Daventry and the boys came home with my brother David from the farm in Wales. To complete our family, his Doberman Dog "Gerda" came too. David had argued, inevitably, with Dad and came back to the Midlands to start his life afresh too. We agreed that it seemed sensible for the foreseeable future that he should live with us, find himself a job and help me with the boys, till he knew in which direction he wanted to go. We had always got on, and the arrangement worked well, David on permanent night shifts at Jaguar in Coventry, and me working during the day at Fords and, of course, we shared the overheads. We settled into a reasonable, if unusual, stable lifestyle. I also passed my driving test and bought my first car, a Ford Corsair, which I adored. It felt sleek and it made me feel sort of 'sexy' when I was driving it and the mens' heads turned as I drove by, a nice feeling for a change.

Chris kept coming over and spouted more of the same old routine, trying to get me to give him one more chance, we could get married again and start afresh – have another baby! How romantic that would be he thought, to re-marry the same girl and start all over again. I don't think so, not this time. It broke my heart to do it, I still so desperately loved him but I absolutely knew, once and for all, that this man had a terrible illness and he would never get better, he could only get worse. For my own sanity and for the boys, I had to move on and build some kind of future for myself and for them from this awful mess. He never asked for proper access, he said he would see them when he felt able, emotionally, to handle the situation, and he never wanted to take the boys out anywhere, something for which I had never been able to forgive him at the time, but with the passage of time and my understanding over the years of this dreadful illness with which he suffered, normal procedures like access and wanting to be there for the boys was not even in his mind – his mind did not work that way then and never would.

We did agree that if he left us alone to try to get on with some semblance of a normal life, then I would not ask for any maintenance payments from him at all, despite the Court Order on my custody document making him financially responsible for their maintenance. True to form, he never sent any money either. With hindsight, I should have made him pay something, but I wanted him to just to go away and leave us all alone to be able to move on with our lives and release me from this never ending nightmare that I had been living in alone for so long now. It all just felt so much 'cleaner' that way and somehow more final.

After a while, he simply stopped coming and his parents, firmly believing it was all my fault, also stopped coming over. They completely abandoned their grandchildren! I must have another man, they said. Their accusations hurt, but I knew the truth and I never, ever told them what had really gone on for all those years, the womanising, the lack of money, the breakdowns, the drinking – nothing. What none of them ever knew either was that I have never, ever stopped loving this man, this mess of a man, this wretch – my beloved Christopher.

At work I sat at the head of a group of young men called 'merchandisers'. I relayed incoming calls to them in turn and they dealt with the problem of locating, obtaining and forwarding wayward parts and components for vehicles considered 'off the road'. There were maybe six or eight of them. One of them was called Peter. He was about the same height as me maybe a couple of inches taller, and he had a shortening in his left leg for which he wore a raised shoe. He was quite swarthy looking with dark wavy hair and a very warm smile. He obviously fancied me from the pure body language that went on. There were others who made suggestions, and I knew that they had sexual encounters with no strings in mind, but I was not like that. My children and their future came first for me and I had no intention of becoming one of those women divorced and available to every caller who wanted a quick fling, but not the package that went with it. And at that point, I was definitely not looking for a replacement husband either, that was the furthest thing from my mind.

Peter chatted me up, made jokes and seemed a thoroughly nice person. Ultimately, we started going out together on a casual basis and, apart from family outings, he took me to functions, cinema, out for a drink etc., while David babysat. I made friends too with one of my neighbours, Bunty, who lived in the house opposite – she was to become known as the 'Welsh Witch', because she was small, very blonde hair and came with the deepest of Welsh accents, the most gorgeous infectious laugh and warm, warm smile. She was such a good friend and we never seemed to stop laughing. We could make a funny situation out of anything. She too was divorced and had three children at home.

One day she asked me if I could go to Coventry with her and run her uncle's pub for the day. Of course I said yes and

Peter and Jacqui Jones – 1976.

so off we went in my car. It was an extremely busy pub and we were both kept on the run behind the bar. Every time I passed her, I would ask if she was alright. "Alright Ja-a-ack" she would say in her broad Welsh accent – "I've got this lovely man who keeps buying me aniseed cordial – he is so nice". After we called time, we cashed up and locked the money in the safe. Outside we got into the car and for some reason, Bunty got into the back of the car and sat right in the middle of the back seat. All the way back to Daventry, every time I looked in the rear view mirror, she was staring blankly straight ahead, eyes glazed, like someone who has been hypnotised. She made no attempt to speak, it seemed as if she was just either completely in a trance, or simply did not wish to talk to me. When we got home, I opened the rear door of the car, she got out and, to my astonishment she crawled on her hands and knees to her door, unlocked it and just closed it behind her – not a word. The next day, after drinking several pints of water, she came over to see me.

"Bunty, are you alright. Did something happen to you last night, did you take anything that I don't know about?"

"Nothing Ja-a-ack, honest only that lovely aniseed cordial that nice man kept buying me".

"What kind of bottle was it in and where behind the bar was it?" I asked her, because I could remember clearly what was on the optics. We discovered that she had been drinking Pernod all night, then drank all that water in the morning and the whole process had begun all over again! Bunty never drank in those days, certainly not spirits of any kind. That hangover I did not envy and whenever I see her, to this day, the name Pernod is definitely not up for discussion.

Bunty was good at getting herself into fixes, which certainly kept life interesting. A little while later, she went into partnership in a shop in Kettering with a man she had met through her sister. She had not met him many times. She hardly knew anything about this man and I questioned the sense of this move. However, she pooh-poohed my misgivings and carried on and after some time things went terribly wrong and they parted company on bad terms. It turned out he was something to do with axes, with prison sentences and with the Kray gang. David used to patrol round her house at night with Gerda the Doberman till it was all settled and he stopped stalking her! Bunty was certainly never conventional, but she was a great joy and support to have as a friend and you could always guarantee a bundle of laughs, however serious the situation.

One afternoon having just returned from work, Bunty came across and asked me round to her house that night. She had some guests coming from Coventry, one of whom was the leading medium in the town, and she wanted a reading from him. Bunty said that I should have one too as I was in a really unhappy frame of mind over Chris, I really was finding it so terribly hard to get over him. I reluctantly agreed, after some persuasion by Bunty, although I confess to having been really nervous about it. He really was a very warm and kind sort of man and he proceeded to tell me my fate.

He said that I was, at present, in a deep black hole which I was having difficulty getting out of, but that I would come out of this period in time. He said that I would have four children in total, which made me doubt him immediately, as I had no intention of going down that road ever again, the two I had were enough for me to handle. He could see me in a very large white house, with a flat roof, standing in its own grounds in a place that was surrounded by water. There was a man with me and this man had very distinctive wavy, white hair. This man would be good to me and it would be a relationship that would last. After he had gone, I told Bunty what he had said and what rubbish it all was, there was no man with white hair in my life and with my finances, what chance would I have of being in a large white house in huge grounds, surrounded by water and four kids in tow! I dismissed all this as quickly as I had heard it and, in truth, I forgot about it completely in time.

And so, I was coping. I had never envisaged life permanently without Chris, but I was moving on as a person and, I thought, very in control of my emotions. I had been persuaded by Peter to go down to meet his parents in Dagenham, London – John and Ann, delightful people, true Cockneys. John was always a very happy little man, he could laugh at anything. He had been a docker and Ann – or 'Mum' as I was encouraged to call her – never used a sentence without the word "bleeding" in it, and loved her tipple of gin. Alan, Peter's brother, and Peter used to tease her unmercifully. It was a very happy and secure family circle – I envied her.

The following weekend, it was suggested by Peter that we should visit my parents, so we went down to Wales to see my Mum and Dad. I must have been so preoccupied with my situation, and Chris still completely absorbed all my thoughts and dreams, that I did not see the implications in all of this 'getting to know the families', nor that it was all moving in a direction in which I didn't really want to go, and now, I just don't understand how I missed it, maybe because it was the furthest thing from my own mind. However, blindly, I rang Mum to tell her that we were going and she said that they were just about destitute. I went to a supermarket and filled the car up with groceries to fill their freezer and fridge and gave Mum enough money to pay off Daddy's stamps for his pension.

My parents liked Peter immediately. I asked Daddy why they were in such difficulties as they had a few cows, pigs, chickens and so on. They had intended to be self-sufficient. He said he would simply show me. He took me down to see all the farmyard animals in turn. Of course there was Willie the bull calf, Mary his mother, calves Jacqueline and Gill, pigs and piglets all with names and row upon row of hutches containing the most beautiful, enormous black rabbits you have ever seen, and the jewel in the crown, on the top of each rabbit hutch a plaque with each name, Hilda, Martha, Sam, Alf, Win, May, Simon, Bob, need I go on? Remember the gazelle in Kenya – he could not bear to part with any of them if they were going to be killed, let alone kill them himself. So their supposed food source became, in fact, a large and unaffordable millstone round their necks, as all these animals had to be fed.

We returned to Daventry where life returned to some semblance of normality. I began to notice that Simon was showing traits and signs of disturbances that I disliked. I have to admit that in those days, little was known of genes and chromosomes, nor any heredity factor; but something was lurking at the back of my mind. Simon deliberately smashed Rob's toys at Christmas, and I knew that he was stealing from my purse. He was also obtaining things without my permission from the shops and putting them on my bill. He was becoming increasingly naughty and disruptive. More worryingly, he was becoming more and more devious and deceitful.

Peter had been continuously pestering me to marry him. I was flattered in a way, possibly because he liked the boys and didn't seem worried about 'the package', but I really didn't want to. My brother was all for it, however; in fact he went out of his way to bring us together by engineering some of the chance meetings and dates etc. The boys wanted me to. They wanted Peter for their Daddy and my parents wanted me to take the plunge again. Bunty was also urging me to go ahead – of all the people around me at this time, she knew how lonely I was for Chris and, well, everyone thought Peter was great and would be good for me. Nobody asked me what I wanted and I felt pressurised, but stupidly, I didn't say what I wanted and I should have. However ultimately, though not really doing any favours for Peter, (because I truly can say that I did not come anywhere close to being in love with him) I agreed to marry him because I believed that my children were in great need of a father. It was pure selfishness on my part, no maybe about it, but nevertheless the date was set for the 20th July 1974.

In the car on the way to the Registry Office, I turned to Peter and said:

"I really don't know what I am doing here; I don't want to do this". He said that he wanted me just to give it a chance and if I ever really felt that it had been the wrong decision, then he would call it quits and let me go. I took him at his word and on that day I grudgingly became Mrs. Jones. Well Mum, I had certainly gone one better, hadn't I? Ashton, Brown and now Jones! The sexual side of my courtship by Peter and our married life was hardly worth mentioning. If he could be bothered at all, let me just say "there was 'little' to it" and it did not particularly matter; I have no great and lasting memories of warm and wonderful nights with him.

I then concentrated on where we were going now after this wedding, Peter's bungalow was too small for us all and so he sold it and we moved to a new house in Weedon, not far from Daventry, but Robbie began to develop asthma and excema badly (he had had it when he was a baby) and it was found to be an allergy to the gas blown air central heating. We therefore had to put the house on the market and find somewhere more traditionally heated and cooled.

I had long wanted to go back to Hinckley as a lot of my family were there, David had moved there also. Mum and Dad were also selling the farm, for which they received a handsome price and they were buying a bungalow in Hinckley too. They were in their late sixties now and Mum especially was worn out. I had always liked Hinckley, especially after my eighteen or so months with Tetty and Jack, and I wanted for us to be a family unit like other folk. Peter was happy about this, as he too wanted for us to be a true family and he certainly did not want to live back down in Dagenham again, so we came to a mutual decision that Hinckley was perfect.

So, we bought a house on Sketchley Hill, Peter stayed on at Ford Motor Company and I got myself a job as a personal assistant/secretary to the sales director of a fabric producing company. I was thirty years of age, I was proud of my stature and appearance, I was more confident than I had been in years, and I knew how to make the best of myself. This was a super job, dealing with the fashion trade. I went to London to the big fashion shows and I even met famous designers such as Paco Rabanne. I loved being involved with the fabrics. That was the want-to-be-designer in me, I suppose, and seeing the fabrics right through from production to the make-up stage was so satisfying. I used to receive wonderful gifts of outfits from the designers, and of course, Paco Rabanne perfume, it was wonderful. My boss used to follow me around like a puppy dog, sometimes hard to shake off, but every week, there was a fresh orchid on my desk, with a card from him saying 'Just because..... ' . I realised how he felt, but I'd seen this before with my boss in Birmingham and I could handle that.

Apart from having serious worries about young Simon's increasingly erratic behaviour, I loved the house that we had bought and being back in Hinckley and I was as happy as I could be, given the circumstances, although in my heart, I felt like 'second hand Rose', a feeling that never went away. Where was the passion, the butterflies in the tummy I used to feel whenever I saw Chris? They simply did not exist for me any more without him, so life with Peter just went on from day to day. Sometimes you do get into a rut and don't stop to think and try to do something about it to prevent it being a rut; but in my life so far, fate seemed to be totally in control and it still had plans for me, plans which I could do absolutely nothing about.

CHAPTER SEVENTEEN

The Licensee again

Peter had set off to drive to Daventry as usual one morning and he rang me later on at work and said he had the most awful pains in his chest and found it hard to breathe. He came home and we arranged for him to go and see the Doctor. After all the tests, it was said that there was absolutely nothing wrong with him, it was just that he had to admit that he could not cope with Ford Motor Co. any more and that he wanted a change. Suddenly I was gripped with the thought – here we go again, something like *'deja vu'* – in fact I think the word 'psychosomatic' was mentioned at some point and I really needed to hear that word like a hole in the head!

We sat down after the boys had gone to bed to discuss the matter. One thing I had made up my mind about, no matter how callous it may have been, I would not, could not contemplate continuing with this second marriage if psychological problems were to become an issue. I waited for it and, sure enough, here it came. He said he had been thinking about our future and he felt it would be a good idea if I contacted my former management at Watneys and see if they would consider us for pub management, he thought it could be a good life for us. To say that I have felt as if I was being used once again would be an understatement at this point. Would it be anywhere near the truth to say that I believed that he had pursued me and married me just to get him to where he wanted to go? After all, just a few dates with me, and he knew pretty much all about me and what I was capable of. I have discovered that sometimes in life, it is much, much better to keep your mouth shut, but hindsight is always so cheap...

Peter claimed that he had got the idea watching me as I worked at our local Social Club when they needed relief management. I gave in to their pleas for me to work for them and said yes, not really thinking that Peter would see the social side of it, and would then hanker to do the same, so that we could work together. He thought how easy it looked just to pull a few pints, as everyone does – little do they know!

"Peter, do you realise that the highest incidence of divorce is in the licensed trade"? I asked him, but he kept on pressing me and reluctantly, and for the life of me I don't know why, I caved in and agreed to try.

Before finishing at the Social Club, I was there one Saturday when a Rolls Royce pulled up outside. Out of the limousine came an old lady who, I was told was a Mrs. Smith, and she was a true and very wealthy Romany gypsy. She came up to the bar and ordered a schooner of sherry. We began chatting and she asked me where I came from.

"Why, Hinckley" I said.

She asked me about my family, and after telling her about Daddy and the family, and the Nan I had never met from Brick Kiln Street, she went on to tell me that she could remember my Dad's mother clearly. She told me that my Nan used to sing in pubs in Hinckley on a Saturday night for pennies for her gin – she also remembered my Dad when he was about nine years old, working in the local slaughterhouse and looking after the undertaker's horse, and the hearse. This bore out what my father had told me himself but it made me realise that my father, the Major, was ashamed of his slum background and that was why I never knew his mother, my Nan. It also explained his pride in having got himself out of this kind of world and into making something of himself. My father's gin and tonics at Sundowner time would have seemed so different to seeing his mother belittling herself in his eyes and selling herself for pennies for gin. However, I was thrilled to learn something of my family history, and all of this from a gypsy!

Having given in to Peter, I contacted my former District Manager, Gordon Shrive, at Watneys, who agreed to interview us. They took us on there and then with the proviso that Peter did a basic pub management course, whilst I was to run the business. He said he was taking us immediately because of my past performance and especially for the way I handled things at the Rose and Castle. He said that he trusted me and was impressed with my natural ability to run the businesses and he had a location in mind. I was going to have to learn to do the bookkeeping too though this time, they were prepared to trust me personally. It felt as if they were insisting that I be a kind of guarantor for my husband, until they knew he would not be another Chris and I can't say I blamed them.

When the written offer of employment arrived, we were asked to go to Peterborough and look at a pub called The Paul Pry. It was yet another large, fabulous public house and the living accommodation was stupendous. The business itself needed about twenty or more staff. It too had a restaurant on the side and I suggested that we should also do bar snacks ranging from Ploughman's lunches and sandwiches to a completely new concept of hot food to be eaten in the bar and served from the bar itself. The Brewery were very impressed with this idea and the requisite equipment was fitted during extensive renovations that were being planned for the establishment. We had, however, to remain open and fully operational during these building works. We managed to remain open, and we were re-launched with a grand opening. Very quickly we built up the reputation for excellent food served quickly, efficiently, and very well presented. We were booked up in the restaurant, lunchtimes and evenings, sometimes up to weeks ahead.

In quirky repetition, I was to end up as chef again along with everything else to do, but we had three magnificent waitresses, the like of which I had never worked with before nor have I worked with since, Sheila, Betty and Maria – insatiable when it came to increasing our numbers record for meals served each day and evening. They really were something else. Betty and Sheila were both married ladies and into their fifties by this time and Maria was much younger and carried a baby to full term without any of us realising she was even pregnant, and continuing to work full time at The Paul Pry. They were all three remarkable ladies. I never did get to meet their families, work was work and their private lives away from the pub were their own. This was a sort of unwritten law of the Brewery that you did not get personally involved with the staff, you had always to retain that management position above theirs.

At least, realising that if I took on the role of chef, this would cement my recognition by the brewery again, it would keep down overheads which would impress them, and I managed to negotiate myself an extra separate wage as chef to supplement the pathetic amount I was paid as the wife of the manager; laughable, considering the work that I was required to do. I also won a catering competition being the busiest food outlet with the best presentation within the brewery. I won money for that and I put it away in a savings bank determined to have something which I, nor the children, had ever had – a proper holiday. Peter had done his initial training; he could now slice a lemon better than anyone in the pub trade! He commanded very little respect from the staff, in fact the waitresses, to whom I was particularly close, used to get so annoyed at the amount – or lack of – his input into the actual running of the pub. Let's face it, Peter was bone idle, just plain lazy.

Also, at this time, Simon was proving to be a continuing major problem. In Daventry, he had been destructive, stolen from my purse and put things I could not afford on my account at our local shop, without my permission. Now I was noticing some serious behavioural problems and a defiance of any kind of authority. I did not consider this to be normal teenage puberty-type problems. They went much deeper than that. He was devious, he told lies, he was smoking, and he would change out of his school uniform as soon as he was out of eyeshot of the pub into jeans and despite all my efforts to make him wear the school uniform, he lied about changing. I was getting seriously worried.

The next problem I was in no way prepared for. It came when he stole a customer's motor-cycle and hid it in the lock-up garage. How long he thought he would get away with it, I do not know. He had given no thought to the fact that we might lose our jobs, our home and our reputations. He was thirteen and old enough to know right from wrong and that what he had done was criminal. It was a stupid theft and was quickly detected and for which he was prosecuted by the Police, receiving a severe ticking off from the judge and a fine of £30, which Peter and I had to pay. The whole incident just seemed to wash over his head and he carried on as if nothing had happened.

I was so ashamed. He was smuggling girls into his bedroom and no-one seemed able to hold any control over him. Peter held no authority for or deterrent over the boy he hardly even tried, and I certainly couldn't do anything with him, he had this attitude of sheer defiance towards me. I approached the school for help but received a pathetic reply from a very weak-willed headmaster who seemed to feel that the times we were living in were a '*fait accompli*' and there was no point in trying to fight for what was right from wrong and no point in trying to even administer any authority whatsoever. He even condoned the teachers borrowing cigarettes from the pupils! Robbie, thank goodness, attended a different school and he gave me none of these problems.

I also became aware at this time that Simon was showing some traits very similar to his father, such as failure to acknowledge or accept any rules and the right ways of doing things generally. Honesty did not seem to be a part of his vocabulary. I know that I was very strict with the boys, but that was the way I had been brought up and I felt nothing but benefits from my father's rigid handling of his children.

One afternoon, when Simon should have been at school, I was fetched upstairs by one of my waitresses. She had found Simon at the foot of the stairs and she said that he appeared to be delirious. We managed to get him into bed and I realised very quickly that he had consumed a vast quantity of alcohol. One of the strange things about his bad behaviour generally, was that even with the easy accessibility to the vast volume of all our alcohol on display in the bars and in the storerooms, the one thing he had never done was to abuse this and help himself to it. He was obviously past being just drunk, he was very seriously sick, but we eventually, slowly, nursed him back to consciousness enough for him to tell us that it was one of our regular customers, Gerald, who had a business next door who had tipped neat whisky into Simon till he was comatose and then dumped him back at the door of the pub. He could have killed him, as it was, he had severe alcohol poisoning. Really, with hindsight, I should have reported him to the police there and then, but the Brewery had hard and fast rules about bad publicity and customer relations. If we put the pub in jeopardy, we lost our home.

Every Tuesday afternoon I used to drive over to my parents in Hinckley and spend a few hours with them. Mum was ecstatic at being back in Hinckley and Dad was heavily into his rose garden and vegetables, all laid out in beautiful straight rows, like a battalion of soldiers! These rows reminded me of my proudest moment as a child, watching my father at the head of his troops, marching them through the streets of Nairobi. His life was run in the same way and, on thinking back, so was our family life as I have said, one did not disobey orders. Funny how these thoughts run through your head, but sadly, I did not seem to be successful in passing any of this discipline on to Simon.

I was driving to my parents' house on one of these Tuesday trips and the whisky problem and Gerald still rankled with me. Simon was only just recovered from the alcohol poisoning. What he had done was stupid and dangerous. Then I suddenly realised why he had done what he did, because on one of these previous trips to see my parents, I became aware that the same car had been driving along behind me since I had left Peterborough and was attempting to keep as close to my car as possible. I began to feel very uneasy and somewhat afraid. When I got to the outskirts of Uppingham, the car behind flashed his lights, overtook and forced me into the lay-by at the side of the road.

All sorts of things were going through my mind, when out of the car got the driver and came to my window. It was

Gerald, of course not my favourite person. He told me he had followed me deliberately, and that I would be meeting him for dinner that evening. What he wanted, in a nutshell, was to have an affair with me. I told him in no uncertain terms to go to hell! He threatened that if I did not agree, then he would tell the Brewery that we were already an item and would broadcast the news to all and sundry. Had it been true, it would most certainly have cost me my job and us a home and income. I told him to leave me alone and drove off. It must have been then that he hatched the plot of getting Simon drunk to get back at me, but he went far too far and almost killed him. I could not mention it to Mum and Dad, but I did leave them earlier than usual to get back home in time to ring the Brewery and speak to our General Manager. I told him exactly the events of the past few days, including the whisky incident and he said they were coming over immediately to see me. Of course, I had told Peter first, and we awaited their arrival. After long discussions on the whole matter, especially with regard to the implications, we all agreed that my problem would be treated as a complaint against Gerald, but that it would not come to light. The Legal Department would be informed and, if he tried to implicate me, they would handle it. Apparently this situation was not a new one to the big brewery chains, although not at all a common one.

Having been spurned and suitably warned off, and being the kind of person he was, Gerald did try to besmirch me. I suppose I gloated inside knowing that he did not know that the Brewery were prepared for whatever went on, but at the same time, not saying a word to him nor treating him any differently. In other words, his ploy had failed and the Brewery was behind me one hundred per cent. It seemed it had all passed over successfully and things went quiet for a while.

Apparently, however, his little ploy had failed miserably, I had got the better of him and he didn't like that – not Gerald, and he was resolved not to let things end there. From then on he did and tried to do everything and anything he could to try and make me look a fool. One lunchtime, I had prepared the hot bar snacks and was carrying a large heavy and extremely hot container full of lasagne to the bar servery area. He walked up behind me and pushed my white hair band down over my eyes. It was an extremely dangerous and stupid thing to do. I was furious and after the barmaid took the dish from me I went over and officially warned him never to do that again. He challenged me and wanted to know what I thought I could do about it (little me!) I told him to grow up and walked away.

After I had filled up the servery with the goodies of the day, I went around the other side of the bar into the seating area to clear tables. I was then approached by someone at the bar who had a question, and whilst talking to them, Gerald came up behind me and, in yet another stupid and childish gesture, he pushed my hair band down over my eyes again. This time he had gone too far. I did not lose my temper. I completely kept myself cold and calculatingly cool and made an instant decision by way of retaliation. I did no more than my old trick, I bent down, legs apart, and pulled his trousers through my legs, just like at the Rose and Castle, and down he went with a loud thump. I then simply picked up the soda siphon from the bar and with my foot planted firmly on his chest, whilst he attempted to regain his equilibrium, I squirted him from top to toe – his immaculate, expensive, Italian silk suit was all soaking wet. All his sales team that were with him fell about in fits of laughter and he dashed out of the pub, totally embarrassed and very sheepish. I merely shouted after him:

" I warned you never to mess with me Gerald! I am not

the wilting rose you seem to think that I am, there had better never be a next time, or else it is a complete ban for life – and that comes from my heart and from the Brewery – they know all about your antics. Carry on and so will your wife!".

After that incident, he could not have been more co-operative and, in fact, he apologised to me for all the unpleasant incidents he had put me through. After that I was merely pleasant to him on the surface, because I had to be.

Dramas like that were not the norm, of course, and running a pub and restaurant has its lighter side, like the time a passing lorry driver came in for a drink and asked me for a pint of shandy (beer and lemonade), with a very large dash of peppermint cordial in it. All of the bar staff, with open mouths, took a 'double take' and watched him down it. He turned to me and, before I could utter a word, he said:

"Before you ask, I am a lorry driver and I was thirsty. The peppermint kills the smell of the beer, just in case the coppers stop me". He paid up and left – we were all still open mouthed! What a combination, peppermint and beer.

Mum and Dad came over frequently to the Paul Pry and stayed for weekends. I think my father was over-awed by my ability to cope with such a busy business and the sheer volume of it, controlling all the staff etc., and, for once, I truly believed that he admired me. The unfortunate part of this was that he kept hinting to Peter that we should be doing this for ourselves and not for the Brewery, but I was really happy there. I felt secure because I had come to realise that I myself was good at what I had achieved over the last two or three years, I had found a new talent in being the chef and taking control of the running of the pub that showed that I could cope – on my own if needs be- in a business that was usually male orientated and not only that, I had all the staff and most of our regular customers behind me too. They liked the way I ran things and so, it seems, did the brewery. Our home was good and guaranteed, we were well fed, bills all paid and we received a reasonable wage too because I was paid as the chef, and our only expenses for ourselves were our clothing and personal items. We had achieved a tremendous reputation, not only locally but especially with the Brewery.

However, these hints from Daddy eventually turned into heavy discussions with Peter and these discussions were only with Peter, because my father still believed that the man of the house ran things. He could see Peter sitting there able and free to talk to him, whilst little me did what I did best, kept silent and worked away – just like at the shop and all my life I suppose. I did have a very solid point of view on all these issues, but I was never able to put these to my father, the security of a paid salary, no overheads with the home, all cleaning and laundry and food included and so on, and so on. Pretty soon all the talk between Daddy and Peter convinced him that, with the backing of my parents, we could be our own bosses and to Peter that then became much more attractive that working for the Brewery – Daddy had succeeded and the seed took root. Peter started to send away for catalogues and the like from the Pub Agencies. He approached our bank but because we had no sizeable savings, they were not prepared to help us with the ingoing for a tenancy. This made me very relieved, but Peter would not let it rest there. On one of my usual Tuesday trips to see Mum and Dad, Peter asked me to approach them for a loan. At this juncture, I took the bull by the horns and I told him, point blank that I did not want a tenancy, I felt perfectly safe where we were and our income was more or less guaranteed. (Somewhere from the back of my mind came all those memories flooding back of incessantly moving from one place to another with Chris, and me, never seeming to have a say in whether or not we came or went). He insisted that I talk with my Dad and get his advice. Little did I know that my father was already streaks ahead of us and, with hindsight, I should have stopped it all there, I should have stood firm. My Mum loved her little bungalow in Hinckley, it was all paid for as they had made good money out of the farm, and she really did not want any changes to her now perfect lifestyle, neither did I. However, the men had different ideas. Dad offered me the loan there and then without me asking and my heart sank. I saw my Mum's face turn pale.

When I got back to the Paul Pry, I told my senior barmaid Vi what had been suggested. She had been a pub landlady herself and was a good confidante and I was hoping that she would see where I was coming from. I did not want to hear what she had to say next, because she felt that I was wrong and that I should back Peter, he was the man of the house – ha! bloody ha! – and I should at least have a look at any likely places that were to be found. It all felt a bit like another of those *'fait accomplis'*, to me and I knew my Mum would not be happy. However, Peter and Daddy had their own plans firmly in place and they duly went off that weekend down to the West Country to view a few places that they thought worth taking a look at.

To be honest, I was glad to see Peter go because he was becoming a pain to live with and he was extremely lazy. It was like having three boys to look after, not two. He was not in the least concerned that this would mean yet another move for the boys, thus disrupting their home lives yet again but even more important, their schooling. The fact that I was adamant that I did not want to leave our management position did not even come into the equation. Mum came and spent the weekend with me and we commiserated together over the whole problem. Let's face it, she and I wanted things to remain the same and the two men had firmly resolved to go. Somehow, though I really did hope that we could persuade them out of it all. When they looked back at what we had at the Paul Pry and the secure financial future that had been built up there, then they would come back and say that really we would be better off to stay put.

There was, however, the ultimate problem to face on their return if they liked what they saw there, I knew that Mum would ultimately give in to Dad, if he thought that we should take the pub in Somerset, and I knew that because of my father's attitude towards me that I would have to be seen to be ending up having to do the same with Peter.

My worst nightmare was realised when they came back; Daddy was so excited, he was almost ecstatic. They had seen a village pub south of Bath in a village called Stratton-on-the-Fosse. It was opposite Downside Abbey and the Public School and although small, apparently there was nice accommodation upstairs, including letting rooms, a tiny restaurant and two smallish bars. Dad and Peter were both so over enthusiastic, but Mum and I had had a heart to heart and we both realised that this was the absolute last thing that we both wanted, we were both happy where we were and nothing was broken in our circumstances, so why try to fix it? We really did not want this. She was worried because they had little spare cash to lend and they were going to have to mortgage the bungalow to give us the loan, I didn't want to do it because I preferred being employed with all the perks and a guaranteed home and future and we knew where we stood with the brewery. If we stayed where we were and went on up and up in the breweries' eyes, we could have landed up with an absolute money making machine in a prime location. Why spoil it to start all over again?

I was obviously very negative when Mum and Dad went back home and Peter asked me to go down to Stratton and see the pub. Vi, my barmaid, was all for it and offered to come with me. Reluctantly, I gave in to all this pressure and booked us in for bed and breakfast at the pub and off we went. After all my misgivings, I have to admit that it really was a lovely little pub and the landlord had been a Downside boy himself. He told me that the parents and visitors to the Abbey and School brought in quite a reasonable amount of the overall trade, plus it was the only pub in the village. It had an old, large inglenook fireplace, low beamed ceilings and was really a very pleasant little old country pub. However, this was no temptation in comparison to our secure situation as management; I loved all my staff, pub and clientele that we had built up in Peterborough. I already had a good name for catering there, and at the end of the day, I simply just did not want to go, somehow to me it did not seem like a forward step, it seemed like going backwards and I had this utter feeling of doom and gloom and total failure.

We got back to Peterborough and after closing that evening, Vi and I sorted out all the troubles of the world through the eyes of a nice drop of scotch – how else do you sort out a problem thoroughly? Despite all she said on the plus side of taking this little pub, I could only feel minuses and I realised that I really did not love Peter that much. I felt, yet again, that I was being taken for granted and being forced to go somewhere I did not want to go. Again, I felt totally used and someone else was deciding my future, not me. Why, oh why, did the men in my life never listen to me and my point of view from the pure working aspect or ever put my feelings into the frame for a change?

The following week, matters were taken right out of any control that I may have had. Mum was absolutely beside herself. Daddy, without a word to her, had put their beloved bungalow on the market and he had decided that they were not only coming with us to Somerset, but they were also going to live with us – what a recipe for disaster!!. Once again, my heart sank. Here I was at thirty four and my father was still ruling my life. No choices. I was overcome with the distinct feelings of impending doom. For Daddy, of course, his ambitions were soon to be recognised – from shop, to farm and now to pub. He wanted to lend us money called 'the ingoing', which is the amount you have to pay to the Brewery for the fixtures, fittings and stock. He also wanted to live in and help with the business. I was devastated – I well remembered his attitude towards me, and how he treated me with regard to work in the shop in Leicester. To live with my father would be one thing, but to work with him again I could only see as a total disaster just waiting to happen from moment one. By now, I knew my job, I knew where I wanted to take my businesses and I had my way of working, and, to boot, I was very successful at it – daddy would never be able to work along with that situation, he would have to be in control; and I was so used to being in control, I could never give up that position. I knew what was best for the pub and business and I knew how to perform and do it. He did not know this profession at all and his old ethics would not come into play here – he was totally out of place and out of his depth before he started. However, it seemed that despite all this Mum and I had lost the battle but in the back of my mind, I hoped that we had not lost the war too, maybe, just maybe, I could win that back somehow.

So, it was with a heavy heart I went to the interview with Peter and, despite my reluctance, my menus made a huge impression and we were offered the "Kings Arms" there and then. Peter accepted immediately, I remained strangely silent. I had thoughts I could not discuss with anybody at this time. Looking back I think that not maybe, but definitely, I was putting some future decisions into place.

A leaving party was planned, with great sadness and devastation, by the staff at the Paul Pry. They were totally gutted at the news. We had had such a wonderful success at the Paul Pry and we were all reluctant to let that go – except Peter. It was decided that it was to be a fancy dress party. I wore a *sari* that I had previously bought in Leicester and Peter borrowed my Dad's old army uniform. The two waitresses loathed Peter for his lack of concern for me and the end of our time at the pub and they asked me if they could "custard pie" him. I chuckled to myself and found myself agreeing gladly, but they had to get him out of the uniform before they could do it, Daddy would have been devastated and very unforgiving if his beloved uniform were spoilt. Somehow we managed it and Peter was duly well and truly done. They went on rubbing in the pies with great relish. I never did tell him the truth, that they had been waiting to do it for such a long time, but I know that he never realised, and to some very small degreee, I felt that they had taken a humiliating revenge for me – too bad he didn't see the significance of it all.

Well, we may have been moving on to pastures new and all those old clichés, but I was coming to a realisation that things between Peter and myself were not going in the direction he was thinking and I had my own very definite ideas on the matter.

We would have to see how it all worked out …

CHAPTER EIGHTEEN

The Demons return

By now, despite going into this new venture with Peter, our marriage in my own heart was definitely in serious and irrepairable trouble. I was definitely not even liking him as a person. I hated his treatment of the boys, Simon especially, I could not agree with, and as for love, well, that had gone out of the equation altogether for me, if indeed it had ever really been there. I shouldn't admit to it if I am absolutely truthful, but I was still missing Chris so much. I always had, always have and I always will.

We moved into the Kings Arms at Downside in October

Barmaid Val at King's Arms – 1978

1978, Mum and Dad having given us a loan of six thousand pounds. One advantage, in fact to my mind the only one, that may have come out of it was that Simon was now out of that awful school in Peterborough and had a fresh start in much more tranquil surroundings, maybe at long last he would begin to see sense and settle down – just maybe .

Our very first day in the pub a girl came in from the village and said her name was Val and she was looking for work. She liked her village pub, knew everyone and had done bar work before. She was quite a chubby girl with a lovely warm face, a beauty of a Somerset accent and a lovely dimple in her chin. She had such a bubbly personality and seemed so full of life that she immediately seemed to 'fit in' with the King's Arms and to somehow belong there from day one. I most certainly took to her immediately and set her on there and then. She proved to be everything you could imagine a good barmaid would be – an absolute treasure and we worked very well and extremely hard together. I told her my plans for the food side and she was very excited about it and more than willing to give it her all – and in the fullness of time, she most assuredly did that.

I decided we needed a special 'lure' for the local business people to come out for lunch. This would not be as easy as Peterborough, because they were all on the doorstep there. Here we were out in the country, but we had a regular trade of local young professionals who needed to have a good lunchtime outlet and soon we became 'it'. I decided to put on a lunch time menu of ten portions each of four specials of the day, different each day, like pork in cider, my own *paté*, to my own secret recipe plus lots of unusual dishes that no pub in the district had done before. When the specials had gone, we always had a full rump of rare roast beef with homemade horseradish, ploughman's lunches with my own pickles – and all for £1 per head! We were soon packed to the hilt every lunch time, sometimes the specials all sold out over the phone before we had even opened. We did sixty plus lunches every day and that was really some going for a tiny village pub.

I am proud to say that we were spotted by an Egon Ronay Scout and made the Good Food Guide for Pubs for that year 1980 – unsolicited, and that I have always been really proud of. I also used to give gourmet dinners for a select few of the Masters from Downside and we had some gorgeous evenings, Val, bless her, and her cousin Julie ran the pub whilst we entertained. We even went with three of them to Rome for a weekend and went to a service when the Pope ordained three new bishops. I especially loved St. Peter's and the Vatican, it was all a very moving experience.

One section of our business lunch trade was a group of young men from the Midsomer Norton Cricket Club and they too became regular daily customers. They were a great crowd and came in the evenings as well. We were also privileged to have many members of the Somerset County Cricket Club and I even did a benefit lunch for Hallam Moseley during the Ian Botham era, though he Botham, in person, couldn't attend to be with his friend.

After a few months it became very difficult to function with Mum and Dad in the pub. Dad had his very rigid ideas on how the timetable should run and on what we should or should not do. It was almost like being in the army. If we were not up and about by a certain time, then, when we did come down, he would go around the place doing his little throat clearing act, to make us feel totally inadequate and uncomfortable. If we were having a few late drinks with friends who were always 'the selected few' with even, sometimes, a few songs around the piano, then he would send Mum down to tell us that it was time we were in bed and to keep the noise down! Peter and I were both in our thirties, in our own home and still my father wanted to rule the roost. There was always an atmosphere if he could not get his own way. Mum loathed every minute and missed her own home. They were both living for free on us and at the same time, we were paying Dad back a large amount off the loan every month, which became all too much for such a small business to carry. So, when our accountant came to visit, having discussed this huge burden we were carrying, he suggested we purchase a house, with Mum and Dad, in all our joint names. Their share would take on board the amount we owed and Peter and I would pay the mortgage. This would mean that when anything happened to Mum and Dad, the house would be immediately and totally ours, and it would not only solve our debt to my parents, but apparently help our income tax situation and be a good way of securing a future home at the same time.

Unbelievably, Dad and Mum agreed, I think by this time their picture of life in the village pub had become completely tarnished and I know Mum longed for her own home again and Daddy missed his garden. Boy were we relieved when it was all agreed and one of our good village customers, a very reputable builder, offered us one of his new houses in a village called Coleford, just a couple of miles from the pub, and we could buy it for just fourteen thousand pounds (it was a huge bargain at that time). This would have been an absolutely superb buy, Mum and Dad would have been only a couple of miles from the pub, but when I tried to talk to Dad about it, he became really angry and accused me of trying to decide his future. The peace had not lasted long.

Nothing was further from the truth, I was trying to help them with their future, but you didn't argue with Daddy and because I stood my ground on this one, we had not done anything underhand or suspicious, which was how he was making me feel, and it all ended with him picking up his fist and knocking me from one side of the kitchen to the other. This was a situation I would never have believed if you had told me it was going to happen – I was absolutely and totally devastated in that one blow. This was the second time that a man had hit me, and for this I could never forgive my Father. I idolised him for the 'correctness' in him as a man, and, above everything, as my father. This was a total and irreversible destruction of all that I held in esteem for him, including the incident with Mr. Best at the shop and my unrequited 'honour'. Now it was gone, completely shattered. Why do all the men I love seem to want to destroy me and take enjoyment in doing it?

The result was that Mum and Dad went off in high dudgeon and deliberately looked at houses as far away from Somerset as they could get. Eventually they chose and and gave instructions for the purchase of a house in Whittlesea, way up in Lincolnshire, an area we hated, but they obviously wanted to be as far away from us as possible, and to top it all, this house was nineteen thousand pounds, five thousand more than the one we were offered in Somerset, which again was going to stretch us to the limits. In effect, I suppose, Dad was really calling in the loan and most certainly on his own terms and conditions and I honestly could't believe that he never even stopped to consider that this extra five thousand pounds added extra to us on top of our end of the bargain, would cripple us. There was obviously no option and so we went ahead with it, I felt Mum was owed this much for her loss of her beloved bungalow in Hinckley, but again, she was being forced to go to an area of England which she loathed. She hated the place till the day she died. Mum and Dad ended up paying only a five thousand pounds deposit and we were lumbered with a fourteen thousand pound mortgage which was huge repayments for us given our circumstances.

It was now 1979 and waiting for finalisation of their move, one weekend, totally out of the blue, I received a call from Chris. This came as such a complete shock, as I had not heard from him for such a long time and he hadn't asked to see the children since after the divorce, in fact he had kept his word and left me and them very much alone. However, he still had the ability with just one phone call of stirring up all those old feelings in me and I felt apprehensive but at the same time disturbingly excited at the prospect of seeing him again. He had been working in the Bahamas for a couple of years, he said, and now wanted to see the boys. I would never, ever have refused him and so, when he arrived, looking as self confidant, debonaire and handsome as ever, Mum and Dad sat with him on my behalf whilst I continued with the lunch time service. Of course, he was accompanied with the usual beautiful, raven haired and glamorous young woman on his arm. I remember him pointing out her gold necklace that she was wearing, he had bought it for her in Bermuda he said. That hurt me a lot as I remember thinking to myself that he had never bought me anything except my engagement and wedding rings and the cheap bracelet when Simon was born, when we were together, this lady must have had something really special. Her name was Katherine and it became quite obvious during that visit that she was totally besotted with him. It was almost like looking in the mirror and seeing the repetition of my past staring me back in the face.

Simon flatly refused to even see his father and went off somewhere, but Robbie sat with them and they stayed till after the lunch time session was over. Peter was not too pleased about the situation and my Mum said that she wished that I was still with him, instead of the wimp I had married – I know she loved Chris too, despite everything that had happened and she knew he was still the real love of my life, but even for Mum, that was quite a statement to come out with to me. I also believe that my mother truly felt that other women were par for the course where married men were concerned and maybe I had made too much of things and should have stuck with him. I have to admit that I loved seeing him again, deep down. All the old feelings, the butterflies, the heart thumping, yes, he could still do it to me and no, my feelings had not changed. How I longed to just rush straight into his arms and make things up. Why the hell did I not do it? Why? Because it would have all ended in tears all over again, and in my heart of hearts I knew it too well. He hadn't changed, I knew that also, and, if I had been truthful with myself, I knew that I did not have the strength to go through all the heartache all over again. In my own way and on my terms, I had come to accept Chris how he was and I definitely accepted by this time that he could never, and would never change. I was also in enough of a mess with my marriage to Peter and things there would have to come to some kind of a head before I even looked at my personal feelings again.

Katherine was with Chris for quite a few years and she used to ring me regularly after their visit and tell me what he had done next and how would I have dealt with him? It was quite quirky really but I truly felt very sorry for her because I knew exactly the turmoil she was then going through and why. I tried to help her as best I could and I never ran Chris down to her, how could I? I still loved him. There has not been a single day in my life that I have not wished we could have made it, especially because he never got to know me or his sons properly, nor they him. He really did miss out on a lot, whether good or bad, and sometimes it was so dreadfully lonely bringing them up with no-one to share it with or discuss problems and the future of my children.

While they were having lunch, my friend Grace, a teacher from Downside, asked me who Chris was. I said that he was just an old friend.

"Good Lord, Jacqui" she drawled in her slow, deep velvet, and very posh voice, "how come you let that one get away? He is so suave and handsome, and so utterly you".

I did enlighten her eventually. She and I were good friends and her son and Simon went around together after school and at the weekends. Soon it was time for Chris to go and he came and kissed me tenderly on the cheek and gave me a gentle squeeze, pulling me affectionately and very familiarly into him. Everything in me wanted to hold on to him and never let him go – but let him go I did and I stood in the car park and waved them goodbye. Away they went, and I stood waving goodbye till they were out of sight, warm soft tears running silently and gently down my cheeks. If only – .

Though of course, I didn't realise the visit to Stratton was to be the last time ever that I would ever see Chris ...

CHAPTER NINETEEN

The loss of a son

Mum and Dad left for Lincolnshire and again in my life there was a deep, irreparable rift with my Dad. The last few weeks of their stay were almost unbearable and I was heartbroken but nothing could make me forgive my Dad for hitting me. He tried very clumsily to apologise several times without actually saying he was sorry, words that he obviously found not hard to say, impossible to say, but something died in me that day. I couldn't bring myself to even speak to him or look him in the eye. Mum appeared to be holding a grudge too – it had all ended heartbreakingly in tears, as I had suspected it would and the outcome was exactly what I had dreaded from the outset.

The move to Stratton had not made much difference to Simon and we seemed to go from one crisis to the next. After Mum and Dad left, he became even more surly, disobedient and defiant. Dad had helped to keep him in check. Being the strict taskmaster that he was, he stood absolutely no nonsense, but as soon as he was gone that was it. Peter made no impression upon him at all on the few occasions when he tried to intervene. Simon informed, or should I say *told me* that he had no intention of going on beyond his "O" levels and as soon as he was sixteen, then he would leave home and not come back. He said he could not accept the house rules. According to him I was far too strict. How else should I try to bring up two sons properly? In my mind I had been doing it alone since he was born, both he and Robbie and I wanted them to have the best and be the very best they could be considering all the knocks in their short lives. Simon however, just seemed to take pleasure in doing things the wrong way deliberately, even if it was the right way and was easier, just like his father. I had tried to control and curtail his wayward behaviour, but I had not considered for one moment that just because genes and chromosomes were there, they were not under my jurisdiction. Simon was resolute in his decision that he would be exactly the person that he wanted to be and would not fit into any pattern of self discipline that fitted my dreams and aspirations for my first born son – and these are always special dreams. He would be what he wanted to be and he let me know in no uncertain terms that he didn't need me or want to be with me, or have me in his life any longer than he had to be.

By this time, Peter was no help at all. In fact he seemed to exacerbate the problems as Simon had come to dislike him. One night, when he was about fifteen, he drove a car belonging to one of our customers and wrote it off on a bend. I have to say that the customer condoned this and gave Simon the keys voluntarily so there could not possibly be any come back – but what if he had been hurt or killed or, even worse, hurt or killed someone else? Thankfully he was alright, and even thought it was a huge joke!

On another occasion, he took a kitchen worker home after we had had a very bad snow storm – no vehicles could move. He did not come back till the next day, saying that the drifts were too deep – of course he had slept with her. I fired the girl, she was in her thirties, and should have known better than to have sex with a fifteen year old. She had children of her own and much trouble with her husband, but this was not a good enough excuse for me. I had been up all night, frantic with worry and imagining all sorts of scenarios like him lying dead in a deep snowdrift somewhere. It just went on.

On 23rd June 1979, on his sixteenth birthday, Simon walked out of the King's Arms for the last time and left home – he was never to return. As he began to walk away from me, my heart fit to burst with utter sadness and sorrow, I turned and said to him:

"Simon, if you are absolutely resolute to leave like this, you will force me to go down a route which I would never in a million years have chosen to do. I warn you now, and I mean it, I will firmly close the door in my heart to you forever, I shall have to, to be able to survive, and be most assured, there will be absolutely no coming back".

I was trying desperately, but badly, to frighten him and make him stay. He merely said quite coldly that that suited him perfectly, as he had no intention of ever coming back – he had his life to live and it didn't match my concept of it. I was to find out later that I could have forced him to come back – apparently I had legal custody, care and control of the children until they became eighteen through the divorce settlement, but I would not do that, it was important to me that I gave my children the option to choose. I had not had that luxury at home, and I felt that they had to trust in their own judgement. I also knew that if I had brought him back on that occasion, obviously hating me the way he did, that he would simply have left again – and again. I was absolutely heartbroken, I felt that he was not ready to leave home yet, and somehow I believed that I must have failed him. He went to Bath and got a job in a hotel in the kitchens. At least I had taught both of my boys to cook and so he became a chef. He also proved that he was not afraid of hard work either. Again I was to agonise over his leaving and to mourn my loss, first I lose a husband then I lose his son. I remember thinking, why can't I seem to do it for the men in my life – what on earth am I doing so wrong?

All this did little to improve my relations with Peter. I did not blame him for Simon leaving, but at the same time I did not think he had done anything concrete to try and stop him, in fact it was one of our regular customers, who tried unsuccessfully to bring him back to me. I was rapidly losing all respect for Peter because he did so little of the work. He kept the worst pint of beer I have ever seen, he should have had the barrel in use on the thralls (the wooden barrel supports), with one behind already settled, ready to serve and then the next and so on. He used to change over un-tapped barrels and as a result, and one that was becoming increasingly noticed, we were serving cloudy beer. This was unforgivable and down solely to pure bad cellar management. I used to do the daily banking, request for float (extra change), the vegetable orders and list for cash & carry. I did the bed and breakfasts and I was the chef and barmaid, from breakfast till late at night. All Peter had to order and keep properly was the beer. He even had to be urged by me to clean the pipes more often than not, and I can well remember having to remind him of his lack of his own personal hygiene from time to time – ugh!

On one occasion, we had run out of one keg beer – the kind that is ready to serve – as he had forgotten to order it. We rang round and eventually located a nearby pub that had a spare we could have. So I sent him off with the daily meat and fruit and vegetable orders, which were needed for that particular lunchtime. In his wisdom he decided to go to the other pub first and pick up the beer. He got drunk and on the way back to the pub, he smashed in the front of the car wing hitting a stone wall, on a bend, which he failed to negotiate. It could have been much worse, but it was bad enough as Val and I were full with lunches and no vegetables or change for the till! Of course, it caused a terrible row, especially as in his drunken state, he seemed to find it all so amusing.

By this time too Val, our barmaid, was losing her respect for him. I knew in my heart that I had made a very serious error in marrying Peter; in fact, I had actually begun to realise that he was turning whatever respect I once may have had for him, into utter dislike. However, I pushed these thoughts to the back of my mind and tried to concentrate on making life as normal as possible, because I wanted nothing to affect the business, but more especially trying to assess how Robbie would cope without his brother for the first time. I was also aware of a selfish angle. I did not perform at my best if I ever let things get on top of me. It has always been important to me to be able to carry my head high and be proud of my family, and friends but especially myself – I don't do second best very well, and this was certainly one of those occasions when I needed everything to appear as normal as possible. Customers do not like domestic problems interfering with their entertainment and leisure time in the pub.

As the days went by, I was putting all these thoughts into place at the back of my mind and I made some decisions; but the hand of fate is strange indeed and a completely new chapter, or even era, was about to happen in my life.

Once again, it turned out to be something over which I was to have absolutely no control....

CHAPTER TWENTY

Going one better –
Ashton, Brown, Jones – ?

The Midsomer Norton Cricket Club and its Team formed quite a proportion of our 'regular' customers, especially for our lunch times and the 'specials of the day menu'. We had come into 1980 by this time and one day in April, one member of the cricket team, Jim Smith came in, by himself. He came in most days, and we used to have a good chat. Jim

Ron (bottom row 2nd from right and son Jim 2nd from left) circa 1970's.

Ron and Sarah – circa 1970's

informed me that his Mother was very seriously ill indeed and the prognosis was not good at all, and I said how sorry I was to hear this and that if there were anything I could do, I would not hesitate. Jim then brought his father and mother in for a spot of lunch and introduced them to us. I remember thinking at the time, what a good looking and extremely nice man the older Mr. Smith was. He was about five feet eleven inches, quite portly at the time, but with a very handsome, strong face and white, snowy white, wavy hair. He made an instant impression on me as a very kind and caring man, he was obviously devoted to his very ill and terribly frail wife and to their beautiful Golden Retriever "Butch". It was good to meet them and I understood why Jim was so worried about his mother.

Sadly, a few days later, Mrs. Smith passed away. Jim and his sister Jan then approached me and asked me if I would do a very private and discreet lunch in our little restaurant, away from prying eyes, for the family and close friends, after the funeral. I said that I would of course do so and help in any way I could and indeed, that is what happened.

Ron – Air Force Cadet circa 1942.

After the lunch was over and before the elder Mr. Smith, now a widower left, I offered again to be of any assistance, in whatever way, in these difficult times ahead for him. I made a few trips to Bath disposing of some of his late wife's belongings and doing those tasks that he did not feel able to ask his daughter Jan to do. After all this, Mr. Smith, or rather Ron as we were now to call him, became one of our regulars too and came in most days for a rare beef sandwich with horseradish – his favourite, and a friendly chat. A friendship between us all soon blossomed and we would go to his house after closing time some evenings to have a take away meal which we would pick up on the way – he was obviously extremely lonely, and I suppose afternoons and night times must have been the worst, when you faced life in the empty home you had shared with the person that you loved. We spent many

Ron – "Rugby forever" circa 1950's

pleasant evenings with Ron sharing take-aways from the Chinese restaurant in Midsomer Norton, where Peter and I were always greeted by the Chinese owner as "Mr. and Mrs. Kings Alms". Poor man, he could never pronounce the 'r'. On one such evening, Peter stayed on to clean the pipes before joining us, and Ron and I went ahead to pick up the food. Arriving at the Chinese, I was given the usual greeting:

"Good evening Mrs. Kings Alms, how you this ebening"?

"I'm fine thank you – our usual takeaway please".

"Sure Mrs. Kings Alms – but where Mr. Kings Alms and who dis person wiv you"?

"Mr. Kings Alms is joining us later and this is my sugar daddy", I said rather naughtily, but purely in fun.

"Good ebening Sugar daddy" said the man behind the counter and from then on Ron was always referred to by that name whether he was there or not.

After some weeks, Peter made what was to be the biggest mistake of his life, as far as I was concerned – mind you, maybe not from his point of view, it could well have been planned. Our relationship was rapidly going very much further downhill and I was becoming more and more unhappy, and it showed. One lunch time, Peter had a quiet chat with Ron Smith and asked him if he would mind taking me out for dinner, which he would be pleased to pay for, to cheer me up. Ron said he would be happy to oblige and it was decided that he would take me to a hotel in a place called Blagdon that same evening; it had a good reputation and was in a wonderful setting. It was all arranged between them and I was very happy to go. Ron arrived on time, dressed impeccably in his blue blazor, Bomber Command tie and grey flannels. He escorted me out to his Jaguar car outside and opened the door for me. Such a gentleman, I remember thinking to myself. He was absolutely wonderful company. We had a lovely meal, we shared a chateaubriand and I had strawberries and cream afterwards, I will remember that evening for the rest of my life.

After dinner, we had Gaelic coffee on the balcony, which looked right down the valley and over the lake. Ron was the perfect host and we had quite a long chat about all sorts of things. He told me a great deal about himself and his life with Sarah, how they met and so on. He had been in the Air Force during the Second World War and joined Bomber Command as a navigator on the Lancaster Bombers, and he was in 49 Squadron, flying 39 missions in all. He had loved the Air Force, he was the epitome of the 'quiet Airman'; he did not speak about it very much and was certainly not boastful, and he needed to be prompted before you got any information from him about the subject. He had not wanted to come out after the war, but his late wife insisted, and he now found himself with his own roofing contracting business into which he had taken his son Jim and his daughter Jan's husband Abe, and the rest was history, as they say. We then went on to talk about the predicaments which we were both now in. I was telling him more and more this evening, and subsequently when he came to the pub, he would prompt me to talk about and discuss yet again my marital problems, and Ron confided in me that since Sarah's death he had come to feel old and tired and so, so lonely, these chats taking place over a period of about four or five months. One of his later statements made my heart go out to him when he said that he was afraid of dying alone, this lovely new person, this new friend in my life. When we arrived back at the pub he held me very tightly close to him and kissed me goodnight, a very long and very tender kiss, and there they were, I felt the butterflies in my stomach and my heart was pounding like a drum, for the first time since I had been with Chris. I remember wondering what the hell was happening here, am I letting my feelings run wild a little? Should I put a stop to these feelings before anything has time to happen? We had certainly discussed what was wrong with our present predicaments, but we had never even touched on the subject of where we may be going in the future. I had told him that I wanted to get away from my marriage to Peter, but we never took that conversation any further than that. Ron's situation though lonely with his loss of Sarah, was safe and secure so I didn't suppose that he would be making any changes there. That kiss woud lead to me asking myself all sorts of questions, but not daring to give them any answers…

The following day, I was busying myself in the kitchen with my usual daily chores. It was around mid-day and Val put her head round the kitchen door from the bar and said, in her broad Somerset accent:

"Jacqui, Mr. Smith has just come in for his usual beef

sandwich and half of bitter, he asked me to tell you he was here".

My stomach took a complete double somersault and suddenly my heart was pounding again in my chest. I stopped for a moment and told myself to pull myself together. Where the hell had that reaction suddenly come from and what was this all about? This could not be the start of a new love surely? Ron was twenty years older than me, we barely got to know all about each other, and I was still married to Peter. However, from that day, whenever he came in, I knew in my heart of hearts that I was slowly falling in love with this nice gentle man who had come into our lives by accident, and it suddenly occurred to me that this man had strikingly white, snowy, wavy hair. My memories of having my fortune told in Daventry came flooding back into my mind and Ron certainly fitted the description. The rest of his predictions – well, we would have to wait and see. I had no intention of manipulating the situation into where I wanted it to be, we would just have to see how things progressed for themselves.

Time went on and in the August of 1980, a group of mutual friends suggested we should all go on holiday together to North Cyprus, to our friends' villa in a place called 'Ambelia Village', just above Bellapais and near one of the main towns – Kyrenia, and take Ron away from it all for a while as he was still mourning Sarah very much. I had never, ever had a proper holiday and, of course, I had my savings of my prize money from Watneys, so we didn't hesitate in agreeing to go. There should have been four couples and Ron. We were well on the way to completing the final arrangements when the others, couple by couple dropped out for one reason or another. All this left just the three of us still wanting to go, and, determined to take this break, off we jolly well went. Val, her cousin Julie and another friend Peter King had kindly offered to run the pub whilst we were away for the two weeks, which we gratefully accepted.

All the arrangements were made with the help of Maurice and Diana Davis, who owned the villa we were going to use in Ambelia and we flew into Ercan Airport, Northern Cyprus for a two week holiday, on the 24th September 1980, landing at about one o'clock in the morning. As I stepped out of the plane, onto the staircase, I took a deep breath of the lovely warm night air. In an instant, I could have believed that I was back in Nairobi. I knew at that moment that this was a very special place and I was going to love it, whatever it held for me. We had a taxi waiting for us, which Maurice had also arranged for us and off we set for Ambelia Holiday Village, above the quaint little village of Bellapais, nestling up on the side of the Kyrenia Mountain Range.

Villa No. 6 was all neat and crispy white, delightfully furnished in royal blue and with a view over the lights of Kyrenia and the Mediterranean to die for from one end of the island to the other, as far as the eye could see. It was stunning and almost mystical. Once we had sorted out our rooms and unpacked necessary items, we went downstairs to enjoy the night air.

"Who's for a gin and tonic?" asked Ron. Peter and I heartily accepted. Peter and I were in the lounge and Ron gave him his drink and sank himself down on the sofa with his legs up. When Ron gave me my drink I looked at it quizzically and asked him:

"Where is my slice of lemon, you do not serve a g. and t. to a landlady without a slice of lemon!"

Ron said that we did not appear to have any but we would get some in the morning. Reluctantly accepting this I slid back the French windows to step out into the night air onto the balcony. Not three feet away from me, growing in the balcony garden, was a lemon tree. I picked a lemon off the tree, took it inside and sliced it, popped one slice into my g. and t. and one into Ron's and immediately I turned and whispered to Ron so that Peter could not hear:

"That was just magical, I am going to return to England at the end of this holiday, sell the pub and come back to live and work here, I have decided". (I must confess Peter was not even in this equation in my head as these words came out!)

The next morning, Ron and I set about discovering the village whilst we waited for Peter who, lazy as ever, had not even got out of bed. Our hire car was to be delivered and, of course, we ended up at the bar in the pool and restaurant area. We introduced ourselves to the manager Cemal and met his Chinese wife Cathy. I was to find out during the course of the holiday that Cemal and Cathy were going to live in Kyrenia in about two months time, to start a Chinese

September 1980 – Ron and Jacqui on holiday in North Cyprus.

Restaurant and then to Istanbul to do the same. I asked Cemal whether he would have any objections to me applying for the next managership of the complex and he said he would be delighted and kindly gave me the telephone number of the owner of the complex in London, a Mr. Glynn Welby-Everard. This gentleman was going to get a call from me within about a week. I was very excited.

When the hire car did arrive, Peter chose to stay at the villa and left us to set off to explore a beach recommended to us by Cemal. We had moved the patio furniture out from the lounge and onto the patio before setting off and apparently, whilst we were away, Peter chose to move it. We discovered on our return, to our horror that Peter had not been able to hold the table, which fell over and smashed the marble top. We found out from Cemal where they were made and sent Peter off to Nicosia with the measurements to find the factory and replace the top. It was as if fate had played a real hand here and Ron and I spent a very romantic afternoon together, with the radio softly playing and, as we began kissing, the song "Me and Mrs. Jones" came on. We looked at each other lovingly, we laughed a little and then we made love. It was a kind and gentle love really, and that song became our song for ever afterwards. Ron was to tell me later that the physical side of his marriage to Sarah had ceased some years previously and, because of her illness, they had shared separate bedrooms for some considerable time; no wonder he was lonely.

This was the most tender, but wonderful love that I had experienced in a great deal of time and now I really knew that I loved this man very deeply, it was all such a new, refreshing and most welcome kind of love, it all felt so safe and so very right, but I knew that whatever the outcome, I would always have feelings for Ron.

Peter spent the majority of his holiday on a day bed

outside the bar, sipping gin and tonics – he'd earned the rest he said! That just about summed him up. Both Ron and I continually asked him what he wanted to do for each day, but he seemed to have no enthusiasm at all to do anything except stay where he was. In fact, he would tell us to go off and enjoy ourselves and go wherever we wanted, apparently "it was not his kind of holiday really", and I had to wonder to myself just what kind of holiday he would have preferred – perhaps one that didn't include me at all, who knows what was going through his mind. This was making a rather uncomfortable atmosphere – there was no pleasing him and so Ron and I set about making the most of the situation, completely created by Peter himself, who continued to give the impression that he was pushing Ron and me deliberately into each other's arms. We just decided to set about enjoying this precious time in Cyprus, seeing as much of the island as we possibly could, and especially the beaches, and making love at every opportunity that presented itself, which was wonderful. If there were more than two people on the beach, we used to say that it was crowded! We even swam in the nude, and sunbathed, we went sightseeing and on one occasion, Cathy and Cemal made us a barbecue on the beach. We were invited to parties in some of the other villas after meeting the owners at the pool.

We met a couple, Arthur and Benny Fishwick from the Isle of Man, staying, like us, in a friend's villa. He was so funny he had us screaming with laughter. Arthur had one of those scarred by time and lived-in faces, just to look at him made you laugh. He regularly drank quite a lot of whisky, and would pretend to drink it through his ear! We have some great photos to prove it. We asked Arthur and Benny where they came from and Arthur told us that they came from a little rock out in the sea with seventy thousand drunks hanging on to it – he said he was describing the Isle of Man! Benny was a tiny lady with very black short hair, and she always wore the same little 'golfing type' hat. She also had the most impish sense of fun and obviously enjoyed every minute of Arthur's high jinx. At the end of the evening, Arthur would turn to Benny and say:

"Come on sugarmitsu, put your hat on, Sonia Heaney has just walked in". We never really understood why he used to say that, but he was funny, you felt like you had had a "feel-good" treatment or a tonic, after a bout in their company.

On several evenings we visited a Restaurant called "Abbey House", situated behind Bellapais Abbey and it was the only non-Turkish Restaurant in North Cyprus. This Restaurant was owned and run by two young guys, Graham and Bryan, who had been British Airways cabin crew. Graham was a very dapper young man, he had a Van Dyke style beard and gave the appearance of being very elegant, suave and in control at all times. Bryan was much more impish, he had very well groomed blonde hair, again his appearance was always elegant, but Bryan was always at the ready with the risqué jokes and was full of laughter. Together as a Team, they were tremendous company and extremely talented and good hosts. We struck up a friendship with them and went back on several occasions.

Ron and I had a wonderful, loving holiday and Peter took many photographs, encouraging us to be together, even insisting that we kiss and be photographed doing so on many occasions. As for Peter, well I assume he enjoyed himself, as only he knew how. I have to confess to being exceedingly bewildered by his behaviour, but maybe our feelings for each other were mutual, and maybe he wanted rid of me as much as I did of him, and if that were so, then I was more than happy with that. We seemed to be going into a set of naturally flowing 'happenings' leading us and our marriage into its own downward spiral. Ron and I used each of our days discussing everything there was to discuss, and I began to use him as my *'confidante'*, especially with regard to the situation with Peter. I knew I could not last out with him for much longer and, during these discussions, I came to realise finally that my marriage was over and I had to start making plans for the rest of my and my sons' lives, if Simon were to come into the equation.

In my mind, this holiday had become a turning point in my life. However I did not know where the future would be going with my decision to come back and I dared but hope! I knew Ron had already got deep feelings for me, but we had not talked at all about the future or any kind of commitment, to eachother or otherwise, at that stage. Time came to go back to England, the holiday was over, and still Peter had no idea of what was going through my mind. There was just no communication between us at all, I had given up even trying and he was not interested any more.

Back at the Kings Arms, Val, Julie and Peter had done a wonderful job. We were so grateful to them, as it is a

Bryan and Graham at Abbey House – 1981

responsibility to look after a business for someone else, and it is demanding in terms of time and energy.

I now had my plan of action, I had to find a way of putting it into effect, and then to make the whole thing work for me. I had raised two sons virtually alone, I now had what looked like being two marriage catastrophes under my belt and I came to realise more and more that I was now thirty six years old, and it was time, time that I did it for me.

I had no idea where this would go, but I would certainly soon be finding out. A new determination was festering away inside me, positively desperate to burst out – hey world, this is me, this is Jacqui Jones.

I have places to go and things to do and now is *my* time…..

CHAPTER TWENTY ONE

Cyprus Time

Having thought long and hard about the whole situation, I spoke to Peter at length and it was decided that we would give in our notice to the brewery just as soon as I had been down to London to see Mr. Welby-Everard. Peter, thinking that we would be doing this together, asked whether he should be there with me, but I just said that I could handle the matter better myself and that he would be of much greater use at the pub, handling the busy lunchtime with Val. At this point he had no idea that my plans from now on did not include him. Just like Peter, he readily agreed because it suited him better not to have to make the effort.

So, on Wednesday the 15th October 1980, I drove down to London alone and had my meeting. I was offered the complex immediately the interview was over and rental terms agreed, starting on the 1st January 1981. I drove home to Somerset absolutely elated and stopped at a call box and gave the news to Ron. I had no idea at this point what would go through Ron's mind either at this time. Val was not thrilled with the news, but she was living in the village and had, of course, seen landlords come and go and I promised her the highest possible reference with the next landlord.

It was agreed with Peter's Mum and Dad that Robbie,

Peter and I would stay with them, Peter would find a job and Robbie continue his schooling till after his O level exams and I would go out to Cyprus and get the business up and running as soon as the complex was vacated by Cathy and Cemal, the planned flying date being 31st December 1980. All our belongings went into storage in Frome till they could be sent for. When we left the pub, despite all the sheer hard work and effort, we were overdrawn at the bank and our £6,000, the money the brewery had charged for fixtures and fittings, which we had paid to go in, was now worth about £600 when they came to pay us out! This meant immediate employment of some kind to bring me in some funds to go out to Cyprus, plus the fact that we were still paying the mortgage on the house in Lincolnshire for Mum and Dad. Of course, Peter said he could not go out and do menial work, he would have to stay at home by the phone in case a suitable job appeared in the papers. To fund myself, I took a job at a restaurant in Theydon Bois in Essex, called "The Rodings", as a silver service waitress for the evenings and I worked jolly hard too.

I used to drive home to Dagenham in the early hours of the morning, but in one month, including wages and huge tips, and it was November by now, I had saved over £1,000 to take to Cyprus with me, and there was Christmas still to go. Peter was still sitting by the phone! Ron phoned regularly just to keep in touch and time marched on nearer and nearer to New Years Eve and my planned departure date.

On one of these phone calls, Ron had spoken to Peter first and then asked to speak to me. He asked me to call him from a phone box on my way home from the Restaurant that night and not to mention it. I agreed and so, on my journey home, having wondered all day what Ron wanted to say to me, and in typical Jacqui fashion, expecting the worst, I phoned. Ron said how much he was missing me, and how did I feel about him coming out to Cyprus with me. I could not begin to explain the joy I felt at that moment, my stomach was doing leaps and bounds, it was exactly what I had been hoping and dreaming for. I didn't dare ask any questions or presume too much, in case it was all for nothing. How were we going to get Peter to agree to this I wondered. It had to be handled, I needed for Robbie to stay where he was and finish his exams so that he would be free to leave school and join me when the time was right. I did not want to confront Peter at this stage and upset the applecart, and I have to admit to subtifuge on my part in getting this part of my plan through. I didn't feel guilty about this, as Peter obviously didn't care. Ron solved the problem by suggesting that it would be best if he broached the subject with Peter and so I waited for that phone call too. Of course it came the following day and I couldn't believe my ears when I heard Peter saying what a good idea Ron had thought of to help our situation, he had suggested to Peter that he could afford to take the time and, of course, the money to go out to Cyprus with me and help me to get the business set up and earning. The next thing I knew, the tickets were booked for the 31st December and all the arrangements were made. Jim, Ron's son, was to drive him to the airport and Peter, Robbie, even Simon, my sister Gill and her children were to come to see me off. I kissed Robbie goodbye, hugged him very tightly and tried to reassure him that he would definitely be coming to join me very soon. I wasn't ready to tell him anything else at this stage, because I certainly couldn't be sure myself what the future held for us. I said goodbye to Peter and said something to the effect that I would be in touch and that was it. No long, lingering goodbye with Peter holding me and hugging me , kissing me and saying how much he would miss me, nor me him for that matter. He just gave me a peck on the cheek and I walked away. Ron and I boarded the plane and then, there we were, up and away.

I was feeling exceedingly nervous and excited at the same time, if not a little bit wicked. I had never considered another man before in either of my two marriages, but here I was, doing things which went against my whole nature, but I seemed not to want to take any control over. It all felt as though I was functioning as in a dream. Ron was sitting next to me, holding my hand very tightly and we were taking off back to Cyprus and my whole new life was starting from this point. I suddenly felt very much in control, I knew where I was going and what I wanted to achieve with the rest of my life. More than that, I knew I was in love with this wonderful man sitting next to me and I realised that I had known this for some time, but I had, and could only hope that in time, it could be, it would be reciprocated.

So far, I realised, he had never actually mentioned it specifically, so I would have to let things develop for themselves day by day. Ron could be a very quiet man when it suited him, and only time would tell the outcome.

This could turn out to be a very interesting journey or the greatest disappointment of my life...

CHAPTER TWENTY-TWO

A New Decade begins...

We arrived in Ambelia shortly after midnight on the 1st January 1981. What a wonderful start to a new decade. We were taken to Mr. Welby-Everard's house, which he had instructed his staff to get ready for our personal use whilst the apartment above the restaurant and bar was being decorated and cleaned up for us. This was soon finished and at last we could plan our move into our first 'home' together.

It came as a complete surprise to me when Ron then set about arranging for some of his belongings to come out from England to 'start us off' as he put it. So we now had to start buying the necessaries to turn this lovely apartment into a new home. Still Ron had not mentioned any commitment to me, nor him contemplating starting a new life away from England and his family and business. It felt strange, and yet I could not bring myself to question him about his motives in case he felt that I was trying to manipulate him to where I wanted him to be and he seemed to be taking it purely for granted that it was what we had both had in our minds and it was also what we both wanted. It was, of course, but I was to learn, in the fullness of time, that Ron always did things without the need for lots of pre-amble. If that was the case, why question it, or one of his favourite sayings 'if it ain't broke, don't fix it'. I was here

First day at Ambelia – 1981

and going to get my new life up and running, no matter what. I decided to just let things drift on into their natural course – the words could come later. This was my way of trying to make sure that I was 'safe', that I wouldn't be hurt – no broken promises, no misunderstandings and, above all, no recriminations.

In the meantime, we stayed on at Mr. Everard's house till the container arrived. Several evenings, until Ambelia Restaurant kitchen was completely functional, we went back to Abbey House for dinner and rekindled our friendship with Graham and Bryan. Their faces were a picture when Ron and I walked in without Peter and, of course, we soon enlightened them. They both seemed genuinely thrilled that we were together and neighbours, and that I had got the business at Ambelia. Mine was a holiday village enterprise and theirs was an elegant, sophisticated restaurant, but Ambelia would do for now, as I had long term dreams. This was merely the beginning, I firmly and resolutely believed that North Cyprus had a lot to offer for the future. It was a relatively new country and was very beautiful and unspoiled and I so much wanted to do something here that would make my mark on it and make it our new future.

I made lots of enquiries and asked lots of questions, because prior to coming on holiday to North Cyprus, the only things I knew about it were from the news broadcasts on the B.B.C. years ago at baby's bath-time in front of the fire, when I would watch the news about the EOKA terrorists and the last of the British conscripts Britain sent over.

Just to give you a little of the background of Northern Cyprus, there had been trouble all through the 1960s as the Greek Eoka terrorists (who by 1959 had forced the British colonial government out) then turned their attention against the Turkish minority on Cyprus. The Greeks were attempting to ethnically cleanse the island of its Turkish Cypriot population and force "Enosis", or union with Greece. There were some nasty atrocities against the Turks, and eventually in 1964 the UN was called in. From 1964 to 1974 there was an uneasy peace between the two sides. In 1974 it all blew up again. The Greeks launched a coup against President Makarios which quickly turned into a nasty civil war, with Makarios fleeing for his life. This was really the final straw in the long-running problem on Cyprus. The Turks intervened to stop the fighting. They had guaranteed the Island's constitution and swiftly overran the north of the island. A buffer zone, often called the "Green Line" was drawn in autumn 1974 to separate the warring factions with the Greeks moved to the South of the island and the Turks to the North. The island still remains divided by this UN 'border'. The North became 'The Turkish Republic of Northern Cyprus' in 1984, and is isolated by much of the rest of the world. However, this does not detract from the total lack of pressure, the easy pace of life, the stupendous scenery, and glorious unspoiled beaches. Cyprus enjoys a climate that can be predicted, which makes forward planning easy, and a good standard of living. But the biggest gem is the warmth and sincerity of the Turkish Cypriots and Turkish people. The welcome is unbelievable, their sincere love of you once you become friends, and their generosity cannot be matched anywhere.

Kyrenia is dominated by a backdrop of the Kyrenia mountain range and is absolutely breathtaking. Ambelia itself nestles into the side of the mountain above the picturesque village of Bellapais, made famous in the book "Bitter Lemons" written by Laurence Durrell. It is a purpose built holiday village comprising villas, apartments and studios all set round a central bar, restaurant and swimming pool with private management accommodation in the form of an apartment above the restaurant and bar.

There was an enormous balcony to the apartment and when you stood out there, you had a complete vista of the whole of the coastline in front of you, the blue of the Mediterranean and the smouldering Kyrenia range of mountains at your back. Wonderful scenic countryside, tremendous atmosphere, the sensation of the freshest clean air and that glorious perfume of the pine trees, wafting in the evening breeze.

We had done all the sightseeing we could do on our holiday back in September/October and now was the time to look at this new project. I was so keen to get this on the move and I immediately set about stripping and cleaning the restaurant kitchen, working out my menus and recruiting staff. I had to get the restaurant up and running as quickly as possible as every day that we were not trading was money lost. This was achieved within a few days and life in earnest began in Cyprus.

On the first day on the island, I was feeling very unwell, I put it down to something I had eaten. We needed transport urgently, so we phoned our newly found friend, Namik Ramadan of Atlantic Car Hire, and a vehicle came up to collect Ron and take him down to Kyrenia to arrange for a hire car until, Ron said, we could make long term plans for a vehicle of our own. Ron duly collected the car, which was a left hand drive Renault 9 and probably ten or twelve years old, and which he was definitely not used to driving.

On his way back up to Ambelia which involved a climb back up the mountain on what was almost a single track road, on both sides of the road was rough track on which you could just about drive by getting your nearside wheels off the tarmac area. However, despite putting his nearside wheels on the rough portion of the road, he took the spare wheel off an approaching Army jeep which failed to pull over far enough to avoid Ron. As a result, Ron had to telephone our friend Namik at the car hire company. The civil and military police arrived and took measurements etc. Ron was advised by Namik that although it was not his fault, if he took the Army to court it would probably take four years to get them into Court and then he would definitely lose. Namik took Ron up to Ambelia to get his passport, then took him to Kyrenia Police Station to meet the police officer who had done the measuring.

Namik, at that time, imported a Scotch called "Cream of the Barley" and had put a bottle in his briefcase before they went to the Police Station. When they arrived at the Police Station, they met the Officer who attended the accident. A conversation took place in Turkish, which of course, Ron didn't understand. Suddenly, with the conversation now at an end, in silence, Namik took the Scotch out of his briefcase and put it on the Officer's desk, who then opened his desk drawer, again in total silence and took out the case file, ripped it in half and put it in the waste bin and then put the Scotch in the drawer. Namik turned to Ron and said:

"That is the last you will hear of this matter. Pay your excess, about £80 and forget this ever happened".

On the following day, the bug that I had picked up was still bad and I was still vomiting violently, so I decided that around food was not the place to be. The next day I was much better and went down to begin working in the kitchen. We had inherited a couple of waiters and one of them, Shener, who had a smattering of English, asked me where I had been the day before. I pointed to my open mouth and gestured that I had been vomiting and told him that I had been very sick. I suddenly realised that he had the most horrified look on his face and he scurried off, muttering in Turkish under his breath. Not understanding this reaction, I told the story to Graham and Bryan at dinner that night and they too looked horrified.

Bryan said:

"oh f . . k me darling, you did not say the word 'sick' did you"? I told him that I had and he and Graham started laughing. When I asked what was so funny, they told me that in Turkish the word 'sick' was the f . . k word and that Shener must have thought that I was explaining that Ron and I had been practising oral sex all night! I never made that mistake again and went on from there to learn all the Turkish swear words and rude sayings so as never to land in that kind of trouble again. All this drama – and it was only the first few days, but what an impression I must have made on my new staff!

The next night, I was up in the apartment, putting the

finishing touches to my furnishing talents and when I surveyed my achievements, and it did look great, there was something obviously missing. I stood in the middle of the room and looked round at everything, then I realised what it was. We had this wonderful fireplace, I had had one of the boys place a basket of logs and kindling beside it, but the fireplace was empty. It needed a fire to put the finishing touch. So, I lit the fire. It was all warm and cosy and I went down to one of the empty studios of mine and brought a beautiful long haired, furry white rug up to our apartment and laid it out in front of the fire, perfect. We had a nightcap and started to kiss and cuddle and before I knew it, we were making passionate and tender love on the rug, in front of the fire. We spent one of the most romantic and wonderful evenings I think I have ever spent in my life, with a man I had come to know that I would always be able to trust, who I could be sure would not go off with the first good looking woman to pass him. I now had a new love and everything in the world to look forward to. However, there were things to sort out before that time could come.

Ron and I had a great discussion the following day. I could not afford to let Peter have too much time to make plans to join me, he was definitely no longer any part of my future as far as I was concerned. I plucked up the courage to bring up the subject that had not yet been discussed or even hinted at and I asked Ron where I stood with him and the future and he told me:

"I thought you had realised Darling, that when I came away with you, that it was going to be a permanent commitment. I am staying with you, I thought you would have realised that for yourself. Of course, I shall have to go back at some stage and sort things out with the 'kids', but that will come later, when I have seen you alright."

I was at once so ecstatic, so happy and, at the same time,

Relaxing at Ambelia between customers – 1981

so relieved, but of course, I hadn't taken it for granted. We chatted on and it was decided that I would phone my Solicitor in England and ask him to act on my behalf, which he did, I told him what I was thinking of doing and he said he would await my instructions, Then I plucked up all my courage and rang Peter. I kept reminding myself of the conversation Peter and I had had in the taxi going to the Registry Office, when he said that if ever I changed my mind and did not want to be married to him that he would accept that. The conversation went like this:

"Hello Peter".

"Hi babe"(a name for me which he knew I hated).

"Peter I have come to a final decision".

"What about babe?"

"Peter, I don't love you, I never have and I would like a divorce".

"O.K.babe, I will see a Solicitor in the morning".

That was that, no trying to reconcile, no hope for more chances, nothing. That was what I meant when I said Peter made no effort at anything, he always managed to make me feel like Chris did, that I was worthless and that he just didn't care, but equally, at the same time I was relieved and grateful that he had kept his word and did not try to drag things out. The divorce was finalised later that year. I came to find out eventually that Peter made no effort because whilst I was working hard and paying money into our account to pay the mortgage, he had been steadily drawing it all out to live on, he had made little or no effort to find immediate employment and we were now overdrawn and I was overdue with the mortgage. Ron helped me out with that and, with help from Ron again, I bought Peter out of his share of the house in Lincolnshire. He was out of my life now and I never heard from, nor have I ever seen him again from that day to this.

By way of a celebration of our newly confirmed 'union', Ron suggested that we go down to Kyrenia that evening to celebrate. I readily agreed and we decided on dinner at Abbey House first, which was wonderful as usual, and we gave the boys Graham and Bryan our news of a future together without Peter. They were delighted for us. We then set off for the casino and disco to round off our evening in style.

When we got into the casino, I had never been inside one in my life, much to Ron's amazement. We went around all the tables and watched people playing 'black jack' and some of the other games for a while. Then Ron turned to me and handed me a £10 note and said:

"There you go darling, go and try your luck on the roulette wheel."

I must have looked very worried and unhappy as he looked at me and said:

"Go on love, have a little flutter, it is just a game, don't take it so seriously".

I went over to the table and watched other people for a little while, then gave my ten pounds to the croupier who used a special pusher to put it down a slot in the table and then pushed my chips over to me. I played numbers 4 and 9 as 49 was always Ron's lucky number, and to my amazement I started to win. I started to win but at the same time, I started to shake from head to foot. It got to the point where I was genuinely becoming distressed and I pulled all my chips off the table and went over to the cashier and cashed them in. When he gave me the money back I had over £100 in my hand. Ron came over to me and asked why I had stopped playing and then noticed that I was actually distressed:

"What's the matter darling, why did you stop, you were on a winning streak?"

"I have never gone through such a frightening experience", I said to him, "I have never ever held £100 in my hands in my life, bringing up the boys, I didn't even know what spending money was all about, and the thought that you can stand there and throw money away on that table like that just terrifies me".

Ron thought it was so funny, and when I tried to give him the money back he said:

"Why are you giving it back to me, it is yours, you won it you spend it on yourself and enjoy it".

"It is not my money Ron, it is yours, and I don't want it" I said, I was still shaking.

He insisted I keep it and go out the next day and spend it on myself exactly how I liked. Then, that drama over, it was time to go on down to the disco. We used to love the Dome Disco because when we used to walk in, they always played "Me and Mrs Jones" first and then all the oldies but goodies, great for us to smooch to, and smooch we did. It was wonderful to feel Ron's strong arms and hands pressing me close to him, he made me feel so safe for the first time in my life.

The next day, back to reality and we set about decorating and cleaning in the Restaurant and bar and to this end Ron bought himself his first ever pair of denim jeans. He absolutely hated them and quickly despatched them off to one of the staff. We had begun shopping for the bar and Restaurant but found out that my beer deliveries would have to be deposited at the cafe in the centre of Bellapais because the road up from Bellapais to Ambelia was far too steep for the delivery lorry to make it. This was all duly done and we were so pleased to strike up a friendship with the owner of the cafe Rafat, who was a hero of the 1974 conflict with the Greeks, which had left Cyprus a truly divided island. Whilst we were clearing out the bar storeroom, we found some bottled Guinness which, although dated pre-1974, was still able to be used by me in my steak and kidney pie recipe.

I had brought with me from England, amongst my belongings, a special mixer/blender that cooked whilst blending. It is a wonderful machine, just like another pair of hands in the kitchen. Unfortunately I discovered that the blade assembly was cracked right through so that the machine could not be used. I rang to England and ordered a new blade assembly and they forwarded it at a cost of £29.00 for the part plus postage. Whilst waiting for it to arrive, our friend Behcet arrived at Ambelia and I told him my plight. He took the blade assembly away, to my cries that it was a sealed unit, a specialist part and it could not be copied. Behcet said:

"Don't worry Jacqui, you wait and see what we can do in Cyprus".

He was right. Two days later he came back up to Ambelia and gave me an exact replica of this blade assembly. A little old man in Kyrenia had tooled up especially and copied the part, for which he wanted the princely sum of £2.00. I was thrilled, my mixer was in use again and that piece has lasted twenty eight years so far. My eldest son still uses it.

Along with the bar and Restaurant, included in my rent, for my own use entirely, were three of the studios below the pool. However one of them had a sitting tenant called Sezai, and Mr. Welby-Everard instructed me to have him removed. Sezai flatly refused to move out unless I could find him similar accommodation at the same rent and in a similar location. Impossible. I decided that in his case, discretion was much the better part of valour and I would let sleeping dogs lie.

I was to find out later exactly who and what Sezai was, but more of that later..

CHAPTER TWENTY THREE

And so to Court

We had settled well into our new life in Cyprus and had by now met all the residents of Ambelia. Some of them became special friends, like Janet and Evelyn who were elderly ladies and cousins. Janet was a doctor. There was also Millie and Dick Perkins, who were a wonderful couple, Millie was a large lady with short blonde hair and she was always smiling, Dick used to remind us of Ghandi, he was tall, very thin and very bald. We all became close and visited each other for dinner and lunches sometimes. There was also a lovely couple at number 4, Emine and her husband Engin who were very wealthy Turks and who came from Istanbul. Engin had the gambling 'bug' and we were to watch him many times as he lost several thousands of pounds. It never seemed to worry him unduly for some reason, but a lot of the Istanbul Turks are extremely wealthy families, and gambling is part of their culture.

Ron had completely redecorated my three vacant studios and I had managed to fit in making new curtains and bedspreads, by hand, for all three. There was nowhere in those days where you could buy ready made items such as bedspreads, curtains, cusions, lampshades and the like – you had to make them yourself or get atailor or dressmaker to make them for you. I put in new vases and as equally, there were no florists either I went up into the mountains and picked dried flowers to make arrangements. I also went to Dizayn74 workshop in Kyrenia – all traditional Turkish Cypriot pottery and new ornaments and plates. They all looked so fresh, clean and pretty now.

A few days later, Ron went down to Kyrenia to shop and pick up any mail from our P.O.Box. He came back with a letter from two friends of his and his late wife, Iris and John. I had never met them whilst I was at the King's Arms, but apparently they would like to come out and stay with us at Ambelia. Ron was very keen because in his mind, they had been quite close friends. He asked me how I felt about it and, of course, I said they would be very welcome, I hoped that any friends of his and Sarah's would become friends of mine too. I suggested to Ron that they could have the largest of my three studios free of charge. Ron was delighted and wrote back immediately, inviting them to come. This they duly did and Ron went to Ercan airport to meet them and bring them to Ambelia. They stayed for two weeks and every day started the same, with them on our apartment balcony and me cooking them a full English breakfast each. I also fed them in the evenings, all free of charge. They seemed pleasant enough, though it was a little strange for me as I had not met them before and they knew Ron so well.

One evening, we took them down to experience the Dome Hotel, Casino and also the disco. After a little flutter in the casino, we went into the ballroom and Iris immediately grabbed Ron and pulled him onto the dance floor. John and I sat at the bar having a drink and a chat, but I noticed every time Ron and Iris came passed us dancing, Iris was crying, streams of tears were flowing down her cheeks. At the end of the holiday, after Ron had taken them back to the airport, I told Ron what had happened whilst he was dancing with Iris.

"She is in love with you Darling" I said to him, "I am convinced of it".

"Don't you start" he said, "Sarah always used to say that, and I always told her she was imagining things and talking absolute rubbish".

I let the subject drop. It obviously embarrassed him that his late wife and his new lady should pick up on exactly the same thing, and life just went back to normal but I didn't forget the incident. At the end of their holiday, they thanked us profusely for having them, they thanked me for my hospitality in cooking for them every day and after all the niceties, Ron took them to the airport and off they went back to England.

About ten days later another letter arrived from Iris and John from England. I saw the look of horror on Ron's face as he read his way through the letter. He let out an awful moan and started to weep bitterly. Ron, despite his happiness at being with me, was still mourning his loss of Sarah, he used to sob during the night and during the day, each time he told me a story about their lives together, you could see his pain in his face and eyes. It was his way of coming to terms with his dreadful loss, they had been married a long time, and by listening and just being there for him, I felt as if I was actually helping him through all of this, it is a privilege to be in that position, especially if you care very deeply for that person.

I asked Ron what was wrong and, silently, he handed me the letter. I was horrified as I read through the sour, bitter and vitriolic words that she had written to him, words like "coming away and sleeping with that slut of a woman, so soon after Sarah's death". I immediately took the letter over to Janet, the doctor, and after she had read it, she said:

"This demented woman is in love with Ron: she's jealous".

I was so furious that I had gone out of my way to wait on those two, hand, foot and finger as we say and all at no cost to them, and then for her to write that evil letter. It was vile. I did no more than to sit down and write to her husband John, enclosing her letter and asking him if he knew that his wife could write those kind of things and that his wife was, in the opinion of an expert, definitely in love with Ron. I said that I hoped she would be punished in such a way that she would regret it the rest of her life.

The story has a sequel. Some while later, the jealous Iris wrote and apologised to Ron. She added that her John had dropped down dead in the street and people had walked round him thinking he was a drunk, and then she added that, oh, by the way, she had met someone else just a few weeks later and was now living with him! We were ultimately to find out that this man too died suddenly, not long afterwards. God works in mysterious ways.

Ron slowly, but surely, got over the whole incident, but needless to say, Iris was never invited back. What we also did not know at that time was that when she and John got back to England, Iris went round to see Ron's daughter Jan and told her that she believed that Ron and I had been having an affair before Sarah died! We now know that is the reason why she would have nothing to do with me and still will not, to this day.

In about March of this first year, Ron received another letter from England. This time it was from his neighbours in Midsomer Norton, Jean and Don Wiggins, and they asked if their daughter Jeanette could come out and live with us for a few months and help me in the Restaurant. I knew Jeanette because she had gone out with my Simon for a short time and he had brought her to The King's Arms. She was a lovely girl and I didn't hesitate in saying 'yes'. Jeanette finished her A level examinations and came out to us in about May. Besides helping me, Jeanette was a beautiful and elegant young lady of seventeen, she had long blond hair that she used to style very carefully every day and she was very particular about her makeup and appearance. She also had a tremendously healthy appetite to say the least and soon earned her nickname that Ron christened her – "Tubby". All our male Turkish Cypriot friends soon tucked her under their wings and despite teasing her unmercifully, (including a ducking in the pool after spending hours doing her hair and getting ready to go out) they protected her fiercely because European girls are much pursued by the young Turkish Cypriot men. She soon met and teamed up with a young Turk named Hasan and they went on to have quite a long relationship, which came to nothing in the end.

Shortly after this, Robbie came out to me to live with us till he knew what he wanted to do with his life. We picked him up at the airport and immediately, in a totally surly voice, he said:

"I don't like it here, I am not going to school here, and I am not going to learn Turkish". Just like that.

Well, of course, he was at what parents have, since time immemorial, called "those difficult years in a young man's life". Robbie well and truly had those, on his own admission. I merely told him that he could make his own choices in life, up to a point till he was eighteen, but that whichever paths he chose would reflect on his later life. I also insisted that if he did not want to continue school, then he would have to learn a profession and go out to work. In the meantime, he would work with me and we set about running Ambelia with him now on the team.

Ambelia was mainly a holiday village but a few of the houses and studios were occupied and indeed owned by people that I have already mentioned like Dr. Janet and Evelyn, Hasan Ramadan Cemil (a young and prominent businessman) and his girlfriend Eileen, Peter Holmes (the Architect of Ambelia) and his wife, our friends Maurice and Diana, who came out several times a year and the Manager of the village and his wife, Fikret and Hilary. Graham and Bryan from Abbey House came up regularly and we, naturally when we could slip away, went to them for dinner – our friendships with all these people were developing and they were helping us to form our first circle of friends who would fill our days and nights from then on.

Once the restaurant and bar were up and running, in the very early days, I was in the kitchen doing my daily preparation and Ron was outside when I suddenly heard him say:

"B....y hell, what are you doing here?"

I rushed outside to see who he had said this to. Ron had a roofing contracting business in England and this was one of the roof tilers he used to employ. Small world, he had no idea that Ron was out in Cyprus with me.

In about the June of 1981, we received a booking through the Football Association in Kyrenia, for a Mr. Keith Burkinshaw and his wife to stay with us for ten days. They were to be treated to great privacy as he was at that time famously known as the successful Manager of Tottenham Hotspur Team (he had brought a team of youngsters over to play as a touring side against the youth of North Cyprus). As he was being mobbed adoringly by the football-mad youth of Cyprus, I was anxious that they be afforded maximum privacy at Ambelia. Robbie was one of his greatest fans. He was so excited at the prospect of Spurs' boss staying with us; but I warned him that it was not done for him to approach him under any circumstances until and unless Mr. Burkinshaw encouraged the move. Robbie was bitterly dissappointed, but give him his due, he abided by the rule and gazed on admiringly from afar.

At the end of their holiday, having dined with us several times, Keith and his wife thanked us profusely for their stay and our hospitality. Keith asked me if there was anything he could do for us in return. I told him how my son was his greatest fan and that he had wanted to approach him, but did not break the rules, so could he possibly have an autograph. Keith said he could, but only if Robbie approached him and asked for it himself. So Keith and his wife placed themselves on their daybeds beside the pool and I sent Robbie over. He was so thrilled. Keith called me over with the camera and put his arms round Robbie's shoulders and I snapped them – lovely photo. Keith then took his gold cockerel pin, the Tottenham emblem, out of his lapel and pinned it onto Robbie. He was so proud, he has it to this day and the photo.

Below Ambelia was a mainland Turkish Army Camp. We had given Jeanette a studio at the top of the village to give her some privacy and independence. One day, whilst getting showered and changed for the evening, she was frightened when one of the soldiers did a "peeping Tom" at her through a window. The soldier the Army suspected was immediately arrested by the Military Police. They then placed him in an identity parade, and Jeanette had to attend and pick him out. This was a very frightening experience for a young lady of seventeen, especially with a race of people that she did not know very well, and she told me that she found the whole incident extremely intimidating. I could understand that. However identify him she did and he was charged and sentenced to three years hard labour tacked *on top* of his conscription time. That came as a shock; but I learned quickly that the Turks don't mess about.

The summer season for North Cyprus was desperately quiet in those days and having asked around and about other businesses on the island, I knew I was paying an exorbitant and totally unrealistic rent for a business that just was not there. I had talked it through with Ron and we decided I would ask Mr. Welby–Everard for a rent reduction, as he was due to come out to Ambelia very soon. When he arrived, I tackled him and told him that his rent was unrealistic for Cyprus at that time, there were virtually no tourists to speak of, just the odd 'swallow' (the home-owners who came and went each year, and these people usually owned their own holiday homes and used restaurants very little.) Even the pool held very little pull for guests, they had the whole of the Mediterranean to swim in and that was free and a darned sight easier to get to.

I had not been able to do much homework on Glynn Welby-Everard, because in those days, there were so few ex-patriots in Cyprus and so few people to be able to give you information in this vein. Someone did tell me that he was a dedicated drug addict and alcoholic and was rated, by some, not to be the sort of person I should either mix with or indeed to do business with at all, and that they believed that he was was dishonest. It would have been no surprise to me how he would take my approach had I known, but in character, he did not take it like a gentleman. Although he knew the business was not there, he retaliated by locking me out of the bar and restaurant and told me to get the hell out of the place. I was devastated. I had lost my job, our place to live and my income all in an instant. I have always hated being out of control. As long as my requirements for life, a safe home, a steady job and income and the ability to rule my own fate are in place, I am happy and confidant and will work until I have accomplished my goal. I was so used to working for myself and for the boys; I had become a very independent lady.

Ron told me not to worry myself; we would rent an apartment whilst we made our plans for a permanent home.

I suddenly felt much more safe and positive. However, the first thing we did do was to go and see a lawyer, Mustapha Güryel, who happily agreed to take my case on against Glynn Welby-Everard, and we set about gathering all the evidence. Whilst all this turmoil was happening, our belongings had all gone, with the help of friends, to our young friend Said's warehouse in Nicosia, so at least our home contents were safe.

Kyrenia was a very small place in those days and the expat community was a very small, but very strong one. We soon came to know most, if not all of them and the social life was very lively. One of these new friends was Rita Cornwell, who lived in an apartment block called Pallidama. When she knew of our plight, she told us the apartment opposite to her was for rent and helped us to get a short-term rental on it. It was a lovely apartment, very graciously furnished and we fell in love with it. It was now our home till we could find a permanent solution.

I eventually won the case against Welby-Everard in the end but only after months and months of hearings, and him having to fly out to every one. The day of the last hearing, after my damages had been announced – which only amounted to a few hundred pounds after all that time – I walked out of the court with my head in the air. As I passed Welby-Everard I turned round and faced him full in the face and said to him in the most bitter and vitriolic voice that I could muster:

" You lying, cheating, bastard. I will see you dead and in hell for what you have done to me, and I never break my word." He merely smirked.

Ron told me not to bother, he wasn't worth the effort. I have to be completely honest here and say that I prayed very hard and regularly to God for Welby- Everard to get the come-uppance that I felt he deserved. I thought that man was evil, I was told that he even practised black magic, he was a really nasty piece of work and, apparently, I had not been the first he had done awful things to.

Beware a woman scorned. A few months later, on a trip back to Ambelia, Mr. Glynn Welby-Everard dropped dead on the tarmac at Ercan Airport and is buried in Kyrenia Old British Cemetary....

CHAPTER TWENTY FOUR

Changes, more changes

In the meantime, life carrying on from day to day as it does in North Cyprus, Ron decided that we should have our own car, the rental had been going on for so long now and he was obviously content with his decision for us to be together permanently, although, he had still never actually got around to making a positive statement or asking me to be his. This was a situation which still perplexed me, but made me more resolute not to 'rock the boat' or try to push him. We had all the time in the world to make this relationship what we both wanted it to be.

At the moment, he was concentrating on 'our' car. He was adamant that he would not want a left hand drive Renault (all you could get new in North Cyprus at that time), so I offered to phone my ex-boss, Len Miller, at Ford Motor Company and ask him to make arrangements for a suitable car to be shipped out to us. We decided on a Ford Fiesta with a sunshine roof (no air conditioning in those days!) and it was duly immediately dispatched to Famagusta by one of the main Ford dealers that Len had contacted.

This car was allowed into Cyprus duty free in Ron's name, as in 1981 a person could bring in one 'retirement car' duty free. People used to stop us in the street and ask if they could buy it from us, so unusual was a new foreign car in North Cyprus.

Just before Christmas 1981 Ron decided to go back to England and tell the family he was staying with me and that he would settle his business affairs. I did not realise what this entailed, as he still did not discuss matters with me first, but no doubt he would tell me what he wanted to upon his return. Our relationship was not such that I knew his financial details or the exact structure of his Company etc. I took Ron to the airport and returned home heavy-hearted, and with little thoughts of doubt going round and round in my mind about whether he would be persuaded to give up the Cyprus idea and me, once he was back with his children. I couldn't bear the thought and had to push it to the back of my mind till he came home. I would know soon enough one way or the other.

I was very unhappy about spending Christmas on my own in the apartment and so Graham immediately asked me to stay with him and Bryan at Abbey House and be with them for their annual Christmas Party, and I readily accepted. In the meantime, as he could see that I was anxious about being on my own, Bryan insisted that I bring one of their dogs, a Cyprus Hound called "Muffin", home to the apartment with me to keep me safe, which indeed she did.

I was in the middle of making a Christmas cake for the party when there was a ring on the door bell. A Turkish man, whom I had been introduced to briefly at the Airport, stood there and as I opened it, he pushed his foot in the gap in the door. Muffin heard my worried voice and came round into the hall from the living room. Seeing the Turk and his threatening behaviour, she immediately bared all her teeth, all the hackles on her back were standing on end, and she gave out the most fearsome growl. With that, the man ran off down the stairs, two at a time.

I left Muffin for a short time to go out and buy some ground almonds to make marzipan for the cake. When I returned, still so thrilled with Muffin's guard dog performance on my behalf, I could not get cross at her when I discovered that she had nibbled away the front edge of the Christmas cake which was being soaked in lots of brandy. She lay on the carpet in the lounge in a drunken stupor, moaning loudly whilst I trimmed it all off. Now it was elliptical in shape not round, and I covered it in apricot jam and put the marzipan on, iced it and took it and Muffin up to Abbey House for Christmas with "the Boys".

Whilst we had dinner, unbeknown to us all, their cat had got into the kitchen and nibbled all the icing off the top! Fated was that cake – it ended up in the bin.

I helped Graham in the kitchen and we had a lovely cocktail party for their friends and a super private Christmas Day, enjoyed in true traditional manner. I was missing Ron very much and looking forward to his coming home, but I returned to the Apartment, with Muffin, and awaited news of his flight home and prayed that the news would all be good.

When Ron returned, he told me that he had severed all ties with England and now we would be together. Of course I was absolutely elated, because now we could make proper plans for our future, not "maybe" plans. However there was a down side because whilst there, Ron decided to not only give the business to his children in it's entirety, but also to sell his home back in Midsomer Norton.

The business was at that time continuing to be run by his son Jim and son-in-law Abe. Ron signed the whole concern over to them lock, stock and barrel, keeping only for himself a small piece of land adjoining the business and no income or pension for himself at all. Selling the house I could understand, but not to buy something smaller to go back to if or when everything maybe did not work out, that I could not understand... Later he was to realise that this was the biggest mistake he could make, for reasons which will later become clear.

I desperately wanted to plead with Ron not to sell the house, at least till he was sure where we were going both for now and in the future. I still had to earn a living, but Ron was retiring and his old age was a long way off. However, I did not feel strong enough in my side of our relationship at this time to insist or talk strongly about matters, which, in reality, were not any of my business – we were not even engaged nor had there been any talk of being, let alone married. More importantly, I did not know how Ron would have felt if I had tried to have an input into his own family decisions. In my own heart I would have loved it if we could have kept a home in England and, ideally, a small house or bungalow in Cyprus. At least, those were my heart's desires at that time. That was not Ron's way of thinking then, and I would find out in the fullness of time that it was never going to be.

After returning, Ron and I set about discussing where we wanted to be and what I needed and wanted to do. Finding somewhere permanent to live became the priority, it was now well into 1982 and I needed to be earning and so, after long discussions we decided that we liked the Pallidama apartment life and we would buy a top floor unit in a new block being built right up at the top of the High Street in Kyrenia. We got the usual assurances that there would be a tenant's agreement, we would not be built in front of, communal areas would be kept clean etc.etc.etc…. Of course none of this ever happened; however, it was completed. We went to have a viewing once the workmen were off site, and we found to our amazement that every flat had a multi-coloured bathroom suite, i.e. we had a blue basin, pink bath, yellow toilet and white bidet, our neighbour Harber had a pink basin, blue bath, yellow bidet and white toilet! That is one of the loveable sides to the Turkish Cypriots' character, they had not realised that each colour was a bathroom suite in its own right. However, the flat was finished, all paid for and we could move in.

We sent for our belongings from Nicosia and commissioned a carpenter to make us all the rest of the furniture that we needed, whilst I set about making curtains, bedspreads and other furnishings. The flat had three bedrooms, so Ron and I had the main bedroom. I furnished a nice bedroom for Robbie in blue and grey with white, summery furniture and the third room I did, in holiday style with twin beds, in case Ron's daughter and granddaughters came out to stay. Jan, his daughter, was not in favour of the match with me but I hoped against hope that with time, she would come around. During one of his phone calls home to her, it was agreed Ron would join her and her family for a holiday in Turkey – I was definitely not invited. Ron never did discuss with me what was talked about nor how much he had told them about our situation, in fact he avoided the subject and made it clear he had nothing to discuss with me. I know this was because Jan would have been so totally anti me that nothing Ron could have said would have made her change her mind, otherwise she would have lost face. So, he came back to the identical status quo of that before he went away and, though I did not know it then, this was never to change. I never let this situation bother me, though had her attitude changed, I would have done anything to make the situation right for Ron. This would not preoccupy my mind for long though; there were apparently other developments in the wind.

I was in my kitchen one day when there came a ring of the front door bell. When I opened the door there stood

Jacqui Jones aged 37 years on the balcony of
our apartment in Kyrenia.

Tamer, from Atlantic Cars, one of a group of young Cypriot friends, who we met with regularly, and he was with an older gentleman, carrying a large bunch of red roses. Tamer said this man was his future father-in-law Abdullah and could they come in and talk some business. The gentleman gave me the red roses for which I thanked him. It appeared that he was the new owner of the Café Chimera right on the front in Kyrenia Harbour, one of the busiest tourist spots in Kyrenia, and it had been closed since 1974. He wanted me to set it up again for him and get it open and trading for the summer.

We agreed a salary and I set about this task with great vim and vigour, working out an original and different menu – café food, but with things like home-made pizzas and home-made burgers and so on, things that had never appeared on a menu in Cyprus before but were good strong café fare. These would be quick and easy for staff to do once I pulled out of the business, or so I thought. In time, I had completed the menus, and staffed the place and we set about getting all of the stocks for the bar and kitchen.

On one of these days, I was out shopping with Behcet and we happened to be in a large supermarket opposite to our apartment, shopping for cases of wines and spirits. I was standing at the till, having carried over some of the cases, paying the owner of the store when I suddenly felt my legs getting warmer and warmer. Behcet looked down horrified. Suddenly he took off his jacket and wrapped it around my hips and the top of my legs.

"Quickly Jacqui", he said, "we have to get you to the apartment immediately".

The apartment block was actually opposite this shop, thank God, and by the time I got up to the apartment itself, I knew why. I was absolutely gushing blood from between my legs. Behcet laid me down in the bath and called the doctor immediately. Within minutes I was rushed to Kyrenia Hospital where, after a clinical procedure to clean everything out of my womb, I was told that I had suffered a miscarriage.

I was absolutely heartbroken. This had never happened to me before, and the sight of all that blood and the thought that I had been nurturing a new life, one that was touched with my lovely new love and certainly all of mine, made me feel inconsolably sad. Although this was going to gnaw away at me and hurt for a long time to come, inwardly I had to have the acceptance that Ron insisted that we have no more children, as he was absolutely petrified of any of his offspring having Downs Syndrome. This was because this had happened to his brother and wife, and Ron and Sarah had seen the affects it had had on their lives for many years. I really did understand and if this was the only request or demand that Ron would make of me, then I felt it was right and proper to accept it.

So I sadly made up my mind that I had to put all this

behind me, and I decided to go to Communion at our little church St. Andrews in Kyrenia. Yet another shock in the roller coaster of events could have made anyone doubt the idea of a loving God. I saw it as a different sign. I went regularly to Sunday morning communion. After my personal prayers, I came to the conclusion that God had decided things for himself for my own good. Eventually, after a few days recuperation, life was running smoothly again, but I would never, ever forget.

After almost one year running, we had a good catering business going on at Café Chimera on the Kyrenia Harbour waterfront. We were even doing boat trips with food from the café but, of course, this was too good to be true. The blow fell when I came in one morning to find Abdullah and a young fellow standing waiting for me to arrive. As soon as I got there I was informed that he had given one of my pizzas to this young fellow to take apart and see what went into them, and he now felt that this lad could make them himself. The upshot was that my services were no longer required.

To be honest, although I was shocked to be treated this way, I was not totally surprised. I was not sorry as I never felt that either Abdullah or his wife completely trusted me. It was not something I could not put my finger on, but there was always an atmosphere behind the scenes in his café, it may have been something to do with the fact that his Turkish and very traditional wife did not like the idea of me, a younger woman, working and earning her living for her husband and I could be a possible threat. If she had looked long and hard at her husband, she would have known that she had nothing to fear from me.

So I went back to being a housewife once again till I could find something more suitable. The trouble was, time was going on and we were well into 1982 by then. I was not to rest on my laurels for too long, however, nor was Robbie. He had been working for Namik Ramadan helping to put an effective system in for the car hire business, at the ripe old age of seventeen, and a very effective system it certainly was, but this would by no means be a good start for a career.

Going back up to the apartment our paths crossed with our neighbour Harber. He asked me what I was doing at present and I said 'nothing' and that Robbie needed the start of a career. He told us that he was opening a new Restaurant in the old harbour with a local businessman called Hasan Ramadan Cemil, whom we already knew from Ambelia, and it was to be called "Ma Cuisine". He asked me if I would help to train his chef and if Robbie could be trained as waiter and *Maitre D*. I readily agreed and Harber asked me to come up with some menus. This I did with great enthusiasm and a final menu was agreed. Harber

Robbie under training as maitre d'hi
with friend Harber at Ma Cuisine.

undertook Robbie's training and, at what seemed like record time to me, Robbie became an excellent waiter. He had great hospitality skills and he was good to work with.

We did a grand cocktail party for the opening night, which was a roaring success. The only problem was that when making the food for the party, most of which I did at home, "The Cyprus Syndrome" came into play. Taking in the pickles and relishes that I had made, I had said to the chef, when you have put all of these food items into dishes, give the jars to the washer up for me, I wish to take them home and use them again. At the end of the evening, the washer up gave me a clean bag with all the gleaming jars in it, but, oh dear, he had thrown away the lids! Of course, I was told:

"You did not ask for the lids to be kept, only the jars". Silly me!

Ma Cuisine was to be the new shining light in restaurants, and it was fast becoming the place to be, in the Harbour. Reservations were good and so was the trade in general, but sadly, it only lasted six months when the partnership between Harber and Hasan came, literally, to a bitter end. Ma Cuisine was never to open under that name ever again. So here we were, about to enter 1983 and Robbie and I were out of a job, yet again, thinking we had seemingly little prospects of any that we could readily see, that is when we found out that the Harbour Club, one of the most prestigious restaurants on the harbour, was becoming vacant. Working for other people and at their mercy, had now lost its' appeal, if it ever had any. We needed a business of our own. I felt quite positive about these prospects.

I knew the owner of the Harbour Club; it was Ramiz who used to come regularly to Abbey House. We knew him and his wife very well, they came to our flat warming party. I took the bull by the horns and telephoned Ramiz and asked him of I could go into Nicosia and see him. He readily agreed, I knew he had a soft spot for me. Ron wanted to go with me for that reason, but I told him that I could handle Ramiz quite well on my own. He reluctantly agreed.

Ramiz was waiting for me when I arrived at his office and stood up to greet me. I have to say, in those days, he was a very statuesque and handsome Turk, very proud of his Ottoman background, and reminded you of it at every opportunity. The warm greeting over, he returned to his seat behind his desk and I sat and faced him:

"Well Jacqui my dear, and just what is it that I can help you with?" he charmingly asked.

"Ramiz, I will come straight to the point, I have heard that the lease on the Harbour Club is available in the next few days. I would like to know if this is true and would you consider letting me have first option on the Lease?" I enquired rather nervously.

He looked at me intently for a few seconds, giving a very wry smile as he did so, and I got the distinct feeling that something was racing through his brain and he was trying to assess my mood at the same time. Just as I began to feel a little uncomfortable and thinking to myself, 'I wonder just what the catch will be.' Ramiz opened the top drawer of his desk, took out a bunch of keys and pushed them slowly over the desk towards me, about half way. Then he removed his hands, sat himself back into his chair and crossed his arms on his chest and looked straight at me, sitting there in total silence.

"That's fantastic Ramiz", I said enthusiastically, "and, now Ramiz Bey, how much for the Lease and how much for the monthly rent"? I asked nervously. I think I already knew what the answer would be. Ramiz still said nothing, slowly uncrossed his hands and leaned slowly over the desk and pushed the bunch of keys till they lay right in front of me.

He said nothing. I looked deeply into his large brown eyes, pushed the keys back a cross the table till they were in front of him and said:

"Thank you so much Ramiz; but that is a price I am not prepared to pay". I got up and as I left his office I turned and added:

"But thank you so much for your time and for the compliment Ramiz. I will not forget it".

So I didn't take the Harbour Club, but just a few weeks later, I was to contact Ramiz again and I was able to get the keys of the Harbour Club for our friend Harber who was branching out on his own after Ma Cuisine. For him, the keys had a monetary price tag. To this day it is still run by Harber's family and sadly, Ramiz has suffered a stroke and is not a well man. However I did see him just before he became ill and he was just the same proud Ottoman Turk that he always was, a very suave and elegant man, and, like so many Turks, a man with an eye for the ladies. But not this one...

That all was certainly an experience but the lack of the Harbour Club did not bring us down at all, for it was glorious here in Kyrenia, and if you had to be out of work somewhere, why not here in paradise? I should perhaps add that Ron was not pushing me to work, he never did, I could have been an ordinary housewife if I had chosen to be one. No, it was I who insisted that I by myself, do my own thing and always, always do more than to pay my way – we both had a certain standard of living and I for one was adamant that that situation would remain for as long as I could help sustain it.

A few weeks later, we were in Kyrenia to get some money and spotted our car hire friend Namik at the entrance to the Dome Hotel. He invited us in for coffee and we graciously accepted. As we were sitting sipping our coffees, a man came over and spoke to Namik. His name was David Hamilton–Grant and he asked Namik if he knew of anyone reliable who would be prepared to house and dog sit for him in his house, right out of Kyrenia along the coast road to the west, in a little village called Kayalar, about eighteen miles out. Ron and I looked at each other, nodded and immediately agreed to go and see the house. It was gorgeous, right on the edge of the cliffs overlooking the sea. We agreed terms and came back to Kyrenia to sort out Robbie and the apartment.

Our friend Behcet, who was a policeman in the C.I.D., agreed to stay in the apartment with Robbie till we returned. We packed up all the things we needed for our stay and set off the next day for Kayalar with Behcet and Robbie following on. When we eventually arrived at the house and went towards the back door, this little black and white poodle type dog with long totally matted fur came running out to us, she was in an awful condition. So this was our doggy sitting task we thought. "She will have to be completely tidied up," I said to Behcet and Robbie – "that will be your task."

As we came through the gate, tied to the back door, the only door to which we had a key, we were stopped by a huge Alsatian dog; and he was ferocious.

"Now how are we going to get in?" said Ron.

I said "If I go back to the butcher's shop in Karsiyaka and buy some beef, we can keep him occupied feeding him whilst you let yourself in".

So that is what we did. When I got back with the beef, we found that even though the dog had calmed down, his rope was too short to get at the door, so Behcet broke a side window, let himself in and opened the door from the inside. He later took the window off and took it to have the pane of glass replaced. We were subsequently to find out that the previous house sitter had abandoned the Alsatian and gone back to Turkey, leaving the dog to whoever would take him. Ron immediately said:

"We shall keep him and his name from now on is Butch" – after his golden retriever that he left in England when he came out to me.

The little dog I called Lady and it turned out a few days later we were to find out that she was pregnant, when she gave birth to four robust little puppies Pugwash, Whisky, Annie and Mimi. They were so ugly but cute and we found homes for all of them. Butch was the father of the pups and so we had Lady spayed. We untied Butch and he came to live inside the house with us all and, day by day, he responded totally to our love and kindness and very quickly reverted back to being a lovely and loving, cuddly big dog. So now our family was complete, dogs and all!

My life now seemed perfect to me and went on day to

Jacqui with Butch our Alsatian

day in sheer bliss. I had this lovely man Ron, my son was with me and he was already forging a strong bond with Ron, we had a lovely place to live right by the sea, we had our apartment and Robbie had his independence there, and now we completed the family with our two new dogs.

Life at Kayalar was idyllic. We did a lot of entertaining, wonderful people like the Turkish Ambassador to London, Rahmi Gumrukçuoğlu and his lovely wife Elçin, who were our next-door neighbours. Elçin was a fabulous cook and they entertained us too, they were truly delightful company. Dear friends Toby and Robin St. John-Caulfeild, ex–Army and terribly well spoken, also lived in Kayalar and came to dinner very frequently. In those days there was a strong expat community in and around Kyrenia and entertaining was very much a part of weekly life, so much so that you were completely unaware of the flight of time.

However, we should not sit with our feet under the table of comfort for too long, after all, that great big hand of fate never left me alone or let me get complacent...

CHAPTER TWENTY FIVE

From Egon Ronay to Michelin Star

It is now the beginning of 1983 and a few days later our lives were to take the most unbelievably dramatic turn. A letter was delivered out at Kayalar, addressed to me from a Mr. Faik Muftuzade. It appeared that his wife had been awarded a property in exchange for her property lost in the South of Cyprus, in the village of Catalköy, some two or three miles east of Kyrenia. He went on to say that he and his wife did not want to spend any money at the moment and the property needed extensive renovation. Friends and family had suggested to him that it would make a nice restaurant, and to this end, Namik Ramadan had given him my name as a *restauranteur*. If I wished to go and see the property, then I could, there was a caretaker there and he told me where to find it in Catalköy. Of course, I immediately showed the letter to Ron and asked him what he thought.

"Well you must obviously go and have a look darling, it could be just the chance you are looking for".

Ron knew that I had a dream, a dream of making my mark in North Cyprus that nobody would forget, indeed to fulfil that one ambition in life, to succeed at something big – "to reach the unreachable star". He was right, that was my dream and maybe, just maybe this was the beginning of that dream..

Mr. Muftuzade also said in the letter that he would not mention the house to anyone else, he wanted me to have the opportunity of the first refusal. So I got into the car and came back through Kyrenia and out to Çatalköy. I took the back road that skirted the village itself and went on towards Ozanköy. I came passed Inci and Tangut's property as instructed and round the big bend at the bottom. As I drove along the road, my heart was pounding with anticipation, I was so excited,and suddenly, there it was, a big white house, standing in about three and a half acres of fruit trees, avocados, plums, cherries, oranges, grapefruit, mandarins and lemons. It was a dream of a place. The house had been built in 1939 by Lady Loch and her family, and legend had it that all the artefacts in and around the house, and there were many, including the pebble paths, had been collected personally and put in place by Lady Loch herself. There is a stone plaque above the front door with 1939 carved onto it.

There was a huge bamboo plant and a giant magnolia tree with flowers so big you had to cup both hands to hold one. There was a beautiful climbing pink rose that grew up into the tree on the bank above it. There was a long pebble path leading to the front steps and the front double doors must have been the archway and doors from some church somewhere. As you walked in through the front doors you were standing on an open balcony that ran the whole width of the house with rooms off on both sides and if you walked to the edge of the balcony, you were physically standing above the tops of the trees in the garden. There was a stone staircase down to the lower level where there were many rooms, including the kitchen and one huge room at the end of a long walk from the bottom of the staircase and this room had a huge archway in the centre. It was breathtakingly stunning.

In true Cyprus fashion there was an open wooden

Loch Manor

staircase up to the top floor. The top floor was one huge room and one smaller one and adjoining the two was an enormous bathroom with walk-in linen cupboard – you could have held a dance in there. It was such an imposing building. All the ceilings were old Cypriot with plaited cane matting held in place by real long timber poles and very high. Every main room had a traditional fireplace, the hearths being about two and a half feet off the ground and a canopied chimney going up through the ceilings. The whole building was in need of urgent renovation and re-wiring, but there was a true magicical atmosphere that was already there.

I drove back to Kayalar in a dream. Ron said:

"Well, did you go?"

"Yes, darling I went", I was hanging it out to keep him a little in suspense, trying not to show my intense excitement.

"Well, don't keep me up in the air like this, what was it like?" he said impatiently.

"Fabulous Ron, just fabulous, it would make a fantastic restaurant. You have to go and see it, and soon before Muftuzade agrees to show it to someone else".

We decided to go together the next day, make a decision on the spot, and then approach the landlady before anyone else got to see it.

The next morning we got up very early and went to see the house. When we got there and had done the tour, Ron turned to me and said:

"Darling, it is unbelievable, it was meant for you, you must have it and have a go at this one. I can feel it, this is destiny, this is definitely the place for you and your talents and I will fund you". I couldn't believe my ears. I was so excited.

"I know what I will call it Ron, it will be named after the Lady who built it, I think 'Loch Manor', what do you think?"

"That's perfect", said Ron, "just perfect". Now we had to contact the owners and talk about the rent. This we did and it was all agreed and signed there and then. Joy of joys, Loch Manor was mine.

So, here was my big white house with the flat roof, my man with snowy white hair and I was on lovely Cyprus, surrounded by water. The medium all those years before had been perfectly right, except for one thing, he had got the number of children wrong. I hadn't had four children, just two and one miscarriage. Close though, so there must be something in these kind of people I suppose. However, at this point, I felt very secure that from now on, I was definitely going to be safe, Loch Manor was going to be famous, but above all, my life had real meaning and purpose, and something great to work for and with my lovely fella and son to work alongside me to build my dream.

I thought that at last I had finally got 'de moon' . . .

CHAPTER TWENTY SIX

A New Era

We made all the arrangements and moved all our belongings from the apartment to Loch Manor and immediately put the apartment on the market. It sold very quickly and we were happy to leave apartment dwelling behind. Now we could focus all our attention to our new venture, Loch Manor Restaurant. Our two lovely new canine acquisitions were coming with us too, now they had a new, very large home with about three acres of garden to play in!

On the ground floor, coming into the hallway, there were two rooms at either end of the long arched balcony. The one to the right I decided would be the bar. The hall and balcony were to be fitted with moveable furniture to make it into the reception area with a table sporting a visitors' book. The left hand room was to be Robbie's bedroom. There was a bathroom with balcony on this floor at the bottom of the staircase to the upstairs level, I decided that this was to be the ladies' toilet and powder room, with two cubicles and a vanity unit, all in a lovely shade of blue, and this was done.

Upstairs, the enormous bedroom became our sumptuous lounge and the smaller room was Ron's and my bedroom. The bathroom between these two rooms, as I said was enormous, so our washing machine would fit in there and it could double as a laundry room for the restaurant – we had

1983 at Loch Manor – the only beard Ron ever grew

to be totally self-sufficient, there were no laundries in Kyrenia then. Downstairs below the ground floor there was, as I said, this huge room with a large, wall to wall, Cyprus archway in the centre and a shelf high up just below the ceiling for decorative plates and ornaments. It had a great atmosphere even when empty and it opened through French windows onto the garden and all of this was to be the all important restaurant. There was an existing small kitchen and another store room, so we knocked one wall out to make these two into a very large "L"-shaped kitchen, storage shelving and serving area. There were two other rooms on this lower ground floor, one of which became my dressing room for changing from kitchen whites into my evening dresses each evening, after finishing being the chef, and the other one was for the waiters. It was all going to work so very well and we set about changing things with as much love and sympathy for the place as we could; but at the end of it all, it all fitted, it all worked, it would flow.

I designed and we had made all the fixtures and fittings, things like the wall lights, which were wrought iron in the shape of a *fleur de lis*, the fire irons and fireguards for all the public rooms. We designed and had made the restaurant furniture and after several shopping sprees in both Kyrenia and Nicosia, we bought tapestry fabric for upholstery, tablecloth fabric which we had made to measure, luxurious rusty coloured carpet, velvet curtains and so on, right through the house. I set about designing the fittings for the kitchen, shelving, work surfaces, hot cupboard and all the kitchen paraphernalia, and sourcing crockery, cutlery, and cooking utensils.

We took on two young men as waiters and Robbie set about training them. We fitted them out in evening suits, shoes, shirts and all those things. We took on Ali, a tall and dark Pakistani gentleman, to help me in the kitchen and Ron in the garden too and our friend Behcet, who had just retired from the Police Force in Kyrenia, was to be my *commis* chef. We had Robbie kitted out with evening suits and shirts, etc. There were several trips to Nicosia's Old Quarter, where I searched out copper trays for small table tops for the bar, brasses and copper ornaments and "nick-knacks", vases, *flambé* lamp and so on. All the pictures were bought by our friend Jean Wiggins from Picture Galleries in Bath in England, and we had them framed in Kyrenia and Nicosia. We ended up with some beautiful pictures and each one fitted into its own special place as if they had been designed or comissioned to be there purposely.

When it came to the tablecloths and napkins, I had, as I said before, been to Nicosia and bought the fabrics and

Behcet my 'commis chef' with friend Tahsin in background – opening night at Loch Manor – 1983.

these were maroon heavier cloths with crisp white cotton over cloths and matching napkins – plain but stunning. I took the measurements of the maroon cloths so that they hung down well over the sides of the tables and had a sample run off at the local upholsterer. When it came to the white ones, I wanted them to be put on diagonally over the top of the red cloths, with the points of the white cloths just touching the hem of the red cloth. I turned to Ron and said:

"There must be a way of working this measurement out darling". Ron, ever proud of his mathematical and navigational skills, proudly said:

"Yes my love, it's called Pythagoras' Theorem".

I had forgotten more mathematics than I dared to remember and so Ron began working it all out. He was absolutely spot on and the over cloths and napkins and maroon cloths were all duly made and delivered back to us. I instructed Robbie to have all the white cloths and napkins freshly laundered because, in actual fact the fabric I had bought, I found out was a complete bale of burial cotton!

When they came back from the laundry – disaster, they had all completely shrunk. We had to start again and kept the first ones as spares in an emergency. We could see the funny side afterwards and it was the subject of many a reminiscence evening with our friends later on.

I had decided that the menu and cuisine would be pure French and immediately began earnestly structuring the menu. This was soon done and I roamed the countryside around Loch Manor picking wild herbs, rosemary, thyme, sage, juniper berries, bay leaves and wild capers, which would set the tone of many of the menu items. I used fresh fruit of the season, and as many from our own garden as I could, to make jams and jellies for the sauces, as in those days, things like redcurrant jelly were not available commercially.

The enormous linen cupboard in the bathroom upstairs (it must have been at least twelve feet square) was already fitted out with shelving and a concrete structure that was perfect for putting on a portable small gas hob with gas bottle. I took up, bit by bit, all the ingredients for the dishes on my menu and one by one, all the dishes on my French Menu were born, all tried out by Ron, my 'official taster' and all done in that linen cupboard.

All of this resulted in what I considered to be an extremely well balanced and exciting menu. A lot of the dishes were of my own creation because of the lack of commercial ingredients available in the North at the time. It worked. I made static silk flower displays using slices through logs for the bases and old roots and grasses and newly imported silk flowers, as there were no professional florist shops anywhere in North Cyprus then. Our neighbour Peter Bevan did grow roses and special flowers in season and I had them as and when they were available. We collected all the old Greek/Roman pillars, which were lying all over the place in the garden and grounds and placed them in strategic places, on landings and staircases and around the balconies.

On the day when everything was to be delivered, we were in the bar, Ron, Robbie and myself and we were hammering and beating the copper sheeting which we had fitted on top of the bar and polishing it. I stood in the middle of the bar and looked around at our handiwork and suddenly I said to Ron:

"What happens if when it is all delivered, it does not work, you know it does not all fit well together, or all my choices of colourings are wrong?"

"Forget that, darling, it will all be absolutely wonderful," he said.

I had a very nervous feeling but this was soon pushed to one side when suddenly they were all coming and going. The carpenters delivering and fitting the furniture, Adem Kaner from Nicosia were busily fitting carpets. My curtain maker was hanging velvet drapes, the tailor was delivering evening suits. The painter was finishing off touching up the balconies and checking toilet cubicles and walls where electricians had worked. It was all happening. I had managed to find and buy, a portable typewriter with beautiful "Coronet" script and I had typed all my copies of the menu by hand. Robbie had gone back to England for me to buy some nice leather-bound menu holders and snail dishes with the cutlery to go with them and other incidental items that I could not source in Cyprus. When he returned, his baggage was overweight by £88 worth of extra items! We paid it with a smile, what else could you do? However it was finally coming together and every day we were closer to that professional touch that I was looking for and it now seemed to be a reality, not just a dream.

As each room was finished, I went from room to room

and marvelled at the results. Every room looked splendid and very sumptuous. I designed a sign with an imaginary coat of arms and it was put up on the branch of a tree overhanging the road outside.

My dream was at last coming to fruition. Can you imagine, at the age of thirty nine, I had overcome twenty one years of unhappiness, sorrow, losses which at times I could barely handle, I had fought back, struggled, managed and somehow at the end of it Jacqui was still intact and still raring to go. Here I was about to launch a French restaurant in the heart of Northern Cyprus which I hoped would be among the best on the island and I stood to make a reputation second to none, anywhere and it was little old me that was doing this for herself. What an enormous mixed feeling of privilege, good luck, fortunate circumstances and I had love, true love in my life at last. My adventure, the one I was born to do, was about to break out of the chrysalis, spread its wings and fly like a butterfly.

All the training and preparations over, "Loch Manor" was at last born. The only final hurdle that we could not overcome was that we could not get a telephone line because there were none available. In the days before mobile phones everyone relied on land lines. The G.P.O. could not give us a date for fixing one either. I did not know it then but it was to take three whole years before we got the phone installed and people devised all sorts of ways of making their reservations.

We had lots of inquisitive visitors leading up to the opening of "Loch Manor" and we always made them welcome and gave them a drink on the house and the guided tour. Many pledged to and did return.

Eventually came the moment of truth. It was time to arrange the launch of this new restaurant and we all decided that a prestigious cocktail party for all our friends and

Robbie operating his bar at Loch Manor 1983

potential customers would be the best way to launch it and I began drawing up a list of names, starting with President Rauf Denktash and his ministers, our neighbours, prominent business people and so on, and invitations were sent out for the 31st March 1983. We were now to find out if the whole thing worked.

I had a long, royal blue velvet skirt and crisp white, high-necked blouse made by my dressmaker for the opening, Ron wore his navy blue blazer and Bomber Command tie. Ever my navigator, he had steered me in the right direction this time! Robbie wore his dress suit – very smart we all looked too. We were having an assortment of newly-devised *canapés* and nibbles, miniature pizzas, choux puffs and all manner of goodies to tempt the palate, including king prawns. Peter Bevan, my flower man had delivered vast bunches of gorgeous roses and flowers from his garden and I had done beautiful displays on all the pillars, in the bar and on the ones going down to the restaurant. It all looked very impressive and was met with great admiration.

Very soon our guests were approaching the front doors down the pebble pathway and the party began. It was a most tremendous night and everyone enjoyed themselves very much from the remarks they made in our visitor's book, every remark from "It is heaven on earth", and a German comment we have never had translated, to "Nice to see the best place in Cyprus eventually exists" – a truly wonderful feeling. Behcet did extremely well in the kitchen, and the waiters performed well too. When it was all over, we sat in the bar with all the staff and went through the Visitors' Book together over a well earned nightcap! At the end of the evening, I told Behcet to take all the fresh flower displays down onto the back balcony and keep them out there overnight in the cool evening air. This he did.

The next morning, I was told that one of our guests, Robin St. John Caulfeild from Kayalar (where we had house-sat the house), was not at the party because she was not at all well and was devastated to miss the evening. I decided to go out to Kayalar and take her some of her favourite food, king prawns, as a get well gesture. I told Behcet to get two packets of prawns out of the freezer and defrost them in some lukewarm water. When I went down to the kitchen to prepare them, Behcet went and fetched the prawns, defrosting in one of my crystal vases that the flower displays had been in!

"What the hell are they doing in the vase Behcet? If the prawns are in the vase, what are the flowers in?"

He took me out to the back balcony and there on the stone floor of the balcony lay all my lovely blooms – out of water and wilting badly!

"Well you did not say to leave them in the vases Jacqui, you said take the flowers out onto the back balcony overnight – so I did!" There I went again, like the pickle jars and lids, I did not cross the "T's" and dot the "I's", but in any event I went ballistic that he would have used something like a vase to defrost a food item. Hey ho – Cyprus….

I had allowed us all one week before the Restaurant opened for bookings whilst we had our final dummy runs to make sure of the menu content, timing, service and, above all, that the ambience and surroundings actually worked. It was as well, because the next day, the two young waiters decided that it was going to be too much like hard work to stay and walked out, just like that. Now we were in the mire, six days to opening and no waiters! I telephoned Mustapha Shah at the Kyrenia Hotel School and he promised to try and help.

I was down in the kitchen doing more preparation when Robbie came down to tell me that a waiter had come for the job.

"Thank God" I said, but Robbie said:

"I don't know about that Mum, wait till you see who it is".

It turned out to be a waiter we had seen in a Kyrenia restaurant we had gone to a few weeks before, and I remember thinking at the time what an idiot I thought he was. However, it really was Hobson's choice as time was now very short, and so Kani joined our team and I just knew the headaches would begin! And begin they well and truly did. Kani was a walking disaster area in every way. Robbie used to have to tell him his routine every day and while in my kitchen, doing my daily preparation, I would hear:

"Kani, you have not brushed your teeth today. Kani you have been eating garlic before service. Kani you haven't cleaned your shoes today. Kani you have a dirty shirt on. Kani, your nails and hands are filthy. Kani you have no deodorant on" and so it went on …..

Then there was the time when serving Prawn Bisque soup in the restaurant. This is a soup made from the heads

Every restauranteur's nightmare – Kani the waiter – 1983.

and shells of the prawns and finished with a tomato sauce. When serving this soup it is normally flambéed, and we chose to do it at the table, for the effect. Kani set alight the brandy in the brandy ladle, and despite being strictly forbidden to carry out this particular task, he proceeded to drizzle it all over the place as he took it to the table without a side plate under it and set fire to the curtains, the dumb waiter, the carpet and onto the tablecloth before floating what was left on top of the soup! He just grinned his inane, sickly grin whilst Robbie flew round and put out the fires. On another occasion he was told to clean the stair carpet down into the restaurant with some soapy water and a scrubbing brush – he used a wire brush and removed all the pile from the edges of the carpet, which then had to be turned! He was utterly hopeless. Robbie used to get so frustrated with him. I could never laugh at the television series "Faulty Towers", because, believe me, it was so near the truth! Manuel was alive and well, living in North Cyprus and working at "Loch Manor".

Time went on and we were getting a fantastic reputation, despite Kani, and much of the credit for that must go to Robbie who was becoming a tremendously skilled "*Maitre D*" and very popular with everyone who came to the Restaurant, especially the President, Mr. Rauf Denktash.

Gradually we noticed that we were getting more and more requests to do a traditional "Sunday Lunch", an idea that I fought off as long as I could, because the one thing I had promised myself when I first arrived on the island, was that I would never try to create a little England here in Cyprus. Then, one day, in our usual lunch time "watering hole" (a bar in Kyrenia run by friends of ours Allan and Jean Cavinder used by all of the ex-patriots), we met two lovely English girls, Carol and Yvonne, who told us they were croupiers in the evening but were also trained waitresses, looking for part-time work, and would love the job of doing Sunday lunches. Two of our other friends, who were English, offered to get me all the pork and specialist things in the Greek South which I could not get in Kyrenia – if I would please do Sunday lunches! A Pakistani waiter called Mohammed, who worked for Allan during the week offered to also help with the lunches and so a Kani-less new team was born on Sundays and lunch at Loch Manor became the in-place. Very successful they turned out to be too, except I think the girls would have liked the waiting-on team to be man free! These two girls could run the whole Sunday show between the two of them and they did this with the same enthusiasm that my three waitresses had had in the pub in Peterborough.

We were headed well towards Christmas at the end of our first year and, despite the intervention of one of the leading Cabinet Ministers at that time, we seemed no nearer to getting the telephone. However to say that this did affect the business would be difficult, because, despite having to come to the Restaurant and book, or do it through a third party, we were exceedingly busy. We even had the disc jockey from the British Forces Broadcasting station giving us bookings over the radio, and we had to have that on in the kitchen just to hear the reservations! He would give veiled messages like:

"Hi Jacqui, Ron and Robert, sweating away over there in the kitchen, how about three at eight tonight?" In addition to that we had ambassadorial cars arriving to make reservations, senior UN vehicles booking for the officers and so on, and there would usually be a batch of bookings for us at Allan's bar in Kyrenia when we made our usual daily trip in, and another couple in Catalkoy who also took reservations for us. It all worked very well really. We had realised very early on in our time in Cyprus, that you have to be inventive and that there was always a way around a problem if you looked for it.

At about this time, the vicar of St. Andrews Church in Kyrenia, Arthur Rider, stopped me after communion one Sunday morning and asked me if I had an hour or so to spare. I said that of course I had and what did he want me to do? He told me to trust him and everything would become obvious to me. He was a truly wonderful man of God, a gentle man, a lovely person and great character, everyone adored Arthur Rider and his wife Doris. He took me down into the old harbour, up one of the little alleyways leading off the harbour and into the garden of one of the harbour cottages. He took me up the stairs and into the lounge and there, sitting on a cream linen settee was an old lady. She was sitting looking out of the window out to sea and listening to the buzz of passers by down below. Upon seeing visitors, she immediately picked up a bottle of perfume from her side table and gave herself a good spraying. It was Chanel No.5, her favourite perfume she informed me. We were introduced and her name was 'Babs' Tyrrell-Martin. She had come to Cyprus to live in 1952 and she lived alone. We became great friends and after that day and a long natter with Babs, I was soon visiting her every time I came into Kyrenia, or at her special request, and I always cooked a gourmet lunch for her to take along with me.

"Thank you darley" she would always say. She loved her food, especially shellfish. She was married to Eric Tyrrell Martin who was, Babs told me, the polo trainer for King Farouk of Egypt. They were great socialites in the 1940's out in California where Eric started his own very prestidgeous polo club. She had a telephone book from their time in California with such names as Charlie Chaplin, and Carol Lombard and Clark Gable, who were two of their closest friends, to name only three. What a life she led, and she had still been a socialite when she first came to live in Cyprus. She was very beautiful in her day and it was rumoured that she really was one of the original 'good time girls' and even had a fling with King Farouk, one among many I was told!

Babs claimed that she was 79 years old, but we were all sure she was much older. After only a few months, during which I became extremely fond of her and she of me, and visiting regularly several times a week, Arthur called me one morning, and asked me to go with him; we had to rush to Babs.

"She has only hours at best, love" he said to me, "we shall have to be quick".

I dropped everything and drove at great speed into Kyrenia, praying that I would be in time to talk to her one more time. We arrived at the cottage and she was lying in bed. I cradled her in my arms and she looked up at me and said:

"You are just like an angel darley, you are surrounded by gold".

Then she just went silent. I kissed her goodbye, sobbed in Arthur's arms for a few moments and he blessed her. I used to visit her grave every week and take one red rose. On her gravestone it reads 'Edith (Babs) Tyrell Martin' 91 years old and gives the dates. She could tell a lovely tale when it suited her and I truly loved and missed her greatly, partly because I knew that, for a short time in a lifetime, I had meant a great deal to a lonely old lady who once had been a force to be reckoned with and had had everything! I felt very touched, blessed and privileged to have known this lady.

About this time, Simon wrote and asked for a reconciliation, he was getting married and wanted Ron and I to go back to England for the wedding. We discussed it and I told Ron that this was my first born son. Despite his arrogance and rudeness when he left and his obvious dislike of life within his home environment, it was decided that maybe he had changed, maybe now that he was going to get married he had discovered what family life should be and so we did decided to lay things to rest and support him and his new wife to be. I had a new outfit made, Ron packed his beloved blue blazer and flannels and off we flew for a very short visit. However despite coming all the way back for the wedding, Simon and his new wife and family barely spoke to us at the reception and so Ron and I left early without any kind of offer of goodbye and thanks for the present and for coming, and drove back to Midsomer Norton, where we were staying with 'the Wiggins' our good friends who came out to stay with us almost every year.

We flew back to our beloved Cyprus feeling a little used, we had gone all that way to be virtually ignored and treated more or less like 'interlopers', we both felt out of place, in the way and exceedingly uncomfortable, to be honest we really did not fit in.

CHAPTER TWENTY SEVEN

Loch Manor thrives...

Loch Manor settled into a good rhythm as a restaurant and we were becoming more and more busy. Reading back through the Visitors' Book today I recall some of the most memorable evenings and people of my life. People like James Scott whose very kind letter to me began "When I came to dinner with Baron and Baroness Twickel on the 13th November"....! Mr. Scott then proceeded to write out for me a full history of the Loch family, including copies of the relevant pages from Debretts' and Burke's Peerage.

We had many diplomatic and protocol guests, and they all left their individual comments and marks in the visitors book. Our then President, Mr.Rauf Denktash was a regular visitor, he was such a gentleman and a pleasure to cook for. Mr.Tahsin Erteruloğlu, whom we had met in the first few months of coming to Cyprus when he was doing his national service, was by this time a friend and regular visitor. He is now a member of the Turkish Cypriot Parliament. Lt. Col. 'Sandy' Mcleod, a very tall white haired man with a wooden leg and proud of it. He was a war veteran in the Indian Army, and a tremendous character of whom Ron and I were extremely fond, wrote – "The best restaurant in Cyprus and would be outstanding in any country". I well remember the day that we were at Ercan airport near Nicosia, waiting for

Robbie to fly in and we saw Sandy striding away at a hell of a pace, his wooden leg held in place with his army "Sam Brown" belt across his broad shoulders, no top on showing his handsome, bronzed torso, his black beret on the side of his head and his longish white hair flowing with the speed he was travelling. He was an awesome sight and a very imposing figure – but such a wonderful character.

I remember those days well: the complete crew of Canadian Customs who came every evening for seven nights and then wanted to smuggle me back to Canada; Steve Coppell of Crystal Palace football Club and his wife Jane, who said "The nosebag was ace!" Lord Ted Willis from the House of Lords; several Chinese or Japanese gentlemen over the four years, all of whom wrote a piece in the visitors book, which none of them would translate for us. We had to wait for the next Chinese/Japanese gentleman to come along and translate. Australians, Canadians, Swiss, Irish, Scots and lots of fine people from Istanbul who were great food connoisseurs all came and enjoyed themselves at Loch Manor. One of my favourites was the late, great Brian Johnston and his charming wife Pauline, who I now still see from time to time, and Brian wrote, " Lovely sprouts and mint sauce, you'd make a great cricket tea lady Jacqui! But the quote that I am most proud of came from Tony Clarke, who lived in Lapta with his wife Maisie and it read:

"EXCELLENT. An excellent meal, most professionally served and beautifully presented, particularly the vegetables. I would rate this in the UK for a rosette in the Michelin. I am Chairman of the International Wine and Food Society for Hertfordshire and Bedfordshire, and Chairman of the British Epicure Society, Chevalier de la Confrere de la Chaire des Rotisseurs de la Confrere du Tastevin & Confradia Riojaxia" (please forgive misreading or miss-spelling!)

One really special occurrence, about four years down the line, was when one evening I had finished in the kitchen, I changed into my evening dress and proceeded to do my rounds. The final table that I called on was out on the terrace in the garden and there sat two ladies. I introduced myself and asked them if they had enjoyed their meals. The elder of the two ladies introduced herself and her daughter and said that they had enjoyed their meal enormously and then proceeded to take my breath away. She told me that she was Lady Loch's daughter and she heard that the house was now a restaurant and desperately wanted to see what I had done with it. I asked her if she approved and she said that she was thrilled with the outcome, having had some reservations to begin with. I was much relieved, and of course I felt very proud.

What truly wonderful memories and times those were, and those I mentioned were only a few of the hundreds of charming and elegant people that we met over the time, who left their most kind and flattering remarks.

Abbey House and Loch Manor were on a par with each other as the only two leading "upmarket" Restaurants in the North of the island at that time. We naturally shared mutual customers but we were both very mindful of each other's menu content and took great pains not to put the same things on our menus and, if we by chance did, always with a little twist of our own that would make them quite different. Abbey House was a more international menu than mine, and mine was pure French cuisine, so between the two of us, we offered the guest a wide variety of dishes, and two totally different, but breathtakingly beautiful settings.

Talking of settings, Ron was in the garage one day, chopping logs for the fires and I was down in the garden trimming plants and picking roses to make *corsages* for the lady guests, a little touch which I did every special occasion and Saturday evening. Suddenly I heard Ron yell out in pain, so loud, it hit me like a ramrod. I dropped everything and ran up the steps towards the garages, only to see Ron with his hands between his legs. As I drew near he took his hands away and the crotch of his grey trousers were covered in blood. I cannot tell you what thought went through my mind! However, he had taken the nail of his left thumb clean out and his thumb was a terrible mess, there was blood everywhere. I ran inside, got a tumbler and filled it with iced water, rushed back to him and plunged his thumb into it. I got him inside, cleaned him up and bandaged it well and put his arm in a sling to keep it up high to stem the flow of blood. The previous day Ron had toppled over the back of one of our chairs, trying to separate the dogs and split the skin on the bridge of his nose, so that had a dressing on too. That afternoon he was due at the dentist to have a bridge fitted to his lower front teeth. I took him into Kyrenia to the dentist and when we came out, I asked him if he would like to go straight home.

'No'! he blurted out of the side of his mouth, his mouth and jaw completely frozen with the anaesthetic, "I want to go to The Dragon and have a whisky with Allan".

So I took him round to the Dragon House and when he walked in Allan just burst into fits of laughter at the sight of my little wounded soldier.

Ron mumbled and blurted out again from the side of his mouth that he had not been in a road accident and he just wanted a whisky. Allan poured him a double and Ron tried to drink it but it just trickled down the side of his mouth and dripped off his chin. Allan laughed again, took his grandson's glass which had been made with a plastic straw permanently attached, winding up the outside of the glass, and Ron sipped his whisky to the last drop. Ron's language was choice, and at the time he was not amused but, to be honest, to see a grown man wrapped in bandages, drinking scotch through a straw was a ridiculous sight, and we dined out on the story for years to come.

However the biggest event to occur that year was that on Christmas day 1986, when we had now been patiently waiting for three whole years for the telephone to be installed at Loch Manor. Ron and I had always stuck to our guns and refused to pay out any kind of "back-hander" for a basic business necessity to be fitted. We had had the conversation with Mustapha the Manager of the telephone exchange who had told us without any kind of embarrassment, that if we wanted the phone, it would cost £100 cash in his hand and then the installation charge on top. However, we stuck to our Britishness and our guns and firmly believed that there were enough important dignitaries from the Turkish Government and the business world who were our clients and wanting to come to Loch Manor with regularity, who had offered us assistance.

We believed that, if that were going to be done, it should have been a subtle suggestion from someone in a good position merely to put a word in the ear of the necessary person in the GPO. For three years however that just did not happen. If anyone wanted a meal at Loch Manor, someone still had to come all the way up to Catalkoy and make the reservation, or leave one with one or two of our designated places. This did happen most days, but nevertheless it was not an acceptable or satisfactory situation.

Mistakes with bookings were happening and causing all sorts of problems, mainly for the guests but sometimes for us too. For example, one evening a coach load of forty people arrived for a reservation they had made with one of our friends, who was regularly drunk and forgetful. The booking never reached us. I managed to feed them all at the same time with a three course meal with some alterations to the menu, but it made us realise that things could no longer continue in this vein.

I was now at the end of my tether and becoming very angry at the total lack of interest and willingness to listen to our problems by the Manager of the telephone exchange. Having talked the matter through several times with some of our closest Cypriot friends, it was strongly suggested that we were being far too stubborn in our attitude of going down the right road to get this telephone. "This is Cyprus", they would say, wagging their outspread hand from side to side.

I took them literally. Next day I stormed into the telephone exchange and straight into Mustapha's office. I told him that his £100 would be waiting at Loch Manor from that moment on. Not in his hand but only when the telephone was connected. That was Christmas Eve 1986. What I hadn't bargained for was that to them, in those days, Christmas Day was just another working day. It was the morning of the 25th December, and we had a special Christmas Day, British style, completely fully booked. We were busily making ready for the first arrivals, hot, salted almonds in place on the bar, Christmas punch at the ready and the main course roasting away in the oven. Then suddenly, from nowhere and with no forewarning, there they all were, we had telephone people all over the place. They were outside connecting lines and inside fitting connections, where they crawled all over the bar, ate all of the hot spiced nuts and helped themselves to drinks, whisky, raki, Cyprus Brandy and even put their glasses under the optics. They did, however, remember to say "Happy Christmas", and so we just decided to let it all happen, we simply replaced the hot salted almonds, rushed around and tidied up and before our first guests arrived, no-one would have known that they had even been there but, we had a telephone at long last. Mustapha the crooked GPO man went away with the money that he had stuck out for for over three long years. That was the most magnificent Christmas present that I ever could have been given.

Apart from that sort of occurrence, time went on in much the same fashion from day to day, but of course, Robbie was now truly growing up. He had formed quite a few friendships among the younger people around us but also some lasting friendships with those people who were our friends at the beginning. He was also now becoming interested in the fairer sex and in that year he met a young girl from the same village and her name was Songul. Although she was seventeen she was really still only a child and could throw a loud, screaming tantrum quite easily, throwing anything to hand at mirrors if she did not get her own way. (And that was within the first few days of meeting her!).

The first time she ever came into Loch Manor, Ron and I stood together and watched her. Her eyes had turned to saucers and we both looked at each other and said, "pound note signs rolling round in her eyes". She was awestruck at the surroundings and both Ron and I, without any prolonged discussions, came to the conclusion that all this young lady really wanted was money and a passport, and that as far as she was concerned, Robbie would do as well as anyone else. That belief over the years has never altered. Everything in Ron and I wanted to warn Robbie, but of course we could not do that, this was his choice of young lady, he was in love and we were there to support him, not to try to destroy their relationship. Uneasily I recalled Chris's mother and her tricks. I couldn't do that to my nineteen year old son.

Robbie and Songul became engaged that same year and subsequently married a few months later. Robbie decided at this time that his future did not lie in Cyprus. He still really did not like it here very much and wanted to return to England and build a career for himself, and above everything else, he wanted to have a family. Of course, despite it being a huge blow, we could see the sense in what Robbie was saying, but it pointed to only one thing, which was the sale or closure of Loch Manor, because Robbie was my Maitre D'hi and very much the other half of our "front of house" magic. Take Robbie out of the equation of 'Loch Manor' and you destroyed the concept of the whole thing. He was so very much a part of it all that once he was removed, the whole thing just fell apart – it was all about personalities in those days in Cyprus, we made the business what it was and simply to just replace him would not have been enough. To replace him with someone from the U.K. or elsewhere was not viable because we did not earn sufficient to be able to pay the wages to lure people from abroad, even if you had the means to go about finding them; in those days, good waiters and front of house staff were not only hard to find, but near impossible, and the restaurant simply could not be run from the kitchen. No, if Robbie went, Loch Manor would close whilst it was at the top, I would not try to run it with numbskulls and slowly watch it slip into mediocrity, as that would have broken my heart. Loch Manor meant the world to me, everything, but I knew my limitations and I knew I could not run it alone.

Robbie and Songul eventually returned to England and purchased a small top floor flat in London. He surprised us by telling us that he was finished with catering and would be going into Public Relations if he could. Of course we were happy for him, but that left Ron and I with the restaurant to pull back together somehow until we decided when to close. The timing had to be right. We had already taken on our two English girls Carol and Yvonne who were our Sunday waitresses with Mohammad. Sunday lunches were doing well, and when we asked them if they could extend their hours so that we could proceed with our plans to close Loch Manor, but run it right to the very end, they agreed, much to our relief.

Robbie and Songul came out for a holiday in September 1987 and we told Rob that we would be closing at Christmas some time. He was sad, of course, but his life was just beginning.

Unfortunately, Songul did turn out just as we expected, sadly for Rob. Songul soon found herself someone else, after only seven years of marriage, Rob lost his home which he would eventually sign over to her completely, and she was off and away. She had got what she wanted, she had made complete use of Rob to fund her own needs and now she didn't need or want Rob any more. What a very hard lesson that was for him, but in true fashion he pulled himself out of it and moved on.

So now we approached the true end of an era, and one which I would always come to think of with great pride and enormous affection; but we had no time to linger over decisions and life had to carry on; we still had things to do and places to go.

CHAPTER TWENTY EIGHT

The end of an Era

A date for final closure had to be fixed and Ron and I concluded that it would be very fitting if we did a grand finale and closed for business at the end of the year and thus, Loch Manor closed with Christmas Day lunch on 25th December 1987.

Every seat had been pre-booked without any advertising, and I decided that if I was going to do it one last time, then we would go out on a high, and so the menu included everything. It was so exciting because we had a *Kleftico* oven built on to the side of Loch Manor which was a permanent fixture, (something which I had never used in my life before) but I decided that I would cook the main course in this the old Cyprus way with hot coals and sealed oven. Brave or completely daft? It turned out to be brave and the right decision. We had a wonderful lunch and the menu was:

Drinks and light *canapés* on arrival in the bar and on the balcony outside it.

Chilled Avocado Citrus Cocktail
(Avocados picked from the garden that morning)

Baby Lobsters from the Lebanon cooked in a Champagne

sauce (Lobsters brought over especially by the Australian Ambassador there) Raewyn and her husband Carl Axel Henelius

St. Clements Snow water Ice
(made with the blood oranges from the Orchard)

A pair of Roast suckling pigs served traditionally on a bed of rosemary and/or Roast Duckling *a la Montmorency* (whole black cherry sauce) both served with Baked potatoes, Brussel sprouts with fresh chestnuts, potato nest filled with Macedoine of fresh vegetables and stuffed, baked fresh apple

Flambéed home made Christmas Pudding with Rum butter and brandy sauce

Truckle of Stilton served with Port

Fine Filter coffee or Gaelic Coffee and/or a good Cognac/Port/Whisky/Liqueur

Mince Pies and Christmas Cake at 6.pm

There was a different wine with every course, including one glass of champagne and the cost was £10.00 per head.

The whole lunch turned out perfectly, especially the suckling pigs, but more than that, it was a first for me and I felt very proud to have achieved all this. Of course, some of the ex-patriots grumbled that it was too expensive, but they were known for their being frugal with their pennies. It was a wonderful day full of nostalgia for Ron and I and for many of our truly loyal patrons and friends. In my heart I felt relieved that I would not have to bear the burden any longer in trying to maintain being one of the two top restaurants on the island without Rob. The staffing was not the same. I tried to look at it rather not as an ending to an era, but to the beginning of a new one for Ron and I, rather more full of domesticity instead of business. I was to find myself a little wrong there in the long term.

Two or three weeks before Christmas, Ron and I were in Kyrenia at Allan's bar when one of our friends told us of a house that had become vacant and for rent below the village where Loch Manor was, but across the main road and on down towards the sea. We were told the name of the owner and we contacted him and went to have a look. It was a wonderful house and we christened it No. 2. Sea Street! It was perfect for Ron and I, lovely garden on all four sides of the house, small garage but the drive was substantial, which was useful because Ron had just treated himself to a new car, an Isuzu Piazza and he intended taking up his golf again – he had not played whilst we had Loch Manor, he had bought me a little yellow mini, which I christened the Yellow Peril and, of course, we still had Maud the Ford (Fiesta) which was to be for visitors to borrow.

There was a large entrance hall, big kitchen, room off the hall for a bar for entertaining, a huge lounge and a folding wall between that and the large dining room, all with double French windows off onto the terraces. There were three double bedrooms leading from an upstairs gallery, wonderful for friends and family to stay, the whole place was ideal and so a deal was struck. We did ask to buy but the gentleman was not selling, as the house was the subject of a divorce dispute. We were then able to move things from the non-public places of Loch Manor at our ease and install them bit by bit at Sea Street, ready for the final move after Christmas.

We had generally been telling people that we were officially closing and that if anyone was interested in buying the business as a going concern, then we had a figure in mind and our landlords had said that they would be more than willing to give a new lease to anyone who purchased. However nothing moved, absolutely not one application, we were obviously not going to be successful at selling the whole business because it was leasehold. We then decided to tell people that we were going to dispose of all the fixtures and fittings, except those of course, which we intended to take with us. Now this did bring a response. Two couples we had recently met, Geraldine and Werner and Jeff and Barbara had decided to go into the restaurant business, they did not want the kind of catering that was Loch Manor, but more of the everyday pub type business with Sunday lunches and the like at a hostelry called The Courtyard. However, they were interested in all of our fixtures and fittings and so a deal was struck – this excluded the wall light fittings, which came to rest eventually on the walls of The Hermitage, the official residence of the Chaplain of St. Andrews Church in Kyrenia. They are still there today. Mr. Asil Nadir bought Loch Manor and it retains that name to this day.

So we began in earnest to empty Loch Manor as quickly as possible and to move completely into No. 2 Sea Street. All three cars were in use and convoys were going up and down, including several of our friends. We took all of the pictures from Loch Manor and, of course, all our own items. We took some of the bar and fitted this into our little room, which we intended to use for parties. However, we had sold all the drapes and carpets and so we proceeded to Nicosia, where I purchased a whole bale of blue velvet and the same lady who made the curtains for Loch Manor, made me all new curtains. Whilst in Nicosia we spotted a fabulous

Turkish carpet in one of the stores and Ron bought it for me. We also had the three piece suite recovered in blue to match and had a lot of fitted furniture made by a wonderful cabinet maker in Nicosia named Mesut Emre. He made a fabulous job and the house looked wonderful.

As all the rest of our belongings came into Sea Street, I put it all where it was going to go and Ron hung pictures and oversaw the placing of the furniture. It took us very little time and on the last journey, we brought down the pets. Ron had Butch and Lady and I brought the four cats in the Yellow Peril, Marmalade, Smokey, Smokey's kittens Misty and Smokey Two, (Tooptoop for short). The kittens opted straight away to stay, but I tried four times with Marmalade and Smokey and four times they returned to Loch Manor. The caretaker asked if he could have them, he would look after them and so they stayed. Butch and Lady made themselves right at home. Ron and I settled in immediately, we were instantly in love with No. 2. and it already had the bonus of a telephone.

A few weeks later, I received a call from England, telling me that Mummy was terminally ill, she had gangrene in her leg and had refused an amputation. She had been failing very rapidly and I should get home to see her as quickly as possible. Ron and I went down and booked the flight. I did not know what to do in my heart as I had had little contact with my parents since my father had hit me at The Kings Arms and they had left with great bitterness. They had both sent several abusive letters over the intervening years and try as I might, and despite the legal documents to support my side of the situation, they refused to believe that I was, in fact taking care of them and making them safe for the rest of their lives. All they could see was that I had borrowed £6,000 and had not directly paid it back – the mortgage of £14,000 they did not even take on board. Looking back this made me angry, but with hindsight, it must have been their old age and the modern ways of doing things and mortgages and the like must have been confusing to them. They just would not accept that the £6,000 was part of the mortgage and had been paid off that way. I was now paying my part of the mortgage for a house that one day should have been mine.

So, going back to England now and facing my Mother and Father with all this bitterness between us I was going to find difficult to do, however I had to do it, she was my Mum. So, on the 22nd April 1987 I took off from Cyprus and I was met at Stanstead airport by Simon and his new wife Sarah, (having divorced No. One, Tracy, very quickly), and I was to learn that Sarah had a baby Emma (not Simon's) and they all seemed very happy. There was something homely and down to earth about Sarah and I liked her immediately.

They took me straight to the Hospital, and with great trepidation I knocked on the door of her room and there in the bed lay my Mum. She looked so tiny and so frail, snowy white thin wispy hair and not the strong forceful lady that was my memory of her. She looked up at me and I took her hand.

"Hello Mum, it's Jacqui. I'm here" I whispered as I kissed her lovingly on the forehead.

"Jacqui, make it up with your Dad, pay him back what you owe him" was all Mum said, then she was gone forever. I was still paying their mortgage, but money was all she could think about at the end, not seeing the daughter who had loved and admired her for years, the one who had worked so hard for her when she herself was having to be half the breadwinner of the family. So much bitterness and hatred – I felt totally hollow and numb. I wept with her for a few minutes and I then called Simon into the room. I sat outside with Sarah till he too came out weeping. Both my boys adored their Nan and Granddad. I told Simon and Sarah about the argument at the Kings Arms, and I told them I would not face Daddy again, especially if he had the same reaction as Mum, I had decided I could not go to the funeral. How much more did my family have to hurt me and each other I wondered. I reconfirmed my flight and set about getting back to Cyprus where I felt normal and safe. This whole incident seemed bizarre and totally dreamlike and unreal. I had wanted my Mum to let me hug her, but, even in death, she was totally bitter, cold and distant. Ron met me at the airport and drove us back to Sea Street, I sobbed most of the way home, I felt guilty somehow and that I had let her down, even at the end.

Life went on once home and one day, after having a large party, Butch had managed to get out (we always kept the gates tied, but one of our guests must have forgotten to re-tie it when they came in), but he came ambling back and the gate was duly tied again. About an hour later a police car drew up outside the gates and a large policeman stood at the gates but appeared reticent to come in. I went out and Butch was lying at the top of the front entrance steps. He made no move to get upset about the policeman, he just lay there with his head on his paws. I got to the front gates and asked the policeman what was wrong. He said he had come to take the " killer dog" away and have him put to sleep. Apparently he had bitten the Hoja (the Teacher from the mosque) on his bottom! I told the policeman that this man regularly poked his walking staff through our fence and hit Butch, but nevertheless, if he wanted to take him away, he had to come in and take him himself. He reluctantly came in through the gate and you could tell that he was petrified. I went up to Butch and I said to the policeman 'hold out your hand and talk nicely to the dog'. He reluctantly did so and Butch just looked up and dolefully licked him all over the back of his hand.

"There you are, that is our ferocious, vicious killer dog", I said to the policeman, do you still want to take him away? And, by the way, you tell the Hoja that the next time he attacks my dog through the fence onto my property, I shall take him to court."

The policeman assured me that he was going straight down to see the Hoja and tell him off for wasting police time, and that he must leave Butch alone, the dog was entitled to bark and protect his masters.

Once settled back into Sea Street, our life returned to normal and was the usual hustle and bustle of lunches, dinner parties and social get-togethers. Ron was concentrating very much on the garden, it was a bit of a wilderness when we arrived, and he already had a vegetable area, he had cleaned out the water feature and had it full with one of the water lilies from Loch Manor's spring floating on top. We had bought a beautifully elegant and substantial cane three piece suite for the back terrace.

We now had a most marvellous home, one of the best we were ever to have and life was good, up to a point. I was sitting on the veranda having my sundowner and Ron came out and joined me.

"Darling, I need to talk to you," he said.

"I know Ron, and I know what you are going to say" I replied, waiting for the inevitable.

"Sweetheart, you have missed two periods now haven't you?" he said quite sternly.

"Yes Ron, I was wishing you hadn't noticed" and a longing inside me wished he hadn't.

"Jacqui Darling, I do not want, I will not have, any more children, I am 64 years old and the chance of a Down's Syndrome child gets nearer and nearer, do you not understand that I cannot undertake my brother's life with his son on a whim of yours to have another baby?".

Jacqui and Ron – "Always"

I said to him that it was not a whim, he had as much blame as me for our non-protection and it was stubbornness on both our parts that we had come to this situation, but when I raised the point that he could go and have a vasectomy, I forgot that I was talking to the generation previous to mine and that was not the man thing to do, I was the carrier of babies, it was definitely down to me. Ron and I never rowed, we really did have a unique relationship, and even in an extremely emotional situation like this, I always had to weigh what we had together with what could so easily be destroyed by being stubborn, however I did have lots of issues going on in my mind, but I kept myself strong and put my brain into gear before blurting out emotional diatribe. I really was looking at the whole picture with total logic.

"Darling you will have to do something soon" he said to me, "I mean it, I will leave you if you are intent on continuing with this pregnancy, I cannot, I will not be party to bringing a possible mongol baby into this world – I honestly and truly couldn't live with it under any circumstances".

This was a bombshell, to put it mildly and brought me back to earth with a bang. I knew that Ron felt strongly – very strongly – about bringing any more children into the world. Because it was Ron's brother's wife who had had a Mongol baby – that's what they called them in those days and that it had changed all their lives for ever could be called an understatement. Ron had seen what it did to their whole family and he was quite determined that it wasn't going to happen to him. He had reared two perfectly healthy children and was absolutely petrified in case he might be burdened with a Down's Syndrome child and everything that that entailed, it was just not going to happen to him, take it or leave it...

So there we are, I thought, my feelings still don't come into the equation – but of course, he was absolutely without question perfectly right, he would not have coped with a Down's Syndrome baby. Would I have been? What am I to do now? I knew what I had to do. I could not bear to even contemplate what my life would be without Ron and he was obviously so scared of the outcome of this pregnancy. I had to end it but, if I have to be the one to give in, and of course it was, I would not have it done in Cyprus, it would have to be a trip back to England.

A few days later, fate stepped in yet again and we heard from Jean in England that Jeanette (our young friend from Ambelia) had become engaged to a policeman in the CID. Jean had now written to say that they were getting married on the 26th May 1988 and they hoped we would accept the invitation that was on the way. I said that of course we would be accepting, after all, we were all family. Subsequently they all came out from England, Jean, Don, Jeanette, David her fiancé, and Jeanette's brother Stephen and his friend, and we had thrown them a tremendous party at Sea Street. When they had gone back, we planned our trip to the wedding and we would have to add an extra two or three weeks or so for me to have the operation before the wedding. We had decided to rent a house in Bath for a month so that we would be free birds and no-one would be the wiser. I hoped I could keep it disguised until after it was all over. Lucky I was so slim still.

My catering life was still ongoing despite my private life, and it was now centred very much around doing parties and dinners for friends and former customers of Loch Manor. I did quite a lot of these kinds of parties and it was just enough to keep me occupied and enough money coming in to help support us. One such party was for the Chaplain of St. Andrews Church and his wife, Arthur and Doris Rider and was held in the cottage belonging to their daughter up in Bellapais, tucked behind the wonderful Monastery and Abbey ruins. Arthur and Doris Rider were celebrating their 80th birthdays and the party was for 60 or so people. I did so enjoy doing it, it truly was a banquet and a resounding success, and I received a lovely card from Arthur thanking me for it.

As I said before, fate only leaves me alone for just so long, it had already dealt me so many big blows and already I was pining for the baby, the fourth baby that the medium had predicted all those years ago. He had been right, but what a time to realise it and I was about to lose it in just a few weeks time and true to form, fate did have other things in mind for me too…

CHAPTER TWENTY NINE

Wedding Bells

A few days later, I was down in Kyrenia and stopped to pick up our mail from the P.O.Box. In it, there it sat, a large envelope, I pulled it out and it was addressed to "Alias Smith and Jones". This habit had been going on for some years now and for some reason, although everybody else thought it was absolutely hilarious, I had been becoming, over some time, more and more furious at this 'no joke' Suddenly I saw red and became exceedingly angry. I have to confess to being rather old fashioned in this respect, and I was definitely embarrassed that Ron and I 'lived together' as they called it and had not got married and to top it all, I was pregnant again – in my day they called that "an unmarried mother" and it carried a stigma with it. Then, of course, it dawned on me that the subject of marriage had never come up for discussion, he had never asked me, not even when these pregnancies came to light! This set me on the road to wondering why.

Driving back, I became more and more mad and very hurt and by the time I got back to Sea Street, I was in such a temper, a state which I didn't usually reach no matter what had upset me. I slammed, I almost stampeded my way through the house till I found Ron. He turned around and, in his usual warm and loving way, he simply said:

1988 portrait of Jacqui

"Hello Darling, good shopping?"

"Don't you *darling* me, Ron Smith!" I said as I threw the envelope at him. "If I've been good enough for the last eight years to wash your stinky socks and scrub your smelly underpants, and let you make love to me and get me pregnant twice, then I should be good enough to be called Mrs. Smith. If you don't intend to do anything about this Smith and Jones business, I suggest that I've done your last everything – including socks. You can pack and leave and we will call it quits". Ron stared open mouthed, looking like a rabbit in the car headlights!

"Oh God, Darling, I'd no idea. I just went on from day to day, sure in our love for eachother, I never thought of changing anything – it was all so perfect. We had better go down and book the flights for England right now, we have to take into account the operation and allow time for you to get over that, then we can be married the week after Jeanette over there. We can have a proper celebration here when we get back, with all our friends. Alright?" He said shakily. I had never seen him look so shocked.

Ron told me that he had never even thought about it, because he thought, and we seemed, so blissfully happy the way we were. He had no idea that things like the envelope and pregnancies would upset me so much, he always thought I was so strong. It wasn't just the envelope, I had been silent about the pregnancy since our initial conversation and Ron telling me he would leave me if I didn't have it done. That hurt me more than words can say, but I loved him and couldn't risk losing the man I loved more than life itself, not a second time.

We went straight to Ankara Travel in the Harbour and booked the flights and then phoned Jean and Don and gave them the news about the wedding.

"We will keep it very quiet Jean, just the four of us if you do not mind" I said, the abortion never two seconds thought away from my mind. We will be doing the big celebration when we get back home to Cyprus."

It was wonderfully exciting to tell all our friends, one by one, the good news and accordingly Allan and Jean at the Dragon House informed us that the party would be on them when we returned. My head was spinning, both with delight and happiness, I could not have been happier, except, I still had my inner sadness too. I loved my Ron so very much, I could not have loved him more, I wonder if he knew just how much. Of course I had thoughts of our being married, but I was always too proud to bring it up if he hadn't thought of it first, or if it hadn't been what he really wanted to do. I was too proud and old fashioned to be the one to ask first, I never had considered myself a 'liberated woman' in the sense of the fads of the seventies and eighties.

We duly flew back to England and Ron and I rented the house in Bath, which Jean had arranged. On the Sunday morning, I went to Holy Communion and asked God to bless my baby and forgive me for what I was about to undertake. This was going to be about the worst experience of my life for me, and it was all building up inside me like a volcano about to pop, I didn't want to do it at all, but if I didn't, I would lose Ron, without question, and there was no-one in the whole world that I could talk to or share this anguish with. It really was a case of the baby or Ron. My God, what an option!

A few days later, Ron took me to Bath, to the Royal United Hospital and he dropped me off outside the doors of the surgical ward where I was to have the operation. He would not, could not, come in with me he said, it was where Sarah had died and he simply could not face it, even after all this time. This was to me the biggest 'betrayal' – not only had I got to go through this operation, but now I had to enter that hospital and face the whole thing alone, not even a girlfriend to share it with me. I have never felt so petrified and so very alone, I didn't think it could be possible. The operation was to include having my ovaries tied off, once and for all, so that this could never happen again.

I came round from the anaesthetic, was taken back to the ward and then proceeded to spend one of the lonliest nights of my life on my own in Bath Hospital feeling bereft of my baby and redundant as a woman, Ron did not visit and that hurt too, more than he would ever know, because I decided that this would all have to be put behind me if I was to get through it, I needed my inner strength today and the forthcoming days, more than I thought I ever would again.

The following day, at the appointed time, he sat waiting

for me outside the front doors of the Hospital and I quietly got into the car. I said nothing. He asked me if I was alright, and I simply said that I did not want to discuss the matter ever again. I knew he was upset as well, that he had been rather cowardly over the whole thing, but then he was very old fashioned too. Maybe he didn't know how to discuss such things as 'abortion', nor the depth to which I know that he knew how much this would affect me. Through the next few nights, I sobbed myself to sleep and when I wasn't sleeping, I was praying – praying for forgiveness and the ability to be and feel forgiven and move on. I will never forget, ever, it haunts me to this day from time to time, maybe it was my Zoe Elizabeth that I had wanted so badly when Robbie was expected.

We still had things to do and places to go yet again, and I tried to come to terms with it all and concentrate on the weddings to hand, it was meant to be a joyous time and other people did not know, but there was no-one that I could talk to about my secret, no-one. All I did know was that I knew I had to be strong.

We attended Jeanette and David`s wedding on Saturday 26th May. It was a wonderful day and Jean had gone to tremendous trouble to decorate their house and the church and reception, something she has proved to be very good at over the years. The day brightened my mood quite a lot, and Ron was trying so hard to make things up to me by being extra nice and attentive. He couldn't find it in himself to say the right words or have a proper discussion though, and never did but I was very aware that he too was hurting very much with me and for me.

Our wedding was now one week away and we decided that just the four of us was not quite fair on some of our friends. So we had a talk with Jean and Don, and told them that we thought that we really ought to invite some friends to our wedding and have a small reception somewhere.

We all agreed and Ron and I went to Bath and booked the Registry Office for the 2nd June, Ron took me to buy my outfit, which he did not see, and we bought the rings.

On the way home, we stopped off at the local golf club and arranged for a small reception on that day and went on back to Jean and Don`s to make our list, which would be quite small. We would invite Jean and Don of course, who unbeknown to us were making plans for 'helping' to make it a little less simple than the affair which we had planned. For us they were going to turn it into a proper celebration, we were not to slip quietly in and out of the registry office. There would be Maurice and Diana, by now close friends having lent us their villa eight years before to come out to Cyprus on holiday. My sister and her family, and of course, Ron phoned his family in the hope that they would attend. I had naturally wanted both my boys to be there, but they both said for various reasons that they could not make it. Ron`s son would have nothing to do with us and his daughter was to attend with her eldest daughter, Tania but very grudgingly.

The best surprise, which made the day, was when I arrived at the Registry Office with Don (Ron had gone in with Jean so as not to see the blushing bride), and there sat Murray and Lorna, two of our close friends from Cyprus who, without saying anything to anyone, had travelled over especially for the wedding. We invited them both to join us at the reception. It made the day, our Cyprus envoys! There must have been some jungle drums going back and forth from England to Cyprus that week, I am sure.

We had a lovely day despite the fact that it rained cats and dogs, and Jan, Ron`s daughter, arrived fully dressed in black leather from head to toe. She looked absolutely ridiculous, a pity someone did not tell her, and she said

Bath Registry Office wedding 2nd June 1988

absolutely nothing to either of us, something which I know hurt Ron very deeply. Jean was resplendent in full wedding outfit and hat and she and Don had been fabulous, there were flowers and decorations and a lovely little wedding cake with an orchid made from icing sugar on the top (I have the orchid to this day). Both Don and Maurice made speeches, it was wonderful. I was on cloud nine, but I carried a great sadness in my heart. However, today I had at last become 'Mrs. Smith', for which I had seemed to wait for ever and which also brought my mother's comment to me on the night before my wedding to Chris firmly to mind:

"You have a lovely maiden name Jacqui – Ashton – and now you are to be a Brown. If you ever remarry, remember to go one better". Well Mum, I have now completed my trio – Brown to Jones to Smith, not bad!

The whole occasion was properly "topped off" when we returned to Cyprus and on the Saturday 9th June, 1988 our reception was held at the Dragon House with drinks flowing, lots of chat, two tier wedding cake – which after the first serving, Allan sent his grandson round with trays to try sell

Reception in Cyprus – June 1988

it to everyone, to make a few bob for himself, one of Allan's jokes, he had always had a wicked sense of humour. The whole day was rounded off with Allan making a speech in which he jibed at me because he knew about my sensitivity on the subject and proceeded to say:

"Alas Smith and Jones, welcome back Smith and Smith". We laughed, it was so appropriate.

There would have been at least seventy people there that day, but the culmination, no-one could ever have dreamed of. "Big Ali", our gardener from Loch Manor, a very tall and elegant Pakistani gentleman, arrived in full ceremonial dress with a box under each arm. He then proceeded to hand to me a white pigeon, which I was informed should have been a dove, and I set it free into the air. He then opened the next box and took out two chickens, one painted red and one painted blue and Ali held the red one above our heads and the blue one up in the air with the other hand. From behind me came a very distinguished voice from our friend Brenda, which said that this was a Pakistani tradition that wished for us that we should be very prolific and bear many children! Ron was 64 and I was 44 – what a time for such a gesture under normal circumstances, but it went straight to my inner soul like a knife – how appropriate I thought to myself, what timing! Thank God no-one knew what was running through my breaking heart at that point. But it was a lovely day, and the whole occasion was put on video tape for us by our good friend Dick Holmes. I still have the tape and play it often to remind me of a very happy day.

Life then settled back into normality and we even managed a trip back to England in June of 1989 and went to Northampton to stay with long term friends, George and Jean Pollard, patrons of the many establishments I had been involved in. George was the Senior Partner of the largest firm of Solicitors in the Midlands at that time. He was a man of some bearing in Northampton and let us know it. They owned a very nice holiday bungalow in a little village called Camlibel, well out of Kyrenia. They had invited us back to stay with them in Northampton many times, and as this was the town dear to my heart after the first pub, The Rose and Castle, the farm at Long Buckby and Robbie being born in the Barratt Nursing Home in Northampton, this time we accepted.

We had a lovely time and George and Jean took us to many eating establishments, took us around and about Northamptonshire and also introduced us as his special guests at his private members club, The Northampton and County Club (or The George Row Club as it was affectionately known). It was very upmarket and you had to have a few shillings to become a member, I can tell you! We had a very nice time, but could not wait to get back to sunny Cyprus.

Life returned to normal until we received a call from George and Jean in the September of 1989 to tell us they were coming out for their annual holiday at their bungalow. We immediately invited them for dinner on their second evening back in Cyprus and they accepted, I don't know why really, but this was something we always did as we thought of them as special friends. I cooked George his favourite dish of Beef Stroganoff and after dinner, we went out onto the terrace for evening brandies and our normal post-dinner chat time. That was when the bomb went up! George came out with it straight up front, no messing about. George looked directly at me and said:

"There is a double reason for our holiday out here this time love, I have come bearing a proposition."

I should have stopped him right there if I had known what was about to come. I thought they wanted a special dinner party doing whilst they were out or something of the sort. Not so. George went on:

"The Managership or stewardship of The George Row Club is coming up in two months time and Jean and I have been talking it through at length. How do you feel about moving back to England and taking the position? There would have to be an interview first of course, and it would have to be approved by the Committee, but as I am Chairman at the moment, that should prove to be no problem"

Whilst he was talking, my heart hit my feet and bounced back up again – I was totally flabbergasted and my mouth just dropped open. Oh please God no, I kept saying to myself inside, please God no. Never in a million years had I ever forseen moving back to England, especially not to work there again. Before I could give George an answer, Ron chipped in with an even bigger bombshell that I could never, ever have imagined. Ron faced me and said:

"Actually Darling, I have been giving a lot of thought recently as to whether I can see me wanting to end my days in Cyprus, or whether we should give home a try one more time".

I could not believe my ears. He had mentioned nothing of this to me at all, I did not even have an inkling. I was totally dumbstruck.

"Personally," he continued, "I would like for us at least to go back for the interview."

"There is an apartment above the Club included in the package, rent free" chipped in George.

Why I didn't just stop everything there and then and say 'absolutely not' I will never know, but I had no idea Ron was thinking in this vein at all, it completely floored me. I wouldn't have shown him up in front of friends, that was not my way. Thank you, I thought, why could he not just have kept quiet and offered the job to anyone else but me.

"Well, thank you for thinking of me, George", I lied through my teeth, "however, can Ron and I have a few days to really think about this huge step and talk it through completely?"

"Of course", said George "we will wait to hear from you when you are ready." Ready! I would never be ready, never, never, not ever.

George and Jean left for Camlibel and Ron asked me if I would care for a nightcap. I was so close to exploding and bursting into tears of sheer anger and frustration, but I quietly accepted the drink and we sat down to talk. Ron and I talked an awful lot always, about anything and everything and we never rowed, not once, but I felt so close to breaking at this point, all my emotions were racing round and round in my head and I just did not know where to begin telling Ron how I really felt. So I just came out with it:

"Ron, there are no circumstances on God's earth that I can imagine that would ever make me contemplate moving back to England to work. Read my lips – I do not want to go, I do not want this job. I am going to turn George down. Do you understand?"

Then came the words that stung me into consciousness:
"But Darling, what if *I* would like to go back?"
This was one reply I was just not ready for, I had never, ever even contemplated the idea, not for a single second. Now I was faced with the worst scenario ever. Previously it had all been about *me*, of course it had. Ambelia, leaving Peter, starting a new life, Loch Manor, Ron's never-failing help financially with my parents, with both my boys at various times and his unending faith and support for me and whatever I wanted to do. For a decade I had been the centre of my man's love and care. He had never asked me for a single thing, except my love in all this time. How could I refuse him the one and only real request he had ever made of me in ten years? How could I not agree to even give it a try, after all that we had been through and had been and were to eachother. I could not refuse, of course I couldn't, and I simply caved in. It was agreed that we would go back for the interview, see whether I got the job offer and then make a final decision; but deep down inside, I just knew exactly what was to come, and I was dreading it.

We booked our flights the next day and got back to England on the 21st November 1990, (ironic really because, true to form, it preoccupied me somewhat, it was Chris' 50th birthday). We stayed with George and Jean and the following day, I duly attended for the interview, Ron with me with a view to being put forward as my caretaker/general helper. What a come-down I thought to myself, how could Ron even consider accepting this? In any event, I did not let George and Jean down and put one hundred per cent of myself into the interview. The result was that we were, as I knew was inevitable, offered the positions there and then. I suppose as George was Chairman of the Committee, it was rather a foregone conclusion anyway, although his second in command, Trevor Hadland, whom I disliked immediately, appeared to be totally against George. This seemed to me to be a prospective problem; or at least at that point I hoped it would be, as, deep down, I simply just didn't want the job.

However, the apartment above the premises was totally unacceptable for us to live in, it required total renovation and refurbishment involving a large amount of money, which the Committee were not prepared to spend, they just wanted to 'do it up'. Even 'done up' it was a hovel really and Ron, by now was sixty six years of age, and I felt we were worth more than that, I felt like we were being treated like a couple of bar stewards, desperate for a job.

We decided to say nothing at this point, take the job, and in our own time, purchase a house of our own in Northampton and then tell them and George that the accommodation was not fit for the position they were offering and we would house ourselves. They would have to make provision for a night watchman or someone to live over the premises, but definitely not us.

We returned home back to Cyprus on the 29th November and proceeded to tell all our friends the awesome news. Everyone was totally shocked, none of them had ever envisaged Ron and I being anywhere together except Cyprus with them, and most of them were as upset as I was.

We then called in a removal and shipping company to pack up the house and whilst doing this, we had to have the ultimate conversation that we had both been avoiding. What about our beloved dogs, Butch and Lady. Ron and I both adored those two wonderful and loyal animals, but Butch was by now eleven years old and Lady about nine. We both instinctively, but sadly, knew that there was no question of taking them back to Britain because we felt that the quarantine and it's restrictions would most certainly have killed Butch and probably Lady as well. We knew we had to leave them behind, and all this was adding to the fact that I could not understand Ron even contemplating leaving Butch, he was so special to Ron, and I still did not want to go back to England at all, and inside, actually, my heart was fit for breaking. We were giving up our lovely home, our wonderful lifestyle but above all, our precious dogs. I wondered if this man I was married to really realised just what he was letting us in for, but a spark somewhere inside him was this time, resolute, whatever the consequences. Now it was his time, he had always given me mine.

Circumstances, however, have a habit of coming right to some degree, because the next day we received a visit from a man by the name of Bill Orchard. We had seen him around and knew him enough to speak socially when we saw him. Bill had heard that we were about to vacate our lovely house and he was hoping to take it, and after being taken round, was very quick to offer to take the house from us with some of the fittings and he offered to take Lady and Butch as well. He promised that Sea Street would be their home till the days that they died. He was so kind and very genuine with this offer. Bill was as good as his word and ten years later, I saw Bill again and he told me that they had both died peacefully in their sleep, at home, when their times came.

At least God had been good to us in that respect, but as for other matters, we would have to see.

CHAPTER THIRTY

Enter "Spengretta Sir Theo"

Our flight date was booked for the 6th February 1991 and we decided that the only way we could leave the dogs at all was to agree with Bill for a day, that we would leave the house and arrange to stay at a Hotel for the one night before the flight. That way, we would leave the house, Bill would move in and we would never return. It was the only way both of us could handle this trauma. We booked a room at the Jasmine Court Hotel for the one night, and had a final dinner with some of our closest friends at the home of John and Brenda Shelley in Edremit, high up on the mountainside.

We were especially close with this couple, and I wept and sobbed all the way through the dinner – how many more times would I repeat that I did not want to go, I was breaking my heart. None of this seemed to move Ron at all, he was resolute that we were doing the right thing. We said our final sorrowful good-byes and we flew to England the next morning. Arrangements had been made by George and Jean that we would stay with them until the apartment at The Club was ready. Now was our chance and we told George that we did not want to move into the flat but intended to purchase a house of our own because, as Ron pointed out, The George Row flat was not fit to live in. George was not altogether happy with our decision, but he should have thought about that before he asked us to live above the 'job' in what was unsuitable accommodation, I had hoped he would have thought we were worth much more than that as supposed friends of long standing. I couldn't help it, but I smelled trouble ahead.

Our furniture was on the way by sea with Ron's beloved Isuzu car and we arranged for it to go into storage until we could find a suitable house. The very first house we looked at, I just took to it straight away. It was detached and stood all on its own at the entrance to a brand new estate in an area called Rectory Farm in Northampton. It was £62,000 and that was a huge amount of money to me, though the agent said that my wages would easily allow us that amount. So we went ahead and purchased No. 3 Allard Close.

Simon very kindly offered to go down to the storage depot and drive the Isuzu back with the furniture lorry. Our lovely new home was soon up and running and I had a new career and I did give it one hundred per cent effort. We were back in England now and I had to get on with it. I set about re-vamping the whole structure of the catering at The Club and bring it back to life. The rules at the Club were rigid, but at least you had a framework within which to work. I soon had new menus and fresh ideas being put into practice and life settled down to a new, but regular routine. Every day that dawned, I missed my beloved Cyprus so much, our friends especially and most of all our much loved and much missed Butch and Lady and our previous lifestyle, more and more.

The 2nd June 1991 was our third wedding anniversary and was only a week or so away. Ron asked me what I would like to have as a present. I immediately said that I would like to have another dog, this time a pedigree. He immediately almost 'snapped back' at me saying that we would never have another dog and would I think again. I was hurt by this, there was no discussion, but I stood firm and said that if I could not have the dog, then I did not want anything. This banter went on for a good few days and I still stood firm, and so did Ron, I knew in his heart that he felt absolutely rotten over Butch and Lady. Then, two days before our anniversary, I came home when I had finished at The Club and Ron simply turned around and said:

"Alright, if it is really what you want then we will have a dog, but it is going to be a Golden Retriever. I have telephoned the Kennel Club already, and they have recommended Spengretta Kennels in Corby. I telephoned the owner today and she invited us over tomorrow. She tells me she has three litters at the moment, which she cannot sell, and because of that, we can have a puppy for £260 if we buy it tomorrow."

I never got a word in edgeways, but that didn't matter, I was so thrilled, it was all I wanted to complete our family again, and we drove off the next day, so full of excitement and anticipation. We were not disappointed, and all three litters were magnificent.

I told the breeder that it was my wedding anniversary present and that I wanted the puppy to be a dog and to grow up to be truly golden in colour and not pale cream or red. She took us to the relevant kennel and I selected the only puppy at the back of the kennel that did not jump and leap around, he just sat majestically there and watched all the other puppies jumping and leaping at us.

"That is the one at the back, I hope it's a dog, because that's the one I want", I said firmly, not even consulting Ron. This was going to be my compensation for England, bloody England and all that I hated about being back.

The breeder said that it was a male, I had made a fine choice, and he was brought out to me to hold. He was so gorgeous, all 'fluffy puppy', and he smelled wonderful. The

Breeder told us it would take two weeks to complete his paperwork with the Kennel Club and for him to be allowed away from his mother. That was fine.

"What are you going to call him?" asked the Breeder.

"Theo", I said without hesitation. When his papers finally came through the Kennel Club had given him the fitting title of "Spengretta Sir Theo", and he truly was! He turned out to be one of the most wonderful things that ever happened to either Ron or myself in the whole of both our lives.

Theo was a joy to have and train as a puppy and a true delight to both of us, he was indeed the baby that we never had, and what a compensation. We had an open staircase in the lounge of the house and Theo would go up about half way and flop onto the top of Ron's head, whilst he was sitting on the settee below. He thought that was great fun, but the highlight of his day was when the ice cream van came round with the tune playing and one of us would run out and get him an ice cream cornet – he simply loved it all.

"Spengretta Sir Theo" joins the family. 1991

Time went by and we were now approaching September 1992. Everything at The Club seemed to have settled down to a nice routine and the chef and I were learning to work together (I think he did resent me a little at first, I am sure he thought he could do just as good a job as me, forgetting the host and hostess part of the role). I left home happily one morning in about the end of August, to be greeted at my office door by the Club Secretary, who had kept his distance from the day I was appointed, and who merely informed me very bluntly that Mr. George Pollard had been voted out as Chairman. Mr. Trevor Hadland – the man I had disliked at the interview –had been voted in, and that Mr. Hadland had, in no uncertain terms, got his own man for the management of The Club. My services, as of that moment, were no longer required. It flashed through my mind, despite the shock, that only weeks before, George, an active member of the Conservative Party was telling me how they were going to go about getting rid of Maggie Thatcher, the original grocer's daughter; and now Trevor Hadland had done the same thing with George, but my head was to roll along with his. I was handed an envelope with three months severance pay in it and told to collect my things – just like that! It all was so ironic.

I was so humiliated, this had never, ever happened to me in my life before. I drove home in floods of tears and in the most frightful temper. When I told Ron, he was dumbstruck! Many years later Ron admitted to me that he had felt guilty about the whole affair, as it was his suggestion that we had come back to England. We had just taken on this house and fat mortgage and now no job. Oh my God! – what next? I rang George and he just did not seem to care at all – the fact that he had hauled us back from Cyprus, two plane journeys paid for by us, and now a mortgage, but no income, meant nothing to him at all, he was nursing his own red face, and the outcome was – he did absolutely nothing about it at all. He was the Senior Partner of the leading firm of Solicitors in Northampton and should have done more. I expected much, much more of him, under the circumstances. He had brought us over to UK and now left us totally in the lurch.

Ron and I sat down and, over a stiff whisky or two, we contemplated our fate. Through all of this we had never had a discussion about whether or not Ron was happy to be back in England, nor indeed whether he really wanted to stay. Of course he already knew my feelings in no uncertain terms, but even now we did not mention returning to Cyprus.

I told Ron that the only way I could see out of this whole mess was for us to buy a pub and for me to get cooking again, that way, I could be earning within weeks and we could keep the house as well. We had very little real capital left but perhaps just enough for a deposit for a business. Ron agreed but said that he would like to move back to the West Country if we were going to do that. I thought that was a lovely idea, I did love Somerset and all around that area, but I suspected that his feelings were moving in the direction of maybe an acceptance by his daughter and son of Ron and I now being a married couple and definitely together for good. Maybe this had been his wish all along and The Club was the first step in achieving what he really wanted, I shall never know.

I went to our local newsagent there and then and ordered the Publican magazine. In the back were all the agents for buying and selling pubs and restaurants. We rang round selected Agents and within a couple of days, we were inundated with details of all kinds of businesses which were for sale, but mainly pubs and restaurants. We carefully sifted through them, and put the ones we fancied to one side and discarded the rest. We then got out the road maps and looked up all the various places and started making an itinerary for each day to go out and about viewing as many as we could fit into each day, all the while heading down towards Somerset.

We had been "hunting" for two or three weeks, by which time, we were becoming a little frustrated with the whole thing. We had not seen one place which took our fancy or was at the right price until one day, we landed up in a little village in Somerset called Burtle. We had details of "The Burtle Inn" which, from the photograph, did not look very much. However, it turned out to be a charming place with a large restaurant incorporated into the pub itself and was fitted out most charmingly with all the traditional horse brasses, old farming tools and the like. It had a lovely atmosphere and I made up my mind there and then, this was the one I really wanted to work with, I could really do something with The Burtle Inn. I was so excited, Ron liked it too and we decided that we would go for it. As soon as we got home we rang the Agents and said yes, we rang the Bank and they said yes, subject to seeing menus and business plan etc. I immediately drew up a set of menus and we set about planning. I should mention that we had offered the asking price, to try and make sure that we did not lose it.

We went down about three or four times back to Burtle taking measurements, photographs, discussing soft furnishings etc. We had telephoned Robbie and told him all that had happened and he suggested that he and our friends Jean and Don`s son Stephen should move into our house and pay the mortgage as rent. It was all coming together, as they say. Then the next bombshell fell! We received a telephone call from the Agents telling us that we had been well and truly "gazumped". Someone had put in an offer that was considerably higher than ours. We came to the fast realisation that we could not afford to go any higher, as we had a ceiling on the monies from the bank and our offer was it. We had lost The Burtle Inn. I was absolutely heartbroken, I had not even pictured us being anywhere else other than The Burtle Inn. What now? I thought.

Ron was much more pragmatic about the whole situation and simply said that we would go off the next morning and start again where we had left off. We had had quite a few more pubs to view when we chose the Burtle Inn. However, I was still left with the feeling that nowhere would match up to The Burtle. The pub business in the U.K. was rapidly coming under extreme pressures, due to the new E.U. regulations, the issue of smoking etc. they were actually in the process of killing one of the oldest institutions in Great Britain and you had to offer the customer something really special to survive, let alone make any profit. We were actually in a very difficult position.

The next set of details on our agenda was in a place called Oakhill, a little village between Shepton Mallet and Midsomer Norton (where Ron was born) and near the area where his children still lived. It was only about four miles from where I had had the Kings Arms, where Ron and I met. Ron seemed very keen to get there and have a look at this particular pub, it was a Bank repossession and was quite a reasonable price and they wanted a very quick transaction to get the pub open again and running.

The Oakhill Inn sits at the end of the Mendip Hills in Somerset and was created about 100 years ago. It is two out of three adjoining miners cottages, knocked into one. The pub had been in the process of being totally refurbished by the previous owner, with all the in between walls being knocked down to make one large through pub, although each of the bars retained their own individuality. There was a public bar with pool table and darts, 'shove ha'penny

The Oakhill Inn – 1992

board and fruit machine, a tiny little "snug" bar with beautifully upholstered seats, and a lounge and restaurant area, which could comfortably seat about 45 guests. Although the outside of the pub was totally uninteresting to look at, it belied what was inside the moment you stepped through the front door. The theme colour for the pub was eucalyptus and bottle green, two of my favourite colours, including the patterned carpet throughout and this gave the inside a very restful feeling and the woodwork was impressive, there was a brick built bar and the dados, again throughout, were in light oak panelling and it all looked quite, quite stunning.

Upstairs the living accommodation was very spacious and would allow us to live very comfortably, with the addition of three double bedrooms that we could use for bed and breakfast, which would produce a welcome additional revenue.

Ron knew quite a lot about the background of the pub and the village itself and it soon became obvious that this was the one that he would like us to have. I felt that as a "second best" choice, it was as close as we were going to get to what I had envisaged in the way of food and amenities etc. So we decided together that we would try for this one. This time I made up my mind that I would not get excited, and to tell the truth, I wasn't at all excited – I was still very homesick for Cyprus, but I knew that God had his plans for me and this was to be. Despite our better instincts, but believing that he owed us something for the loss of my job at The Club, we decided to go to George Pollard and get his firm to do the conveyancing.

Before we knew where we were, we had purchased the Oakhill Inn and the Bank wanted us up and running as quickly as we possibly could. Our friends Jean and Don Wiggins were an enormous help with the alterations and furnishing and they were regular patrons – as always with all our ventures.

Simon had come down on several of the occasions we were coming and going to the Oakhill, and he asked if he could come down to Somerset, join us and help to run the pub. Again, despite our better instincts, Ron and I had a very long and heart-searching discussion, and the outcome was that we decided to give him a chance, Ron was always a very fair man and he knew how I felt about not having been able to succeed with Simon the way I had with Rob. He also knew that I always felt that there was a terrible distance between Simon and myself. We both wanted to trust him but to do that he had to have that chance.

By this time, Simon had divorced his first wife – the marriage had only lasted about a year – and married Sarah and they now presented me with two new granddaughters,

Friends Jean and Don Wiggins, author and son Robbie – 1992

Victoria and Laura in addition to Emma, the baby Sarah already had when she met Simon. I did insist that we keep the rooms at the pub for letting and Simon and Sarah would have to find a proper home for themselves and the children. It would not have worked at all with all of them living with Ron and I – we liked our privacy at the end of the day. This was all agreed and Sarah stayed in the house they were already in and Simon stayed with us temporarily whilst he searched for a home. He registered with the Council and was put on the waiting list, and they did, ultimately, get a house very quickly.

The pub needed new curtains and so I took a trip into Midsomer Norton (Ron's birthplace) to a little fabric warehouse I knew. The signs of the pub, all five of which I had just repainted by hand, bore oak leaves and acorns and to my amazement, I found some beautiful fabric in white with a small pattern of oak leaves and acorns in eucalyptus green. It was almost as if it had been specially woven for

The Oakhill Inn. I bought it all and they came out and measured up and made me the most beautiful curtains, all fully lined and very reasonably priced. I was thrilled with them, what a find!

On our very first day of moving in, a very large, buxom lady, perhaps in her mid forties, came into the pub to see me. She was a real "slappa my thighs" true, blue Somerset lass with a round, ruddy complexioned face and broad smile, and she said that her name was Sue James and she was looking for work as a cleaner. Oh, was I glad to see her, she was one of the members of staff that was a "must have". Sue turned out to be very true and loyal and became a good friend. She had five sons, each one of them as different as could be, Michael who we met only about twice, Dale who was a talented gardener, Gary a real hard worker, Lee a whiz on computers and Andy, the youngest of the five, who was very tall. They were all strapping lads and three of them, Andy, Lee and Gary were regulars in the public bar and were on the darts, shove ha'penny and pool teams. Sue was a blessing to have and was a very hard worker, and she knew how to play hard as well! Sue drank cider by the pint, the strong lager that we sold, followed by whisky chasers, but goodness, could she hold her liquor.

Another regular was a guy called Tony Munn and he had been in the Navy as an engineer. He had a real hard, true, Somerset accent and he loved to talk *at* you – he would say a sentence about something terribly profound and then say "and I will qualify 'dat' statement" in a very determined way and proceed to go on and on at great length and depth, but he did have a heart of gold.

Tony worked in a little factory a few doors down from the Pub. He had been an engineer in the Submarine Service and he sat there every day turning out the most beautiful and delicate lamps and lampshades I had ever seen. They

Regular customer, Tony Munn

were extremely expensive and so Tony and I devised a scheme whereby he came in every day and had lunch and a pint, I kept a running total and when the total came to enough, I had bought another lamp or lampshade. They looked very much like "Tiffany" lamps and the glass came in the most wonderful shades, white, pink, pale blue, bottle green and amber. I bought one large pink lamp, two small pink ones, one large blue lamp, one blue lampshade, two bedroom lampshades one white and the other green and eight wall light lampshades in pink also. I still have them and treasure them. Tony worked with a most unpleasant and rough and ready Cockney man named Tom, who I think was originally of gypsy origin, he certainly looked it. He was a very strange person, he came down once and said that he had a very sore leg. When I asked what was wrong, he said he had got a sore on the leg and poured neat bleach on to it to cure it! Two weeks later he passed away with blood poisoning. I wonder why!

The public bar was quite well patronised and the darts and pool teams were very active. We were in the leagues and on home matches I used to make a good night of it for the boys and treat them and their visitors to very special grub. That used to pack the pub, and the followers were always about double the number of our team when they played away. They were worth it; they were all great guys and brilliant customers.

The snug room and lounge area was mainly food and I had devised some very good menus, which were also on display outside the front entrance to the lounge bar. I turned the eating area into a Bistro and the food was quite adventurous for a sleepy Somerset village. We got two full pages in the 'Pub Walks for the Family' guide book for that year (1994) with a very good commendation for the food, décor and ambience. Every Friday night I did a special night with a different theme each week, Turkish, Greek, Chinese, Caribbean, French, British, Canadian, Australian (I even cooked Roo tails, alligator and emu meat!) and so on.

These evenings were extremely well attended, there were at least twelve or fourteen main courses and about three desserts and it was as much as you could eat for £5. We had one family of mother, father and three children and the father would come in first, and take as much as he could eat and pay the five pounds. Then, Mum would come in and fill the same plate with 'seconds', and finally, one by one, the children would sneak in and go up with the same plate from each other and fill up again for themselves, that way all five ate for £5. I am afraid I had to go over when we tumbled them and ask them for the balance of the money and I let them know for how many weeks I had known they were stealing from me. They never did it again and they did come back.

We had very good neighbours adjoining us and our neighbours to the rear were the village church and graveyard, so they were very quiet! Opposite lived the vicar John and his wife Celia. I attended communion most Sunday mornings and John became a very good friend.

It was on this weekend that I asked Robbie if he and Simon were still seeing Chris, their Dad. Rob said that they went from time to time, but that they were never pleasant visits. Chris apparently had become a complete alcoholic, a tragic mess and even hid bottles and so on. I told Robbie that I really wanted to see Chris one more time. I don't know why I felt this strong urge, but I did. Robbie flatly refused to tell me where he was or what his circumstances were and emphatically stated that the matter was not up for any further discussion. "I am only protecting you Mum, please believe me, you don't want to go down that road, emotionally you would not cope" he said and so I let the matter drop.

It was also on this weekend that it was decided by all of us that Robbie would definitely move into Allard Close and take over the mortgage. The house would then become his and when the time was right, we would get it all put into his name. It all seemed to fit well into place for us all, as we were struggling to pay both the pub and the house mortgages. It was at this point that I was then told by Ron and Rob that I was not to worry about financial matters, I knew we were not making much money at the pub, they would work it all out between them. This reassured me and I set about getting on with running the business and trying to find new and bright ideas to bring in extra customers.

Every evening ended with the same routine, but nothing could have prepared me for closing time the next evening.

The events which were to follow, we could not have imagined in a million lifetimes and this one event changed my life forever!

CHAPTER THIRTY ONE

The Haunting Ends

It was the 20th March 1993, and Ron and I had seen our final customer through the doors, locked them up for the night, and were in the process of clearing up before going to bed. Suddenly there was a loud hammering at the front door of the pub. Ron went to see who was there and came back accompanied by two uniformed Police Officers. I jumped to conclusions, sometimes a bad habit of mine, and immediately blurted out that I did not keep late bars and did not serve after time unless I informed the local Police of the occasion. They said:

"No, madam. Is your name Mrs. Jacqueline Smith?"

I confirmed that it was and they asked if we could sit down quietly somewhere and have a chat. What they had to tell me no one could have prepared me for, you would not imagine it even in your wildest dreams, and it came as a complete and utter shock. I was absolutely pole-axed. Apparently Chris had been found dead in his apartment in Louth in Lincolnshire.

It appeared that the Police were contacted by worried neighbours, after complaints about a stomach-churning stench coming from a flat in Newbridge Court, Louth. Once inside, the police had discovered the decomposing body of Chris – he was only 53 years old. It would seem from the

Last picture of Chris before he died, aged 53

coverage in the newspapers that Chris had been known there as a journalist, though he kept a very private profile.

According to the Police report, the body was found lying in the lounge and had been covered in blankets in the form of a bizarre type of shroud. His head was supported at the neck by a pillow and this had all been done next to a lit gas fire, to keep him warm. Five or six empty litre vodka bottles lay strewn about the floor. There was a woman with whom he shared the apartment, Norah Prendergast, and she had covered him as though he were in a coffin. The Police said that she panicked after Chris died and did not know what to do.

Chris` body had been lying in this state since February 10th – some five weeks! Apparently Norah Prendergast was in a state of complete dissorientation after the death and tried to make him as comfortable as she could and she must have shut it off completely from her mind and, despite the appalling stink of decomposition, carried on living her usual life around his dead body. Her mind just did not work and she could not cope with the enormous emotional turmoil of her companion dying in front of her. She just carried on and pretended that it never happened. The Police revealed that she had no close relatives, so she was absolutely at a loss not knowing who to ring, so she just did nothing, which was the easy answer.

Then, the even bigger shock – apparently he had left a letter containing my whereabouts, naming me as his next of kin. He knew exactly where I was after all this time and still thought of me as his wife. I was devastated, this really sent a blade of cold steel straight into my heart. My mind was racing with questions, in all directions, which I could not let Ron know, but after all these years, had he really loved me all along, and, if he had, why had he not tried one last time to see me and put things right? Maybe his alcoholism, which he would have known I could not accept, had stopped him from doing anything, like Norah, his companion, so easy just to do nothing at all. With this revelation came all the hurt, the missed years, the wasted love and devotion, the longings, and now I could never say goodbye to him, one last time, even if I had wanted to.

The Police said that I would have to go and identify the body and make arrangements for the funeral as quickly as we possibly could. After all this time had gone by, it would be very especially unpleasant because of the decomposition of the body. I immediately phoned Robbie and he said he would be on his way down to us the following morning. He would help me to handle everything together and I was definitely not going to do the identification, he would do that with Simon. Robbie came down as promised and when he phoned Simon, as usual, he had a weak and feeble excuse for not being able to come with us.

When we arrived at the Mortuary, Robbie told me firmly

to stay in the car, I was not to come in. Everything in me wanted and needed to go in and say goodbye, but when I saw his face as he came out, I obviously had done the best thing possible, at least I could remember him the way he used to be. Robbie was positively grey:

"God Mum, it was awful" he said, the tears streaming down his face.

He handed me two newspaper cuttings from the local daily papers and the headings were "**Body found dead in flat after six weeks**", it tore my heart out to read the text, despite the fact that I was now happily married to Ron and loved him so dearly, I was sitting in the back of this car reading about the man I had fallen in love with when I was sixteen, the man I had loved and worshipped for all those years, the man who had tenderly made love to me, the man who had fathered my two children, the absolute love of my life, the man who had, in the fullness of time, completely broken my heart. I thought I could not bear anything more to happen. Robbie brought me back to the real world with a bump:

"Mum, we have got to move on, we have a lot to do today".

We took the Mortuary's advice and contacted a local Funeral Director, Carol Paddison. She was extremely compassionate and very kind and we agreed that, because of the circumstances, it would be best to hold a cremation and as soon as possible. So the date was arranged and we returned to Somerset.

Robbie informed Simon of the date of the funeral two days later and he phoned Great Aunt Daisy, Chris's only living close relative in Leicester and arranged to pick her up on the way and take her with us. Of course, on the day Simon could not make it, he had a burst water tank or some other excuse, so Robbie and I set off alone. Ron had understood completely my need to do this one last thing, to lay my troubled love to lie in peace at long last and so he stayed at the pub to run it for me for the day. He was so kind and understanding about the whole sorry mess.

We picked up Great Aunt Daisy and had our brief reunions, then off we all set for Louth. We briefed Daisy on the funeral and short service and on the way, we started to talk about old times. She asked me why I had chosen to stay out of touch with the family for all those years – nineteen years in total by this time. I told Daisy that, because of things that Mother and Father had said over the years, I always believed that the family and all the relatives hated me and held it against me for splitting the family.

"Good God no, Jacqui!" she exclaimed, "It was quite the reverse in fact – we hated Christopher for everything that he had done to you. You do know that Gerty and I found him in our guest bedroom having sex with that Monica woman the night before your wedding, don't you? We thought you were treated appallingly, especially by Lady Margaret" (the family's pet name for Chris's mother).

All my suspicions had been correct for all that time, in my heart deep down I had known it, the absolute and ultimate betrayal, the night before the most precious day in my life, and now it all came out – the truth at long last, thirty-one years down the line. All that time ago, but how it still hurt, like a shaft of steel straight into the guts; yes it hurt and, by God, it still does. However, I had that final task to perform, one which I knew I had waited for, for eternity…

We arrived at the Crematorium and Chris's coffin was lying in the Chapel, waiting to go through the curtains. On the way, I had asked Robbie to stop at a florist in Louth and we had purchased three long stemmed red roses, one from me, one from Rob and one from Simon. I approached the coffin on my own and put my head close to it and whispered,

"Goodbye my love, my dearest love, I return this red rose to you and will never forget how you gave the first one to me. Please lie in peace now, you are with God".

I wept silently for a few moments and then Robbie went up to say his goodbyes for him and his brother. He too was very emotional. We watched as the coffin went slowly through the curtains and he was gone. I had never been to a cremation before, but as Chris rolled away from me and the curtains closed behind him, an enormous chapter of heartache and turmoil seemed to end for me there. Now I had to learn to live with and control the memories that would inevitably linger on – having someone as complicated as Chris in your life is not an overnight thing to simply 'get over and move on with your life', it had never ending repercussions and would have for years to come – but at last there seemed to be some kind of closure.

Robbie had made previous arrangements to collect the ashes a little while later, which he did and at the request of Chris, his ashes were scattered into the sea in Louth, into the fresh air and outdoors that had been one of his many passions to the end.

The only problem for me is that Chris is like a thorn that has embedded itself so deep down into the flesh that you cannot get at it to remove it, not even in death…

CHAPTER THIRTY TWO

Ron's Flight...

Robbie phoned a little while later to tell me that he and Simon had inherited £40,000 each from Grandfather's Trust Fund that he had set up for them. I was very pleased for them and he also said that he would like to come down that weekend with his new girlfriend Sue, who was half Turkish Cypriot. On this occasion, he asked me if I had still got the video tape of a film that friends had made of Loch Manor with us all in it back in 1983. I said that I had and it was in the bookcase in the lounge. Rob asked if he and Sue could go up and watch it. I told them to go ahead, and I must confess to having forgotten at that point what was in it. There was one scene when Rob was 17 and he came out of his bedroom along the balcony to me in one of those "puberty moods". On the film, he showed himself to be bored and impatient, and very rude.

Anyway, about forty minutes later they came down and Rob walked over to me in the bar and asked if he could talk to me. He said:

"Mum, can I ask you a question? Was I really as bad as I appeared on the film?"

"No Rob" I said with a smirk, "you were a ruddy sight worse". He obviously never realised just how obnoxious he used to be when he was going through that phase.

"Just you wait," I added, "With your kids, you'll have all that to come".

Ultimately, Robbie moved Sue in with him and on the 10th December 1994, my grandson Daniel Christopher Kamil Brown was born. I did not see him for the first few weeks until they felt that they could travel down to Oakhill with him and they came for the weekend. I tried to help Sue with Daniel, she seemed to be having a hard time with him, but she didn't think my old wives' tales of remedies were appropriate to her baby, and so from then on I kept my distance in that respect. In fact, from the beginning really, Sue and I had a mutual dislike for each other and that was to continue till the day they parted, we both knew it and so did Rob, but we all put on a good face for the sake of the family.

January 20th 1994 was Ron's 70th birthday and I was determined that we were going to celebrate in great style. A party would be held at The Oakhill and Ron had invited all of his family, together with some of our closest customers, some of whom had become personal friends of Robbie and Sue. I contacted Robbie and told him that I had been trying to get Ron a flight in a Lancaster for his birthday, but there was apparently only one flying and that was in the R.A.F. ceremonial flypasts. I then wondered if a flight in a Tiger Moth would be a good idea. Robbie decided it would be and took care of all the arrangements. This part of it we decided to keep secret until the day itself. We arranged it for early in the morning and the party for later in the evening. Ron had a great flight and the pilot let him fly the plane over the Oakhill Inn and all the regulars came out and waved at him. He had got his pilot's licence at long last.

In the evening all the guests started to arrive at the pub for the party. Jan, Ron's daughter from his first marriage, and her husband and two children came through the front

"My quiet Airman"
Ron gains his pilot's licence aged 70 years – 1994

door. I immediately went up to them to try and make them feel welcome. To my astonishment, she pushed me away physically and said:

"For God's sake will you just get away from me? I don't want anything to do with *you*. I am only here because my Dad wanted me to be, certainly not because of your invite".

I was shocked but I wasn't prepared to spoil Ron's evening and retaliate, so I went upstairs so that there would be no atmosphere. Eventually, Ron came up to find me. When I told him the reason, he was so upset for me. He knew that I had wanted to make everything right for him, had this not been his plan for us to come back to England and all be one family together? He said he was furious with her, but I persuaded him not to make any trouble and just enjoy his party.

He was never to have contact with his daughter again, nor his son Jim, who did not even bother to turn down the invitation. Even after fourteen years, she still could not come to terms with Ron and I being together. I have since come to believe that Jan was told that we were having an affair before her mother died by the woman Iris; the one who wrote the wicked letter to Ron when we were at Ambelia, Nothing could have been further from the truth. His own son introduced us a few days before Sarah died and he had told us of the situation before Ron arrived at the pub, and it was Jim and Jan herself who asked me to do the wake after the funeral.

Eight days later, January 28th 1994 was my fiftieth birthday. The big five zero, the one I had always dreaded. Ron and Robbie decided that all the family would be invited and we would spend my birthday at the pub altogether with a slap up meal and a party with the locals. Gill, my sister and her husband Charles, had had Daddy to stay with them for

My 50th birthday at Oakhill Inn - Simon back row right – Robbie back row left, middle row Ron, Jacqui, Daddy and sister Gill.
January 28th 1994.

the two weeks prior to my birthday so they were able to bring him with them for the party, and the whole family travelled up from Devon to attend. Robbie and Sue came, and Simon, Ann (his third wife), and the girls came too.

I had been sitting talking to Gill and Daddy and I turned to my father and said "do you know something Daddy, in all these fifty years of mine, you have never, ever told me that you love me".

"Have I not Poppet? But you know, I really do love you". That made my birthday perfect for me. After everyone had gone, Ron and I went upstairs for our nightcap and I told him what Daddy had said. Ron said he had always let his children know that he loved them. They certainly had a funny way of showing things, despite his love for them.

Then one morning, I had another shock, a letter from our Building Society arrived on the mat, informing me that the mortgage was not being paid and we were a great deal in arrears. I explained to them that Robbie was in the house and he was hoping to take it over and that he had, in fact, taken on the mortgage by mutual agreement with Ron and myself. That was neither here nor there to the Building Society, we either paid up the arrears, which were now in the thousands, or they would repossess the house. We paid them a cheque immediately for £2,000 and agreed to pay £100 per month till the arrears were cleared on the understanding that the mortgage would now be paid. What I did not know was that Rob had all this time been paying Ron the mortgage money into our bank account and Ron had been using it for the pub and not paying it to the Building Society. What I also did not know was that when Robbie came down and told us about his inheritance, Ron had borrowed some of that money from him to pay some debts and had not paid it back when promised. It was really Ron who lost us the house and not Robbie, and ultimately

Robbie lost the house too. Ron had been trying to do what he always promised me he would do, protect me from financial worries. My original arrangements with Ron when we first got together was that I could not handle failure and financial problems and still appear in public as the bright sparkling hostess, the most successful chef and with my name over the door, my own personal loss of face. Our arrangement was that I would perform the magic, he would perform the financial miracles. This was Ron's way of trying to get us out of this situation, he was, in effect, robbing Peter to pay Paul but he was digging an even bigger hole to get out of than the one we were in already. The results could only end in heartache, and this they most certainly did. This heartache would not, could not go away for some considerable time, thanks to his actions, but his intentions all along had been with one aim, to protect me.

Robbie then took the decision for him and Sue to obtain a council house and when I phoned him and told him what I had paid off and begged him to pay the mortgage from then on, a huge row broke out between us and both phones were put down with bad feeling between us, although the words were not actually said, Robbie had assumed I knew he had been paying Ron all along. I was broken-hearted and could not understand why this perfect plan had all gone so wrong. Ron quietly said that he did not know the reasons behind it; I just had to hope that we would make it all up and put things right from every angle very quickly.

A few weeks later the Building Society local representative came to the pub and formally told us that the house was now repossessed and any shortfall, once sold, we would be liable for. Unfortunately there was a shortfall of some £22,000 but they merely sold off the house, told us we were clear of debt but, at the end of it all, we lost all of our equity in the property. There was now a rift between us and

Robbie, which was to go on for a very long time, some five years in all, and which caused me not to be able to see my new grandson at all in that time. This length proved to be five of the most heartbreaking years that I have ever spent, unable to see my beloved family – both my sons and I now apart and not talking, and I could not fathom where I had got it all so completely wrong. It was never meant to be like this, I had wanted to be the most perfect mother in the world especially because of the way they had been treated by Chris, the father neither of my sons ever really and truly got to know. I believed I had always been there for them, but I had somehow obviously cocked the whole thing up well and truly.

All this heartbreak over family and money; it is always the same in life I suppose, and the next chapter in my life was to prove all of this to be true.

CHAPTER THIRTY THREE

Daddy arrives

I suppose it would have been about the July or August of 1994 and one morning, I was in the bar and the phone rang. I picked it up, it was my sister Gill and after the usual pleasantries, she told me that she wanted to 'warn' me that she felt quite sure that Daddy would be telephoning me very shortly. She also went on to say that he would probably be asking me if he could come and live with us.

When I asked her why she thought this, she said that he had already rung her and that she had refused and turned him down flat. When I asked why she would turn away her own father, and her always being his favourite through all the years, she said that she was not prepared to make room for him in her home and did not want him ruining her children's' lives with his morbid stories about his childhood spent in abattoirs and funeral parlours and so on, that he had rambled on about when he was staying with them in January. To say that I was 'gobsmacked' would be something of an under-statement, I was absolutely and totally taken aback and appalled at what I was hearing. How could she turn her own father away? I told her that I would discuss the subject at length with Ron but I felt sure what the outcome would be. I also asked about my brothers and where they stood on this issue. She told me that they did not want to know either, under any circumstances. My God, and we dared to call ourselves the Ashton family! I don't think so somehow.

Apparently it had all been discussed between them and their decisions were not shared with me till this point, I felt as if I was being told: 'Ha, Ha just to let you know that you are the one being lumbered'. I was furious, livid and totally ashamed of my so-called family, and how wrong could they be? I had firmly made up my mind that I absolutely would not treat my Daddy in the same way. Ron was appalled too but little did he know, his family would do something similar to him one day.

Daddy did telephone, about two days later.

"Poppet, can I come and live with you? I am so tired of living alone, and so lonely".

I asked him to wait a moment and I held the phone up in the air and with a raised voice, I said to Ron:

"Darling, Daddy wants to come and live with us".

Ron smiled at me and again with raised voice he said:

"Well, what are you waiting for?"

"Did you hear that Daddy?" I said to him lovingly down the phone. "We both want you here with us".

"Yes Poppet I did hear that and how soon before I can come?"

At this point I asked him if he had put the house on the market. He said no that he had not, but he would do it immediately. I then told him all about the Solicitors, his bank manager, all the people he must go and see and tell them of his intentions and give them his new address, and he had to ask his Solicitor to act for him in his absence. He said he understood, but I told him that if he got stuck on any points, to let me know and I would explain to them all what he wanted to do, to come down to Somerset to spend the rest of his life with us.

However, in order to ascertain his frame of mind, and also knowing my father's tendencies to try and be the one to control everything that was happening to him, I insisted that he telephone me every week for three weeks, on the same day, and at the very same time, and tell me that he still wanted to be moved, lock, stock and barrel down to myself and Ron, and I told him that on the third time of ringing, if his answer was still the same, then on that day he would be contacted by a firm of Removal people that I had already primed, and they would come in the very next day, pack him up completely and bring him down to Somerset with them. He was overjoyed. The calls came and they came on time and so, Daddy came down to live with us at The Oakhill Inn.

It was a very emotional 'homecoming' and when Daddy hugged me, I thought he was never going to let me go. Ron poured him a half pint in his very own tankard that we had been out and bought for him. He was thrilled and immediately thanked "Bob" (in his confused mind he must have thought that Ron was his dead son Bobby and my brother), but so as not to confuse him, we did not enlighten him, so Ron answered to Bob from that moment on. They sat together and had their beers and Ron chatted to him and made him feel at home whilst Terry, our barmaid and kitchen helper, and I sorted out his living quarters. We gave Daddy a large double room with its own washing facilities at the bathroom end of the upstairs accommodation, which had a very long corridor, which meant that we could accommodate his bookcases, his record collection in its own stand and various other pieces of furniture that he felt he needed to have around him. We felt that this would give him lots of freedom and make him feel at home. He also shared our large lounge and kitchen upstairs, as we were down in the

Daddy's last Christmas – 1995.

pub working most of the day and evening. He had his own television in his room too, so he would quickly feel very much at home.

The following day, I telephoned the Surgery in Shepton Mallet, our nearest surgery and where we were registered and spoke to one of the Doctors, my favourite one, Dr. Walker. I explained the situation and he said that he would need to make a home visit the next morning, assess Daddy and then he and Social Services would decide what kind of help and adjustments would be needed to enable us to care for him fully at home. They would then handle everything from there on. He duly came next morning and I took him up to see Daddy. He asked him several topical questions which daddy got completely wrong, he then gave him a complete and very thorough examination and then shook hands with Daddy and said that would be all, but he would need to speak to me downstairs.

There he dropped the bomb firmly and squarely in my lap. I did not expect what was to come at all, not of my Daddy.

"I shall not beat about the bush, Mrs. Smith. Your Father has the onset of Altzheimer's Disease, which is a degenerative disease and he will get progressively worse and worse, and he will need constant care and nursing. What are your thoughts on this considering your position and your business, we could at some stage be talking about twenty four hour care?"

I told him that my Father's greatest fear had always been that he would one day be institutionalised, he had seen what happened at first hand when he worked in one as an accountant after he left the Army, and he had made me promise that he would never go into 'an old people's home'. This promise I had gladly given, and fully intended to keep. I told the Doctor that I wanted time to talk with my father about this, he was still very rational, and I would call him within a few days and tell him the outcome.

Over the next two days, Ron and I made extensive enquiries and phone calls and found that we did, in fact, have several options. I had telephoned the private nursing home opposite the Pub called Pondsmead and spoken to the Matron there, whom I knew quite well. She kindly showed me round the whole place, the facilities and the menus and so on. Daddy was right, the lounge was full of people with their heads bowed down and chins resting on chests. Quite frightening, all those people sitting in cabbage-like states in silence, with the television playing for only a few. It was not really an option in my mind, but she offered us a place for him there and then, but I still had to give Daddy all his choices, but this one I knew he would not even take on board, and I desperately didn't want him to.

We were then given first refusal on a one bedroomed

cottage to buy, three doors down from the Pub where I could look after him, but he would retain complete independence as far as possible. We were also offered first refusal on a sheltered accommodation apartment in Coleford, a nearby village, with the British Legion and this had a resident Warden, but this would have removed quite a bit of my input into his care, and this was not a favourite option with me.

However, with all this information gathered, I sat down with Daddy after giving him his 'brunch' and put all these options to him. I explained every one in detail and everything that they would all entail. Without exception, he turned them all down flat and said that he wanted to stay with Ron and I, where he was, he was exceedingly happy and felt very safe, very loved and very much at home. So that was it, it was decided. I felt relieved that I would be there for him twenty four hours of the day, and I think I realised there and then what this would entail, especially with the pub to run as well. I telephoned the Doctor and told him and he asked me to go and see him to put all the 'necessary wheels in motion'. I would have to wait till I saw him to know what that entailed.

I was surprised to learn that 'wheels in motion' actually meant that the Doctor informed the Social Services that they had a patient with Altzheimers that was going to be nursed at home. This apparently was held in much appreciation by them and to that end, they came to your home and equipped it for all the special care that Daddy would need. There was a safety handrail fitted all the way down the stairs, a gate at the top to lock at night to prevent him falling down the stairs. There was a special seat type contraption fitted in the bath so that we could get him in and out easily, a special raiser for the toilet seat and so on. Nothing was too much trouble and the Doctor informed me that I could telephone him day or night and he would come immediately. We really were given all the help and support you could imagine in exchange for relieving them of the burden of care costs for Daddy in a hospital or home. There had never been any real option in my mind, despite our fallings out, I had always worshipped my tyrant Daddy and I always would.

A few days later, my cousin Richard (Daddy's favourite nephew) called me and he told me that his father, Daddy's brother had died of the advanced form of the disease and warned me that it would get very difficult and, at times, very unpleasant. He said that he would come down from time to time and stay a while to relieve the stress, if the occasion ever arose. All those years ago, he looked after me when I moved to Hinckley at the tender age of just seventeen or so, and now he was to do the same thing for his favourite uncle, and for his favourite cousin – me. How lucky was I?

Daddy's life with us settled down to a very pleasant routine, except for the wandering at night and his apparent distress at a lower hernia which was inoperable at his time of life, and for obvious reasons. I talked with Doctor Walker about this all and told him how agitated Daddy became sometimes and I asked him if there were not any placebo type pill he could give me which I could call his 'hernia pill' which would stop him worrying. Dr. Walker said he would give me some 2mg valium tablets and these would help him sleep. I told him at this point that Daddy liked to have the odd hot toddy, especially in bed at bedtime and the Doctor said that one valium and his hot toddy would be the perfect combination to put him at ease and to sleep and for me not to worry. That little pill saved my sanity on so many occasions, though I was extremely careful not to abuse it.

On Daddy's second day with us, he came down for his "brunch" with a bunch of papers in his hand. He proceeded to give me his Will and told me to read it. It left everything to my sister Gillian. I told him that if that was what he wanted to do with his estate, then that was fine with me, I respected him and his wishes, as unfair as it may have been – after all, we had had our fallings out. He became agitated at my response and said that that was not what he wanted at all. He told me he wanted to destroy it and would I please tear it up. I told him that I could not do that, if he wanted to destroy it he would have to do that of his own free will and not in my presence, but I asked him to do it in front of two witnesses who were of no relation to me at all, and that would make it entirely legal and nothing to come back at me later on.

This he did after I had left the room. He also told me that he had moved all of his money in the Earl Shilton Building Society into his bank account and also the proceeds of the sale of 'our' house. He then demanded that I take him to the nearest Midland Bank so that he could move his account from Grantham. So I put him straight into the car and did as he had requested and I took him down to Midsomer Norton and dropped him outside the bank. I waited in the car. He came out after some time and threw a cheque book into my lap.

"What is this for, Daddy"? I asked him.

I had had no inkling of what he had got in mind when he asked me for the trip to the bank. He had always kept his private life so secret from us all. He discussed nothing with anybody, sometimes not even my mum when she was alive – Daddy made his own decisions and told everyone when it was all done. He told me to open it and have a look.

It was a cheque book in the joint names of Daddy and myself. He told me he had done it so that the rest of the family could never ever get at his money, and it was for me so that I could look after him for the rest of his life, and if there was anything left when he did go, then it would automatically come to me and that was what he wanted. He insisted there and then that he should pay weekly for his accommodation and keep from this account at the same rate as the nursing home place that he had been offered, so that I did not lose the revenue from the rooms he was using, that stopped me from doing my bed and breakfast business. So this was all arranged and he was then satisfied and at peace and he stopped agitating about it all.

The Altzheimer's affected daddy in the longterm in a most unexpected way. Not the unpleasantness and nastiness that Richard had described, but he became a very tender, loving and funny man, so much in contrast to the strict Father that I had remembered all my life. He had no concept of dates and days, except on Thursday which was his old age pension day and he would wake up on that morning and walk down to the post office in the village to collect his money. That pension money he always kept for himself and he would often go to the cash and carry with Ron, still "Bob" to Daddy, and always came back with a bottle of Famous Grouse Whisky for himself, one for 'Bob' and a box of chocolates for me. The rest of his money he used to like to spend in the bar and treat the pool team to a round of drinks so that they would play a game of pool for him to watch, or a game of darts. They were absolutely great with him and always very happily obliged. This gave him great pleasure, it would take him back to his early life in Hinckley and going to the 'pool hall' and play a game or two on a Saturday night, when home on leave, but above everything, he absolutely loved the social side of the pub.

He would often ask me for a kiss and cuddle, he regularly asked me if I was married and would I like to marry him! When I used to tell him that I was his daughter and he could not marry his daughter, he would be terribly disappointed and say that it was a shame because he had been looking all his life for a girl like me, and then he would give a little giggle! He did have sane moments though and even tender moments, too. When he first came he gave me Mum's wedding ring and he put it on my left hand and asked me to wear it always, that way he would know his love for Mum would carry on. It is still where he placed it, it helps me think of him every day.

A funny incident happened one night as the last of our regulars were sitting around the lounge bar finishing their drinks. I had called last orders and I was beginning the clearing up. Several of our regulars still sat at the bar with their backs to the Bistro area in the lounge bar, finishing their final drinks. Daddy suddenly appeared in the doorway of the Bistro area and he stood there and said:

"Good morning everyone", as he tipped his trilby at them all and to me. He was absolutely impeccably and beautifully dressed in his thick winter suit jacket, stiffly starched collarred shirt, beautifully toning, highly polished brogues, as always, his walking stick and, to complete this picture of true sartorial elegance, his long johns underwear – but no trousers. He had completely forgotten to put his trousers on! That was not the Major Ashton that I grew up with.

After he went on to tip his trilby to each and every one as they turned round, they all simply said in turn:

"Hello Alf".

None of them smirked, giggled, made snide remarks, nothing. They treated him completely normally as the usual well-dressed gentleman that he was. They turned back to finish their last drinks.

I was horrified, and I came out from the bar and made my way to him. I asked him very gently and quietly where he was going and he told me that it looked like a nice morning and he wanted to go for an early morning walk. I said to him that actually, he had woken up too early, I had not made his tea yet and that it was far too early in the morning to go for a walk because, not only was it still dark but the pavements were completely iced over and you could not walk on them. I then gave him a choice and I asked whether, if I took him back upstairs and gave him his hernia pill and a special early hot toddy, would he sleep for a little while longer till the ice had melted. To this he more than readily agreed and tipped his trilby to all the regulars again, one by one, said 'good morning' to all of them and made his way back upstairs, awaiting his promised temptations.

You could have heard a pin drop in that bar, it was truly eerie. They all turned back around and finished their drinks in silence. Not one of them even so much as smirked or giggled at the sight of my father, in fact they didn't even speak. I took him his hot toddy upstairs and tucked him into bed and kissed him on the forehead.

"I am very proud of you Daddy and I love you" I told him.

"I love you too, Poppet" he said and dozed happily and peacefully back off to sleep.

When I went back into the bar I thanked them all for not laughing at my Dad, and they all looked at me most quizzically. Unanimously they agreed that Daddy was a complete gentleman of the 'old school' and there was absolutely nothing to laugh at, they were very quick to tell me, in a corrective sort of way, even though they were twenty plus years younger than him, they too often forgot between one destination from another what they had actually gone for. They said they all wanted to be as elegant and gallant as he at his age. I was very overcome and flattered for my perfect gentleman of a father.

This particular incident inspired me the next day, to phone my brother Brian and ask him if he had changed his mind about coming to see Daddy. Daddy had forgotten their feud and could not understand why his sons did not want to see him. I told Brian all of this but Brian told me he could not face it at the moment, he had had a heart problem detected and he was going into hospital for treatment. He told me he would phone when he came out. I understood and I accepted this, he actually sounded very frightened, and I decided it would be wise to let matters be for the moment.

Three months later, I was in the kitchen working and Daddy was in the lounge having his brunch. I heard a loud agitated voice coming from the bar and Ron's voice trying to calm the person down. When I went into the bar there stood my younger brother David, whom I had not seen for years, big, fat, grossly overweight and looking like a slob. I had not seen David since we shared the house in Daventry, in fact. I asked him what he was doing in my home and what on earth was he ranting on and going on about.

He blurted out to me, "Where was that old bastard that I was looking after? Did I not know that they had buried my brother Brian three months before and it was all Dad's fault."

At this point, my brain definitely in gear, I showed David a side to his sister he had never seen before. I got exceedingly cross with him, grabbed him up off the seat in my snug and pulled him to the door which went into the lounge area, to look into the lounge and I said in a voice, filled with hate and loathing at his attitude, "That little old white-haired man over there, quietly having his morning meal, is this the hateful ogre that you are talking about. That little old man now wouldn't harm a fly and he has a need and a want to see his sons before he dies".

I ordered him a steak and chips and a pint of Guinness and told him firmly "When you have finished it, get out of my pub and don't come back, I never, ever want to see you or the likes of you again. I am ashamed to call you my brother".

Off he went, slamming the door behind him, leaving me furious. I realised that I had not been told about my older brother's death because they all hated me for taking Daddy in and looking after him, because they all hated him too. I went around the bar and took a huge swig of my cough mixture, a habit I had been forming over the past few weeks. I had this niggly dry cough and when I had been shouting or getting upset, as I had with David, this cough would start and go on for some time, even to the point where it would make me sick. I asked Ron to get me another bottle while he was out shopping.

The following day, David now well and truly out of mind, a young couple entered the Oakhill Inn and asked Ron if we did wedding receptions. Ron asked them to wait whilst he came into the kitchen and talked to me.

"Are you interested in doing a wedding reception, Darling?" he said.

I told him I would come out and talk to them first and see what it was all about. They seemed a very nice young couple and so we sat and discussed the details. They lived in what was known in the village as "The Wendy House", a little round cottage in the grounds of Pondsmead Nursing Home, absolutely opposite to the pub, ideal location, not far to take the food and set it up. I had gathered from the brief meeting that they had approached me because of our local reputation for food and because they thought that 'pub food' would be cheaper than going to a big hotel. They were right, but I was not going to be cheap either, I wasn't doing this for nothing. Outside catering is a great deal more work than doing it on the premises.

They wanted a full reception for about 150 persons,

Gourmet Buffet, continental style with poached fresh salmon, king prawns, quiches, salads and so on. They wanted it to be held in the grounds of Pondsmead in a large marquee. I gave them my menu ideas, we discussed wines and I asked them to give me a few days to make enquiries and come back to them with a price for the whole thing. I went back to them when I had done my research and they booked the reception with me. I set about making all the arrangements and placing the orders. It was to be about six weeks later on a Saturday. This was a good booking for the pub and would swell our coffers quite considerably. Being the person I am, I did not ask for stage payments, as I had taken to the couple very well. However, I should have handled my end more professionally money-wise and learned from the marquee company, who had demanded that they pay for the cost of the marquee up front, otherwise it was no deal – everything was done and paid in advance.

We locked up that night and went peacefully to bed. Daddy had behaved well that day and was now tucked up in bed having had his beloved hot toddy and hernia pill! I kissed him on the forehead and whispered goodnight to him and went to our room. I took another swig of cough medicine from the bottle next to my bed and fell asleep.

If I had known that night what was about to happen next, I wonder if I would have wanted to wake up at all.

CHAPTER THIRTY FOUR

The Bombshells

The following morning I got up and took my shower. As I reached my left arm up to sponge myself down, I felt something "tugging" in my left breast. As I stroked it to ease the painful sensation, my heart skipped a beat and I could hear it thudding in my ears. It was there, I had felt a lump. "Oh please God no, n-o-o," I screamed at the top of my voice, tears falling uncontrollably down my face. This started a coughing fit and I began to have a vomiting attack.

Theo our Retriever, whenever he heard me doing this, which had become more and more frequent, came bounding up the stairs and lay at my side panting loudly, obviously distressed. Shaking from head to foot, and close to collapse, which is how the aftermath of an attack would leave me, I dressed myself as best I could and ran downstairs to Ron.

"My God darling, what's wrong?" he said.

I told him and he picked up the phone and immediately rang the Surgery. There was only a locum doctor available to see, but I would have seen anyone. My appointment made, I jumped straight into the car and went to Shepton Mallet, leaving Ron to run the pub and take care of Daddy with Terry, till I got back.

I entered the surgery and this nice little older doctor asked me to sit down whilst he looked at my notes.

He read my notes carefully, then looked at me very kindly and in a soft but impish voice he simply said: "Are you that nice little bit of stuff that married that old rogue Ron Smith?"

"Yes I am, doctor", I tried to answer cheerfully.

Apparently they were old golf buddies and went way back. He could see that I was in a considerable state of distress and told me not to worry and tell him what was wrong. I told him about the lump and he asked to examine me. After he had finished, he asked me to sit back opposite to him and he looked straight into my eyes.

"I am not going to mince words, Jacqueline" he said, "I don't like the feel of this lump. I strongly believe it is cancer and I am going to write a letter now to one of my closest colleagues, he is one of the finest breast cancer specialists in the U.K. and luckily for us, he works at Bath Hospital. I am going to arrange for an appointment with him for you just as soon as he can fit you in".

A letter came back from a Dr. Maddox's department a few days later with an appointment for tests on the lump. This I was dreading, but I knew I had to face this thing full on and handle it. This was something that I could not hide from till it went away, it would never go away on it's own. I had to deal with it and now.

Daddy always noticed if there was any kind of break in our routine together and when I told him I had to go to Bath for the day, he immediately asked me what was wrong. I could not lie to him and I told him that I had a 'ladies problem' and had to go to the Hospital for the day for some tests. He said to me:

"Poppet, in the jewellers shop next to our bank, when I went in the other day, I noticed a lovely white pearl cross and chain in the window. Please go in and buy it for yourself from me, I know it will keep you safe". I couldn't believe my ears, my father being so kind and precious and remembering something from a few days before, that was very special to me and spoke volumes, so I called in on my way to Bath and bought it.

I arrived at the Royal United Hospital in Bath and a sample was taken from the lump. I was told I would be telephoned when to re-attend for the results. I came home very frightened and went straight to the Doctor's surgery. I told the doctor there was something wrong with my chest and would he have a listen. He said he could not find anything at all, I was just worried about the breast. I was to repeat this trip to the surgery four times and four times I was told the same thing – it is all in your head, you are getting yourself stressed about the operation. They did not know me, I did not give in to stress, I got on with things the way my father had taught me to do.

A few days later, I received a call from the Hospital and the lump had proved to be cancerous, as I knew it would be. They wanted to remove the lump first and then do more tests before going on any further. They sent me a letter to attend Mr. Maddox's Clinic on about the end of May, beginning of June 1996. They removed the lump, stitched me up and after a few hours I was allowed home. I was told to wait for the next letter. I was in a tremendous state of shock and despair at this point in my life, and I now felt so ill with the coughing and vomiting attacks. However, work had to carry on and I pressed on with the wedding reception which was now looming, and running the pub and looking after my men and dog from day to day. The customers must not know anything at this point in time. How I needed my sons and their support at that time, they would never know.

The days went on like this until the morning of the 18th June, 1996 and my helper Terry had come in to work. I told her to get Daddy his morning pint of tea, I had heard him up and about from where I was working in the kitchen. I had started his brunch and would have it ready for when he came down. This she did and took it up to him and when she came down she told me he was complaining that his head felt funny. I told her that I would call Dr. Walker if I was unhappy with his condition after he had had his breakfast.

Then it came, this deafening thud from above in Daddy's room. I ran up the stairs two at a time, my heart beating like a drum and when I got to his room, I hesitated for a moment outside the door, holding on to the handle and listening for any kind of sound at all. There was none, it was all silent. With my heart beating inside like a drum, I opened the door and went in. Daddy was lying on the floor. I ran over to him, knelt down beside him and pulled him into my arms and cradled him there. His eyelids just flickered. I kissed him tenderley on the forehead, and said "I love you Daddy" and he just drifted away, he was gone. I held him gently for several minutes and then decided I must fetch John, the vicar, immediately. Sobbing as I was leaving the room I noticed, there on the bed was layed out all his pristine clothes for the day, his highly polished shoes, his shaving water in the bowl, his toothbrush was still on the sink with the toothpaste on it and his scissors for trimming his side burns and nails. My impeccable Daddy. John came over straight away and gave him a blessing, and then made the necessary call to Dr. Walker who came immediately.

Daddy's instructions on his arrival had been crystal clear. He wanted to be buried with Mum in Hinckley cemetary when his time came, and McCartneys the Funeral Directors of Hinckley, where daddy had worked as a boy eighty years before, were to come and do the funeral. I kept my promise and Daddy would be buried just the way he wanted to go – but not before the whole of my world was to cave in before me, just to add that little extra knock...

I was telephoned by Bath Hospital and asked to go and see Dr. Maddox that morning. This I did amongst all the turmoil of getting Daddy back to Hinckley and arranging the date of the funeral. When I sat in Dr. Maddox surgery, he looked me straight in the eyes and said:

"There is no other way, kindly or otherwise, of telling you this Jacqueline, you have a malignant tumour in your left breast which requires an urgent decision from you. There are options and I want you to consider these carefully."

He told me that they could operate and take more flesh away and clean up around the removed lump, or they could do a complete radical mastectomy, remove the breast completely and the whole of the lymph system on that side, with an option for reconstructive surgery. The tests had showed that the cancer had not reached the lymph system yet, but they needed to act so quickly to prevent this. My decision was instant, I felt as if I had an enormous tarantula spider living inside my breast and it felt creepy. I wanted this intruder removed once and for all and with as much speed as possible, I hated this feeling.

I told him then and there that I did not want cosmetic surgery, I had lost so much weight that there was nothing to cut off anywhere on my flesh to replace the breast tissue anyway, and they would have to use a silicone implant. My reaction was crystal clear in my mind, why the hell take one danger away and immediately insert a foreign body to put something back that should not be there? Dr. Maddox looked relieved and he told me that I had made the finest decision that I could have done for my best chances of a full recovery. He said he wanted me in urgently, but I told him of the loss of my father and that I had a funeral to attend before all this could be done. He was very kind and sympathetic. He asked me when the funeral was and I told him it was at the beginning of July. That was alright, he told me, but not a moment longer.

In the meantime, there were more pressing matters than all of this drama, and me, me, me. I had one precious Daddy to bury. Robbie informed the whole family of the details and it was agreed that my cousin Richard would escort me as a close family member and Ron would escort my first cousin Margaret. We were in the limousine following the hearse, the rest of the family made their own ways there. There was no communication from them, no input, nothing.

We arrived at the cemetery and walked slowly to Mummy's grave which was all prepared. They all stood around not acknowledging either me, Ron, Margaret or Richard. They looked just like vultures – Gillian and her husband, and David my brother. Simon and Robbie were there too, but not 'with me'. The service was almost at the end and then they lowered the coffin into the ground. I had just thrown my handful of soil as had Richard, Ron and Margaret when I heard from someone in the throng:

"Where's the will and do we know how much money there is?"

Richard grabbed me by the arm and said "Come on Ron, let's all go to Margaret's house and see Uncle Alf off in style. Jacqui does not need this".

They hustled Margaret and me into the limousine and we were taken to Margaret's house. I don't think Richard or Ron could take it in. What kind of family was this? No-one had the courtesy to ask me how I was, did we need any help with anything to do with Daddy – just money, money, money!!

Ron drove me home later in a very sad state of mind, both of us knowing that I now faced one of the most difficult days of my life, operation day. I don't remember us talking much at all on that eternal journey.

I had buried my precious Daddy and I now had one of the most unpleasant times in my life to face. I wondered just how much more God had in mind for me to go through…

* * *

The date for the operation then came through and Ron picked up the letter.

"What's the news, Darling?" he said.

I told him the date for the operation was the 1st August, 1996. He was so kind and sympathetic and I really felt for him. His first wife Sarah died in the same hospital with lung cancer and here was his second wife going into the same hospital, with the same disease, but a different part of the body. He knew how hard it was for me too, because I am so vain. I had always had a job where I was 'on show' for the public and my appearance always but especially my figure, were very important to me. There was a lot of love flowing between us but also a great deal of fear and trepidation – on both sides.

I attended for the operation on the due date and Dr. Maddox asked me if I had changed my mind. I said no, I had come to terms with it, albeit reluctantly, I wanted the breast removed. He said he would then fetch his colleague, the anaesthetist to talk to me about the operation. He came and asked me if I had any fears concerning my health in general and the ability to have a major anaesthetic. I told him that I had seen four different doctors in the last four weeks and complained about my chest and coughing. I told him what they had all said and he then told me that they would have to do a series of tests and x-rays before they could go ahead, because if I had anything that was catching, I could contaminate the whole of the anaesthetic equipment.

In a dream-like state, not quite believing that it was all

now getting far too complicated, I was taken down to the laboratories section and given my x-rays. They then took blood samples and sent me back to my ward to wait. I waited and waited and after some considerable time, the nurse came into me and said that they wanted me back downstairs for one more test. When I arrived there a Dr. Alexander was waiting for me, and he told me they were unhappy with the tests so far, they had proved "inconclusive" and the procedure he needed to do involved him snipping away a small part of my lung for analysis, but I had to be conscious when they did it. God knows, if I had known how all this was going to feel, I might well have made them find another way, but there was no other way. I have to say that it was one of the most awful, unpleasant and painful procedures I have ever been through, and one I would never want to repeat, but I took a deep breath, put my bravest face on and gave them a very weak smile and nod and let them get on with it. I was then sent back to my bed to await the results.

After what seemed like an eternity, both Dr. Maddox and Dr. Alexander walked towards my bed. I knew instinctively that this was not going to be something simple, two of the leading specialists in their fields, attending me in my bed, and both at the same time. Something was terribly wrong. Dr. Alexander said:

"Jacqueline, I don't really know how to begin to tell you this, because it seems that you have had and have now got more than enough to cope with, what with the cancer and that operation. The problem is that we cannot proceed with that op. at the moment. It will have to be delayed for two weeks – minimum".

I was stunned. "Oh my God! Why Doctor?" I asked, "what is this all about, I thought the mastectomy couldn't be delayed any longer"?

Then he delivered his bombshell.

"Jacqueline, I am very sorry to have to tell you that you are suffering from acute tuberculosis, which is one of the dormant varieties and comes back with extreme stress. We have to, we need to, bring that under control until it is not infectious, before we can use any anaesthetic equipment on you to do the mastectomy, because you could pass it on to someone else. From the X-Rays, it is apparent that this disease has re-occurred at least twice before in your life. There is extensive scar tissue on your lungs, both from different times. Are you able to shed some light on this for us please?"

I had to think back very hard and then I suddenly remembered, Kenya, six or seven years old and those three months on Auntie Elsie's farm, all the sickness and loss of weight, the never ending treatment with uncle Glynn the Army M.O. Then, the last few months at Loch Manor, I had not realised how ill I had been at that time too, and I took the illness with me to the house at Sea Street, but seemed to get over that quickly myself. All the symptoms, each time, added up and everything about this picture fell suddenly into place.

To say that I was shell-shocked when being told what it was, would be an understatement. He went on:

"The treatment for this – which is a form of chemotherapy – will take about two weeks to make it non-infectious. Your form of t.b. has proved to be responsive to only two medications and if it should re-occur and it should become immune to the treatments, then you would be in a very dangerous situation. Only when we have rendered it non-infectious can the operation go ahead, and it will take about six months treatment in all to hopefully clear it up altogether. I am so, so sorry my dear".

What a double whammy! Oh God! How much more

was I supposed to take. Much more than I thought, it would seem. I had left Bath Hospital T.B.Clinic with all my thirty one tablets a day in a carrier bag and told to report two weeks later on the 15th August 1996 for the final operation to remove my left breast. As I left the Hospital, all the memories came flooding back, I must have been harbouring this bloody disease for most of my life!

CHAPTER THIRTY FIVE

Mutilation Day

Author with full blown T.B. and cancer – 1996

On the Sunday before "Op Day", I went to Holy Communion. I needed this blessing and meeting with God more than I can ever describe. After the service John, the vicar, asked me how I was and would I wait till he had seen the congregation off, he wanted to talk to me privately. I told him of my trepidation at the operation and that things had been very difficult over the last few months, exceedingly emotionally charged, to say the least!

"Jacqui, would you like me to come over later and somewhere very special to you, would you like me to do a healing, I am reputed to be quite successful at it, for you I truly would like to try"?

I was overwhelmed but readily and gratefully accepted, I felt at this low point in my life, that I needed to be touched by the hand of God, there was no-one else to turn to any more.

Later that afternoon John came over to the Oakhill and we went up into Daddy's bedroom, still a special place for me and still in tact with Daddy's furniture and knick-knacks all around us. We knelt and prayed for a while and then John sat me on the end of the bed and stood before me. He placed his right hand on the top of my forehead and went completely silent for what seemed like an eternity. He was breathing quite slowly and loudly and I could feel this burning sensation from his hand at the front of my head and he continued this for some considerable time. After a while, his breathing became more and more normal and he took his hand away and asked me, quietly and gently, to touch his hand. It was burning red hot to the touch, like a boiled kettle! I truly did feel as if I had been touched by God. I kissed him on both cheeks and thanked him profusely. He merely slipped away silently and I knew his prayers would be with me on 'THE' day.

On the morning of the 15th August, Ron dropped me outside the front entrance of Bath Royal United Hospital. He got out of the car with my bag, took me in his arms and tenderly kissed me.

"Darling, I am so sorry, please forgive me but don't ask me, I cannot come in there with you, you know it is the same part of the hospital where Sarah died".

Of course I tried to understand, I did understand, at this point in time he was facing the possibility of losing his second wife to the same illness that killed and robbed him of his first one. But part of me didn't understand how he could not overcome this thing from the past and realise that yes, he could lose me but I was so frightened, and still with the memories of him leaving me there once before, going in with a life inside me and coming out completely and literally empty and so lonely. How was he going to feel if for some reason, I didn't come this time and he wasn't with me when it happened? If there ever was a time when I needed the someone that I loved to be near to me, to have his arms wrapped so tightly around me that I couldn't possibly feel afraid of anything, to fill me full of hope and a life to look forward to, that time was now. But he didn't. He couldn't go in with me, so I undertook that walk alone…

Numb with heartbreak and trepidation, I made the second loneliest walk of my life that morning and booked myself into the ward where, upon arrival, I was prepared for the operation. To describe my feelings at this time is virtually impossible, angry – yes, frightened – unbelievably, hurt – more than I can describe, afraid – yes, lonely – yes, apprehensive – totally. No words seemed to come anywhere near how I felt at that point, but I never did ask God "Why me"? Why the hell not me?

I came round in my bed on the ward and dozily looked around me. I was then to have one of the most humbling experiences of my entire life, my own sorrows were to fade away momentarily. My bed was next to another where a very pleasant lady lay there looking at me intently.

"Welcome back to reality" she said kindly, "are you alright"?

"Yes, I suppose I am and I also suppose that I'm glad that it is all over at long last".

"What did you have done"? she asked me. I told her and, as you do, I said:

"Are you in for the same thing"?

"No, my dear, I am totally riddled with cancer they tell me, and I only have a few months left to live". She said this in a sad, but most matter of fact way, that it left me a little at a loss for words.

How the hell do you respond to that, she was about my age and had a lovely, lovely face and disposition, and there was not a trace of bitterness or anger in her voice, it was so accepting of her state? Oh God, I was so angry at my cancer, how could she not be with hers? Her name was Val and we spent our time in the Hospital discussing just about everything.

The next day I was allowed to take a shower, accompanied by a nurse. When I came back to the ward I decided I had to "do the works" – I had bought some new satin pyjamas and my full make up kit with me and with Val's input in piling and tying my hair high on my head, I tried to make myself look and feel like a million dollars. I had to do this for myself, because if I hadn't, I would have wept inconsolably. No-one had come in to visit me at all, no Ron, no Robbie and no Simon and no-one would be coming. I felt so lonely, so alone and unloved and so terribly, terribly mutilated.

I was discharged on the 25th August and Ron was to collect me. As I left the ward, and said my goodbyes to Val, I walked out of Bath Hospital very, very sad and with a lonely, empty feeling inside. There outside in the car, Ron was patiently waiting and he got out of the car and came over to me. He held me tightly in his arms for a few moments, but all he could find to say was:

"Hello Darling, let's get you home and get you better".

I felt a slight degree of comfort in his words, but my mind was completely overtaken by the sad events of the last few days. Once again I was disappointed that Ron had not overcome his loss of Sarah in this very Hospital, even though I – his new wife – was going through the second of two of the most traumatic events of my life. We drove back to the Oakhill and talked little, I don't really think that Ron knew how to begin to talk to me, and I had little to say in return.

I know Ron felt awful about not visiting me and being there for me, but my heart had to understand and accept just what all this turmoil must have been doing to him too. Not only the return of the awful times during Sarah's last few months of life, but he also had my prognosis to deal with, either of these illnesses could kill me, the mastectomy itself was only the first part of the perilous journey, and of course, it was really unlucky to be suffering them both at the same time. However the infectious part of the T.B. had been brought under control, so I was safe, not only to continue working, even though I had been ordered complete rest and recuperation, but I could even give him a kiss!

I wrote to Val after we came out of hospital, as we had agreed to do, in an attempt to share some of her pain with her. This is an extract from the reply I got from her:

8th September 1996

"My dear Jacqui,

Thank you for your very nice letter. It helps me to know that you are concerned about me as I am about you. As you said, we hit it off straight away and seemed to understand each other, both being in similar and emotional situations.

The tears bubble up some days, just when I think I am having a good day, but there you are. There are some good points to it all – I won't be getting old and stuck in some old people's home gradually losing all my marbles and peeing my pants (ha ha).

I think about you often, remember that awful morning when you were so poorly, but the next day you perked up, put on the make up and sexy pyjamas and looked absolutely fabulous. You were brilliant and very brave".

I phoned Val's number a couple of weeks after getting that letter and her Mother answered the phone. Val had passed away the day before, peacefully in her sleep. I felt very ashamed that I had not phoned earlier, I also felt extremely humble and it had been an honour to know her, I was not the brave lady.

Even whilst in hospital, I had been folding napkins and making preparations for the impending wedding, which was the following weekend after my discharge from the hospital. Despite being told that I must have complete rest and take things very easily, fat chance for complete rest and recuperation in a pub. In fact, when we arrived back at the Oakhill with fluffy toy bunny tucked under my operation arm – recommended by the breast care nurse after a mastectomy, as a comfort – I went straight round into the bar and pulled a pint for Tony Munn. I got through that day with Ron and I speaking little, it was very emotive. I must confess to having been well and truly ready to go to bed that night and have a peaceful rest wrapped in the arms of the man I loved and him holding me so gently, as if he thought I might break.

The next morning, after I had arisen and we had tea in bed, I told Ron that I wanted him to be the one to change my dressing on my wound, we would both share that moment together, the moment when we both looked at my changed body. He was very reluctant at first, but I told him that it was very important to me that he share my mutilation and come to terms with it, just as I had to. My misshapen form was now a part of our intimate life. Ron did as I had asked, took off the dressing and, with hands shaking, he replaced it with a new one and as I looked him in the eyes as he was doing it, he was weeping. He pulled me close to him and just sat there holding me tight and crying.

"Oh my dearest love" he said as he sobbed, "what have they done to you"?

That said it all to me. No more words were spoken, but if it was that moment, and I cannot be sure, but from that day onwards, Ron and I were never to make love again. Neither of us seemed able to bring up the subject, words and explanations did not seem to come into the equation. The moment was the thing. For myself, I could not bring myself to ask Ron if this new view of me repelled him or whether the sheer magnitude of the shock of seeing what had been done to me, with him not there to share it all with me, in other words, his own guilt, took all the magic out of our love making, I shall never, ever know, because I would not allow myself to put him on the spot and ask for a reason. As long as he would hold me and kiss and cuddle close to me, that was all that really mattered. We still had each other for always.

We dressed and went downstairs, expecting the day would be as normal as it could be for everyone. Ron called over to me from the front door as he unlocked it and said that the mail had been delivered. One envelope had the name and address of a firm of Solicitors in Devon on it. The moment I saw it, I knew exactly where this had come from, and from whom, and, more to the point, why.

The letter was written on behalf of my sister, brother, and my two nieces (my eldest brother's children). It demanded that I turn over all relevant paperwork and bank statements with relation to my father's estate. It referred to funds which were not accounted for and other such accusations. I was incandescent with rage. The greedy, cheeky….

I would have liked to have been a fly on the wall when

that Solicitor read my four foolscap page reply to them and my demand at the end for two years storage of my father's excess possessions in our only function room and my time at £10 per hour for nursing him twenty four hours a day, seven days a week, fifty two weeks of the year for two years, all these costs to be shared jointly between them. I think the amount mentioned was something in the region of £187,000. I also told them in no uncertain terms of the steps my father had taken personally and without any help from me, to make quite sure that they did not inherit a single thing for the way he felt he had been treated at the end, and of course, I told them that I had been paying the mortgage on the house and the deeds had my name on them as joint shareholder with my father. My reply gave me great satisfaction, and I felt completely sure that that would be the last I would hear from any of them. How true that was and still is!

The wedding at Pondsmead was now but a few days ahead. All my preparations had been completed in record time but it was all absolutely of the best. Decorated poached salmon *en gelee*, king prawns, smoked salmon, elaborate quiches, salads, home made bread sticks, everything that one could wish to see at their wedding reception, and done with great love and devotion to my profession, of which I have always been and always will be exceedingly proud.

Terry, my helper at the pub and her husband John were helping, to specifically take care of the buffet, do a tidy up and top up and John to do the wine, anyone who could help was there. I was dressed in a green cocktail dress, very suitable, supervising the whole thing and playing 'Madame' as I do, though I must still have been under the influence of the anaesthetic, because I didn't really feel quite 'with it', but I had tremendous support from everyone and it all went superbly well. I was very proud not only of my personal achievement in still being able to do it and actually being there, but in my friends and customers who had all shown their love and warmth and chipped in with their help. It all went off so professionally.

The finale to this story is that, after all this huge effort, and despite my personal circumstances, I submitted my account to the bride and groom, completely satisfied with my own personal efforts and timed it to arrive when they returned from their honeymoon. However, they had disappeared from 'the wendy house' and I had to have them traced and sued for the money. It took forever, but I got an offer to settle and my solicitor told me to grab it. I had been well and truly 'stitched up' deceived and robbed by them.

Gullible – who, me? In respect of this couple, most assuredly.

A few days later, and still feeling exceedingly annoyed at my stupidity, and not listening to Ron's advice to insist on being paid before the event, I was in the kitchen as I had received some orders for food and I was getting them out. After the meals had gone, I came out into the bar and there were several couples eating at the tables around the lounge area. Ron quietly came up to me and whispered in my ear:

"Darling, do you recognise that lady sitting on the left over there, under the big picture"?

"No, Darling, who is she?" I replied.

"Sweetheart, that's Iris James. You remember: the bitch who wrote me that awful letter to me in Cyprus all those years ago?"

Did I remember? Now was my time – now I was to get the revenge I had so long prayed for, fifteen years later and back in England, but here was my day, and this was going to be oh so sweet.

She had walked into my pub with a friend and ordered lunch which she paid for. I have to admit, I hadn't recognised her. She had become old, fat and frumpy but Ron assured me that it was definitely Iris. I wondered did she recognise me, did she know that it was my name over the front door? Just to make sure that she did, I went over to her, took her knife and fork from her hands and put them back onto her plate, put the money she had paid into her hand, grabbed her by her collar, pulled her physically out of her chair and then pushed her through the front door on to the street outside, telling her what a vile person she was to do what she had done all those years before to a close friend, so much still in grief for his beloved Sarah.

She had judged me then and she had judged Ron before knowing his feelings. Dear Lord, I know I should not really have smirked, but it felt really good and I pushed her out of the front door, telling her never to come into my establishment again. She was open-mouthed. I really did hope that, in front of her friend, I had hurt her and shamed her that day as much as she had hurt my beloved Ron all those years before – and, by God it felt really good.

What is it they say? – A woman scorned…

CHAPTER THIRTY SIX

The Crunch comes…

One of the saddest tasks any of us is asked to perform is to sort through a dead parent's personal effects. It's like looking at the secrets of their life story. It's not only an emotional ordeal but it can also spring a few surprises. No child ever knows all the details of their parent's life.

Sorting out Daddy's many possessions was now the next traumatic job for me to go through. All the things in the functions room had to be sorted and moved out and sold or disposed of in the appropriate way. I tried to be logical about the whole unenviable task and decided to start in Daddy's bedroom. I sorted all his clothes out and as I laid them on the bed, including his tweedy suits and, believe it or not, his army uniform, all intact after all those years, including his 'Sam Brown', I decided to contact the Theatre Royal in Bath and see if they would be interested in having any of his things. They were very grateful and came over that day and picked it all up.

However in Daddy's bedroom was a wooden box where he had kept all his little writings and secrets. In one very old envelope, marked "Jacqueline – caul – January 1944" I found this crinkled fine paper-like substance. I had completely forgotten all about it, but my mother had told me years before that when I was born and handed to her by her trusted, and three times used Midwife, whom she called "Mack", my Mother let out a shriek of horror and asked Mack what kind of monster was this baby? Mack, apparently, had burst out laughing, licked the palm of her hand and rolled up and off, what was a complete skin or caul, up over my chin and right to the top of my forehead and removed it completely. She put it beside the bed and told my Mother that to be born with a caul over the face was not only lucky indeed but also a sign of great beauty. My Mother must have given it to Daddy and he had kept it all those years – 52 years. It was in a very delicate state of decomposition, obviously after all those years, but I was very touched that he had kept a part of me in his 'treasure chest'.

Folded up in another very old envelope was a letter which, when I read it, I remembered my father telling me about many years before, when he had explained to me the circumstances under which the letter was written and told me that it was one of his most favourite mementos. Apparently, whilst out in India, one of the servants had been proving to be very tiresome and lazy and my father, he of the short fuse temper-wise, had sacked the man on the spot. In India at that time, the servants would have been those who would not have been to school and so could neither read nor write. However in the main streets on almost every corner in either Bangalore or Poona where daddy had been stationed, would be sitting 'scribes' who, for a rupee, would write a letter on your behalf. Their use and abuse of the English language could prove sometimes to be very funny. This is the letter Daddy received from his dismissed servant:

"*Sir,*
On opening this epistle you will behold the work of a dejobbed and very bewifed and childrenised gentleman who was violently

dejobbed in a twinkling by your goodself. For Heavens sake sir, consider this catastrophe as falling on your own head, and remind yourself as walking home at the moon's end to five savage wives and sixteen voracious children with your pockets filled with non-existent £.S.D.* Not a solitary rupee, pity my horrible state.

When being dejobbed and proceeding with a heart and intestines filled with misery to this den of doom myself did contemplate culpable homicide but Him who protected Daniel safely through the lions den will protect his servant in his house of evil.

As to the reason given by your good self for my dejobbment, the incrimination was laziness. No Sir, it were impossible that myself who has pitched sixteen infant children, six adults and ten adulteresses, into this valley of tears can have a lazy atom in his mortal frame and the sudden departure of Rupees. 60 has left me on the verge of destitution and despair. I hope this vision of despair and horror will enrich your dreams this night, and good angels will pulverise your heart of nether millstone, so that you will awaken and with as much alacrity as may be comparable with your personal safety, you will hasten to rejobbulate your servant. So mote it be, Amen,

Yours dispairfully,
XXX"

* Pounds, shillings and pennies.

I do not know if he was "rejobbulated" but for his sake, I do hope so. I gave this letter to Robbie for him to keep with all the little things he is now collecting together to make some kind of family history for his sons.

In the box I also found a photograph of a young lady, whom I did not recognise. On the back, in daddy's handwriting were the words "*they called her Imogen. She was born in Bath Hospital, why can't she come and live with us*". I did wonder if this was perhaps a sister that we all knew nothing about. I will never know. Those were some of my father's utmost precious possessions. I sat there pondering these few little things that had been so precious to my father and realised that I was exceedingly proud of my Daddy. I still am.

I managed, one way or another, to dispose of everything else and also managed to get rid of the hundreds of books that Daddy had purchased over the years from a book club. I am sure with the number he had, he must almost have purchased the company itself, he had used up six cheque books that I knew of and every single cheque was made payable to this book club. Some of the books had not even been unwrapped, there were thousands of pounds worth.

Life at The Oakhill then returned to some kind of normality, my treatment was ongoing and I was improving little by little every day. However, there were undercurrents of which I was aware but Ron would not talk about. In his own way, as I have previously said it had always been his brief to protect me from the aspects of life that I could not face – not succeeding, not coming up to expectations, not fulfilling my personal commitments, but not even Ron could prevent the phone call that was to come from Barclays Bank PLC the next day.

The pub had been purchased in my name only, I was the sole licensee and the mortgage was also in my name, so when Barclays did indeed call the next morning, they asked to speak to me. Ron tried to persuade them to let him deal with it, but they refused and said only Mrs. Smith could take this call. Ron, reluctantly, handed me the phone and whispered to me:

"We are in deep trouble, darling. The business is not good".

I took a deep breath and said good morning to the

Manager. What he then had to say to me I really didn't want to hear. We had worked so hard and we had a good reputation. But speak he did:

"Mrs. Smith, your husband had described to me the horrors of the recent happenings in your life which makes this call doubly difficult for me. There is no easy way for me to tell you what I have to say, so I will be brief. Your business is in serious financial difficulties and we may have to foreclose on you. If it is any consolation, this is happening a great deal in your profession at the moment, for all kinds of reasons, but can you let me have your proposals, when you have had time to discuss it with Mr. Smith, and Mrs. Smith, sooner rather than later".

I was dumbstruck, I realised that we were not making a fortune, but in my wildest dreams, I never expected this. I looked at Ron and whimpered:

"I presume you know what he has just said to me, don't you? Just what the hell are we going to do?"

Ron and I talked it through and I told him that there was no way I was leaving this pub without handing my keys and transferring my license to a new purchaser, I would not be put out of my home and business, not me, not this Jacqui Smith.

It was all going round and round in my head, over and over again. What could we do, there must be something, some positive action that we could try to make things happen, instead of letting the worst scenario occur without trying to stop it. Suddenly an idea came to me. The week before, the owner of the Oakhill Brewery, a small independent real ale brewery in the village, a Mr. Reg. Keevil had rung me and asked if he could make a brief filmed interview in my bar for a documentary being made on the brewery, which I agreed he could do.

He had said to me himself:

"Jacqui, it is about The Oakhill Brewery, it should be made in The Oakhill Inn, where you sell my ales".

Of course it should and I had agreed. The Oakhill Inn should be the flagship of the Oakhill Brewery. There was my plan, staring us both in the face and we hadn't thought of it, and I made my mind up there and then. I told Ron my plans, but he was very sceptical. I didn't like Ron's reaction one bit but I would not allow myself to be daunted and I picked up the phone and rang Reg Keevil there and then and suggested that I should see him urgently as I had a proposition for him.

He must have been intrigued, because he agreed to see me immediately and I went straight down to the Brewery. I told Reg that because of my illnesses I wanted to get out of the trade, but I firmly believed that the pub and brewery should go together. He mused over my statement for a while and then asked me how much I wanted, I told him, I gave him a sensible price that we, and the Bank, could both work with, and he said he would think about it and phone me later that day. He was as good as his word and called me back a little while later. I was pleasantly surprised and pleased that he had acted so quickly. Yes! I had done it, he had seen the potential of owning the Brewery and the first point of sale of his real ales, in the same village, and the village pub bearing the same name. We struck the deal there and then. It was with the greatest sense of accomplishment and positive delight that I immediately called the Bank and told them my news. I told the Manager I wanted to walk out of my own pub and hand the keys to the new owner, and that would be the only way I was prepared to leave. He was delighted with the news, but not as much as I was!

"Well done, Mrs. Smith, and I mean that sincerely. You really are a fighter" he said.

Things seemed to be going through very well till one

morning Nick Foster, my Solicitor rang me and told me that there was a problem with the title deeds. For God's sake, what now? It turned out that George Pollard – the so called "friend" the man who had lured us back to England to run his social club and then abandoned us – it was his company which had done the conveyancing. They had made a mistake about the car park on the deeds, and by the time it was all sorted out and all the legal proceedings could be finalised, another three months went by with Ron and I working just as hard as we could to make a good job of everything and keep the Oakhill's good name. It was hard for me, the operation and the TB had taken their tolls on me, both emotionally and physically, and it was becoming harder for Ron, who was now limping very badly, as he needed a new hip and would not admit to it but we still carried on, there was nothing else we could do.

I told Nick Foster that when the whole thing had gone through, I wanted to sue George's company and to start the proceedings in motion immediately. I needed to get my own back on the man who brought me away from my lovely Cyprus under false pretences and then allowed me to be 'dumped' and then, for a man at the top of his profession, his company had let me down professionally too. This he agreed to do, but of course it would take time to get it to the court. I understood this and told him to give the sale of the pub priority. Nick immediately went ahead and did just that and the sale of the pub was now nearing completion.

However, this left Ron and I with a problem. Where were we going to live, and what with, we only had the small amount of money Daddy had left me? Like a true spear of justice from God, this problem was solved the next day when I received another call from the Bank Manager. I took the phone from Ron's hand with trepidation, but I was to be totally amazed at what followed:

"Mrs. Smith, I am delighted to be able to tell you personally, that because of your exceptional personal circumstances, and the way in which we admire how well you handled this whole matter, the Bank are going to award you £20,000 for continuing to run the Oakhill until the sale goes through, and for saving the business – we would have lost at least that, and probably much, much more, if the business had been declared bankrupt.

"Thank you very much indeed, it was a pleasure" I said feeling very satisfied with myself. I jumped and squealed with delight when I had put down the phone.

"What did he say, Darling" Ron asked. When I told him he too was overjoyed and much relieved.

"Well done, Darling, I'm really so proud of you" he said lovingly, "but you know, if anyone could have pulled that off, it could only have been you". Those words warmed my heart.

"Right, this has answered our housing problem. This afternoon we will go into Shepton Mallet and find the estate agent and buy the cheapest house we can find" I said to Ron.

We did just that and the first house details we looked at were for a small semi detached pre-war council house, in the centre of Shepton for £40,000. We went round and looked at it, it was a nice three bedroomed house with large garden and that was it; we bought number 11, Douglas Drive just like that. Ron said we ought to take a mortgage, I was horrified at the prospect of ever being in debt again and I flatly refused – no more debts, not for me, just cash all the way.

Simon had started his own building company and I called him for help. I had explained to Ron what I wanted to do in the new house and he felt it was all possible. As you entered the house into the hallway there were two doors ahead of you, one into the dining room and one into the front room. I wanted the two rooms knocked into one but done with archways, Cyprus archways. The dining room door was bricked up and we then had a through lounge and dining room with a Cyprus archway into the lounge area and a Cyprus archway into the dining area. Simon said it could be done and set about doing it and fitting in our existing wooden units and cocktail cabinet at either side of the chimney breast. This I wanted finishing in rough Bathstone, which he did. I asked for the whole new room to be decorated in eucalyptus green and this too was done and suddenly, our little ex-council house became wonderland! It looked stunning.

I proudly handed over my keys to the Oakhill Inn to Reg Keevil and we attended court together for the transfer of the license. When we got back, Simon removed my plaque from above the front door of the pub "Jacqueline Smith, licensed to sell beer, wines and spirits for consumption on or off the premises".

Another era may have truly come to an end, but this girl hadn't finished going places just quite yet.

CHAPTER THIRTY SEVEN

Cyprus calls AGAIN – at last

The time eventually came for the court case and it was to be heard in Bristol. We arrived at the Court and Nick introduced me to my barrister. This case could go either way, he told me and warned me that he was not overjoyed with our particular female judge for reasons he didn't, or chose not to, tell me at the time. I examined her closely. She sat there in her bench, with a completely emotionless expression on her very sour face. I suppose she would have been about fifty plus years of age, passing her in the street I would not have had her marked down as a judge and she gave me no feelings or reason to be hopeful. I was so unimpressed with her, I cannot even remember her name.

My case was well presented and all the evidence put forward. I had had a full medical report especially done for the case, it was a good report which said that the TB. had left me with a loss of one third of my breathing capacity and the trauma of the cancer had affected me greatly, and this too was submitted. I had put in a claim for damages at the rate of ten pounds per hour for the extra time it had taken to sell the pub because of the conveyancing mistake by the original solicitors. This was the normal rate for relief managers at that time, so I was not claiming any amount that could be considered as extortionate. The total came to something like thirteen weeks and the amount I wanted was £15,000, at least.

Then came the time for me to go up into the witness box and give my evidence. This I did quite confidently, and explained to the judge how hard the life of a publican was, especially being the chef as well. I explained that a normal working day was about sixteen and a half hours or so, seven days a week, fifty two weeks of the year, and no time off (for good behaviour) and I managed to do this having just had a major operation and suffering the awful effects of tuberculosis, including the difficulties caused by the continued exposure and inhalation of tobacco smoke for that time. My evidence given, I returned to my seat next to my barrister and waited for the judge's summing up. They both said I had delivered my evidence very well.

The judge then gave her summing up and opinion of the case before her. She proceeded to say that it was quite common and very understandable for solicitors to make the odd mistake; after all, we are all human aren't we? and there was certainly no justification for this case to have been brought to court. To my amazement she ended:

"I am perfectly sure, Mrs. Smith that, despite the cancer and the tuberculosis, you are a perfectly capable woman and more than able to have handled the extra time before completion." She then added, "There are far too many clients trying to sue their Solicitors for minor discrepancies; these are just part of life – Claim denied," she pronounced, just like that.

I was absolutely gutted and told Nick my Barrister so.

"Well, I deliberately didn't tell you before, because I was afraid that this might be the outcome, but she is a solicitor herself Jacqui, so what did you expect? I'm afraid that her sympathies were totally with the other side?"

She then proceeded to ask the barristers what amount of fees they were claiming and when told by the opposing barrister that she wanted £100 per hour, "Perfectly reasonable, very justifiable, I will allow that" said the judge.

That was it, that was great British justice at it's best – I don't think so! To say that I was disillusioned would be to put it rather mildly. I was downright disgusted.

Simon had now finished with his building company and Anne, wife number three, had also kicked him out and was divorcing him. He asked if he could come and live with Ron and I till he could find a flat somewhere near. We agreed rather grudgingly as we were so used to being on our own, but he was good as his word and he actually found himself a job very quickly as a security guard for the only Supermarket in Shepton.

The following day he brought home a girl called Tracy who was very sweet. The next remark floored me completely. After only twenty four hours of knowing this girl, he said that they had found a flat together and could he borrow Ron's Bang and Olufson music centre, our cane furniture and our brand new grill and barbecue that I had recently bought, till they could get started properly on furnishing it. Here we go again, I thought to myself, how long will this one last? I don't know why, except Ron was a big softie with my boys, but we heard ourselves agreeing to the loan of these things. That was the last we saw of them, and I heard a little while later that they had split up and she left heartbroken, as usual. I then got hold of him and when I demanded that the borrowed items be returned immediately, he said that he had sold them because he needed the money. I got so angry with him, because his morals and total lack of scruples had always been the big bone of contention with me, and when I told him that this was not acceptable, he told his own Mother to "Fuck off!"

That was to cause a break up in our relationship which lasted for the next fifteen years. Robbie too, was not in contact and I could not understand why my sons were treating me like this and what was going on, but I reacted the only way I knew how, I took a big deep breath and got on with my life.

I managed to get myself three little jobs, one as a relief chef for the Bath & West Health Care Trust and one as breakfast chef for the St. Ivel factory in a little village called Evercreech, and subsequently one as Second Chef at The Glen Nursing home in the same area. Each of the jobs together paid quite good wages, enough to keep us very well until Ron could get his hip done and until such time as my master plan would then come into being. Once we had left the Oakhill Inn and settled into the house, Ron admitted to me for the first time that leaving Cyprus had been the biggest mistake of his life, and how sorry he was that he had pressurised me to do it and how much he now regretted it. This gave me the opportunity I was waiting for.

I didn't ask his permission first, I merely made the statement "Well, Ron, my Master plan is this; as soon as your hip is done and you are well enough, this house is going on the market and we are returning to Cyprus, where we were happy, and no arguments. Your family still do not want to know us, and it has cost us everything in the world that we had these past few years in the UK. If you decide you do not want to come, I don't know what you will do, but I am definitely going back".

"Darling, we would be there now if I had not got to wait for this hip to be done" he said, "and you're going nowhere without me. The whole damn sorry mess has been my fault and I'm so sorry I caused it all".

It was now 1999, time had rolled on and one afternoon I got a shock. I had just returned from the Glen, having cooked supper for the sixty or so residents. The telephone rang and it was Jean, our very old friend from Midsomer Norton days. She had called to give me the news that Robbie had got married that very day. After giving me all the news about the wedding and I had hung up, I collapsed into the settee and just sat and broke my heart. Not only were my youngest son and I not now in touch at all, but he had actually married the mother of my grandson Daniel who by this time was five years old, and his own mother and step father had not been asked or even told about it.

I was totally devastated and terribly hurt. What with this and both my sons shunning me when I had been so very ill, and not coming to the hospital, what in the world could I have done as a Mother to deserve this treatment was all I could think about. I felt an absolute failure. Two of the people I loved most in the world and neither of them wanted to know me. I began a series of letters to Robbie trying to repair the damage, but always received either 'no' answers, one telling me what a 'sad old lady' I had become, or ones telling me to go away. I decided to let things be and get on with our lives but I would never forget this time or the occasion that caused it, I was so terribly hurt.

Ron knew just how much this business with Robbie had upset me, I was pining for my sons, and Jean and Don had invited me to go up to Northampton for a weekend away. Little did I know that every time I had spoken to her on the telephone and wept over the fact that I had missed Rob's wedding and the rift between us all, and I just could not fathom out what I could have done wrong to cause all that, she had been telephoning Robbie and telling him. Apparently it was decided by Robbie and Sue, that it was time that we had a reconciliation, and it was all carefully planned by them.

On the afternoon that I arrived, I was taken by Jean and

Don to Robbie and Sue's new home. Robbie had laid on a special lunch for us all and we all made it up and I saw my grandson Daniel, who by now was five years old. I was also given the wonderful news that they were expecting another baby and given a copy of the first scan to keep. I was so overwhelmed and overjoyed at the same time. My life seemed so much more positive by the end of this visit, I was so happy. I had part of my family back, though Rob had still not told me at that point why it all happened. It was to be a very long time before I found out.

As Ron's hip got worse, seemingly day by day, he was becoming unable to get upstairs without going up sitting on his bottom, and coming down the same way. As we had only one toilet, upstairs in the bathroom, this posed tremendous problems. From that point on, I began pressurising the two hospitals, where he was registered, for an early date for the operation.

Eventually, an idea came to me suddenly, watching Ron do his usual trip upstairs. I acted on it, literally and immediately. The actress in me that Mum always claimed was there came to the fore. I took a big deep breath and concentrated hard, whilst dialling the first of the Specialists' secretaries, firstly the one in Bath Hospital and then the same procedure at Yeovil Hospital, they had both had him on their lists for the hip replacement, and then the actress took over. I told them both a large, but in my mind, a justifiable fib. I told them it had now become so difficult for my dear husband Ron to get up to our only toilet, that my wonderful ex-Bomber Command Navigator, thirty nine missions over Germany for his country, who was now at the ripe old age of seventy five, having to go outside into our back garden to take a "pee pee" in the outside drain at the rear of the house, in full view of the neighbours! It might even end up in the local newspaper . . . Well, it worked. I really told them a sob story and a half! We had a date for the operation a few weeks later.

The operation was done in Bath Hospital and for a few days after the operation, Ron was supposed to sleep with a long wedge of foam between his legs. He told me that on the second night, the Ward Sister did her last nightly inspection and said to him:

"Mr. Smith, I am very disturbed to see that you have absolutely nothing between your legs".

That was about the most unfortunate statement that she could have made to Ron Smith, with his quaint Somerset sense of humour, because he immediately retorted with:

"I think you had better have a word with my wife about that, Sister!"

She scurried off the ward with very red face. Ron made a wonderful recovery, the matron at the Glen having given me one of their old wing chairs for him, as it was the correct height for his knees and getting out of the chair properly. The difference it made to his life was immeasurable, he was a different man, so much so that as soon as the hospital wrote him off as a patient, the first topic of conversation was, of course, when can we put the house on the market and when can we get home to Cyprus.

I had a definite plan of action for this to happen, the first thing being to talk to Robbie about whether or not he had any thoughts on whether or not we should stay on in England and be near to them or to return to our beloved Cyprus, in our hearts our 'home'. Robbie's reaction was instant,

"Go home Mum, home to where yours and Ron's hearts are, I want you to be happy, we are only a plane ride away, a phone call, a text message. We will probably see more of you there than we have done while you have been in England".

That was all I needed. We first went to the Agent who had sold us the house, and put it back on the market. When we got back, I phoned one of my first friends in Cyprus, Rita and asked her to look for a small villa of some kind to rent from whatever date we got back and just gleaned some information of the state of things, now nine years down the line. It was never meant to take that long, but as always in life, it can be quite impossible sometimes to stick to any plans no matter how carefully made – especially not where my life has been concerned.

The first person who came round to see our little home, fell instantly in love with it. I was very proud of that little house, it really had an atmosphere all of its own which kind of 'grabbed' you as you walked in. We had made an immediate sale – how soon could we complete and how soon could we move out? Our only problem now was that my second grandson was imminently due and I wanted to stay and see him first before we flew.

Our English home was packed up and went away for shipment out to Cyprus so we moved out and went to stay, along with our beloved Golden Retriever Theo, who was coming out with us, with Jean and Don, our friends in Northampton. Our tickets were booked for the 20th May 2000, and Sam Gregory Brown was born in the early hours of that very same morning, just as if it had all been arranged. Robbie was able to drive me to the hospital where I was able to hold number two grandson and I have treasured pictures of the moment. Robbie then took Ron and me to the airport and Theo the dog would be following on two days later, due to one missing piece of paper in his documents.

Our proceeds of sale had now been put on deposit with our Bank in Midsomer Norton and I had given strict instructions to the bank that they were not to play with any investments with it, I just wanted it to sit there safe and make a bit of interest till we knew what we were going to do in the long term, and I was determined at this point to have a lot more input into that. So we flew home to Cyprus with the knowledge that we had a reasonable sum of money and a good future for the next twenty or so years, Ron now of course seventy six, but in the peak of good health.

We stepped off the plane and I took that first big deep breath. The magic was there instantly, as I hoped it would be, completely washing over me, completely enveloping me. I was home. Everything in my world was now almost perfect, and the future looked much brighter. Rita had found us this little detached bungalow in Catalkoy down near the sea, and after two weeks quarantine in Nicosia, Theo eventually joined us there in our new temporary home. It was a nice bungalow, but it was not big enough for us to contemplate living in for the long term, with all the belongings that we still had, including one large Golden Retriever, and we would rather have upsized than got rid of our treasured possessions as they all had wonderful memories attached to them. Luck, or fate, intervened yet again. The problem was about to be solved that very day in a rather unusual set of circumstances.

Arthur and Doris Rider, the Canon and his wife from St. Andrews Church, were about to have their joint 90th Birthdays. This was to be celebrated, like their 80th which I had done for them at their daughter's cottage in Bellapais. Arthur had asked that now I was back, could I please do the catering for them as I had done the party ten years before. However, I did not have a cooker in this little bungalow, and before I could accept, I needed to go and find some kind of oven. When we got to the electrical dealers to have a look around, the cooker salesman asked what I wanted.

I said "Well, I don't know really, as we haven't got our own house yet".

He said, in typical Cypriot fashion, "I have a cousin who has a house to rent at Alsancak, down near the beach and about fifteen kilometres from Kyrenia".

It sounded wonderful, except for the fact that Ron was fighting me yet again on not buying but renting. I desperately wanted to buy, he did not. However, we went out to see the cousin at the address he gave us and we asked about the house. Sadly, it was the last one he had and had been let the night before. He did say though that the piece of land next to it was his and, if we had the plans, he would build us a house on it to our specifications, and we could rent it till we died. Ron was in Utopia, he had the plans with him of his house in Midsomer Norton and steamed ahead. However, this was not built yet and I could not cater for the party from the tiny kitchen in the bungalow, so I had to say "no" to Arthur and Doris, I could not do the party for them.

The house was finished about seven months later and we moved in, complete with new cooker and fabulous kitchen for me, on an agreed life rental of £300 a month, which was far too high back then. Ron assured me it would work out cheaper in the end. That was all very well, but despite the fact that I still disagreed with renting, Ron was now spending money on extras for a house that would not be ours. He spent £2,000 to do up the outside derelict cottage as a storage and laundry room, £250 for a 'wishing well' in the front garden and so much money on plants for the huge garden, not to mention wrought iron archways and all the garden tools, lawn mower etc.

Rita, who had found us the bungalow, took us to find a new car in Nicosia. We were very happy with the little Toyota Starlet, which we chose and which cost us about £6,000 sterling. That wasn't bad, but the cost of shipping out our belongings was another £5,000, so our savings were dwindling already. Something more sinister was going on though between Ron and the Bank, and somehow they persuaded him to go with an investment plan for the remainder of our savings. This plan was to lose us £15,000 in the long run, which we never recouped. We now had the princely sum of £19,000 left out of what started out as £60,000 and not a hope in hell of doing anything with it in the UK. One thing was for sure, I would never have my own house in Cyprus.

This was all leaving me feeling very unsafe and very doubtful about our future finances, and I was now at the ripe old age of 56, so job prospects were questionable, but as with everything else in my life so far, fate was lurking just around the corner to take matters in hand: and what a hand this would prove to be!

CHAPTER THIRTY EIGHT

Enter the Aldridges

The new house at Alsancak was nearing completion now and Christmas was only two weeks or so away and I had all sorts of plans in mind for furnishings and so on. This would necessitate the disposal of some items, such as curtains, and me making new replacements for them myself, to keep down the cost. I was, as I have said of course, still only fifty six, so still four years away from any pension and we were living on Ron's old age pension, albeit for a married couple. It was a struggle sometimes, but as ever Ron always told me not to worry, our finances would be fine, and I in my own sweet naïve way, continued to believe him, despite his less than outstanding track record as a financial advisor. I always trusted that Ron would do the best he could for us, for me, and we would continue to lead our usual lifestyle, one to which we had both become accustomed, holding dinner parties and social gatherings. Also, now we were back in Cyprus to stay I was hoping that we could rekindle old acquaintances and maybe my outside catering would pick up again.

Theo had settled down very well to everything and on his birthday I had bought him a little blonde girlfriend – Lady and they became inseperable.

There was only one thing wrong with all of this, I didn't

Theo and Lady 2002

know why, but day by day, I was feeling, looking and becoming more and more ill and tired. We came down into Kyrenia to do some more furnishing shopping and stopped off at Alan Cavinder's original watering hole, now called Sele restaurant, when from across the road, our old friend Behcet spotted us and called to us to go over. We went to him in the little coffee shop opposite, where he was drinking Turkish coffee and playing cards with friends.

He took one look at me and said:

"Jacqui, sorry but you look really terrible. Are you OK?"

I told him that I had not been feeling very well for some time now actually, and I must do something about it. He said:

"I am giving you the name and address of a great doctor in Nicosia, and I will call him now and make an appointment for you, and you must keep it".

This he did and so I went to see Dr. Ersan at his surgery in Nicosia the next day. Dr. Ersan gave me a complete check over in his surgery and then told me that he was exceedingly worried about me. My eyes had gone yellow and I was in very poor shape and he wanted me admitted into Nicosia General Hospital first thing the next day, when he would carry out intensive tests. He was concerned with my recent medical history and was worried this may be something serious. I was admitted the next morning and then began a series of blood tests, x-rays and so on but Dr. Ersan was completely at a loss to know what was wrong, the symptoms were completely disturbing him.

I got out of bed at one point to go to the toilet and suffered this huge, huge haemorrhage, from my vagina, there was blood all over the floor and I collapsed into the arms of one of the nurses. I completely passed out with the loss of blood, and when I awoke, I was on a drip and people were running all over the place. I had numerous visitors who were exceptionally kind and loving, like Kate Fellows, who I shall always be very fond of, but the ones I remember most would have to be Anthony and Jane Fletcher, the vicar and his wife (I had been taking the minutes at the church council meetings for him and I was a regular in the congregation for early morning communion on Sundays since we got back). Anthony came to my bedside, held my hand and pressed into it a 'holding cross', quite a large hand carved cross that I treasure to this day, and he said prayers over me, whilst I held my cross. I knew at that moment just how seriously ill I really was. Once vicars start holding crosses over hospital patients I knew there was real doubt that I would actually make it. This was scary all over again.

The next day Dr. Ersan had me flown to Ankara Teaching Hospital in Turkey to a leading specialist in the field of the liver and Ron went with me. I was to know afterwards that Ron also thought he was losing me this time. I really was quite out of it all and not really aware of what was happening to me. We were collected at the airport and taken to the Doctor's surgery. It was all very 'dreamlike'.

He gave me a complete examination and then he said:

"I know exactly what is wrong with you Jacqueline, but I have to do various tests to make quite sure. One of them will have to be a liver biopsy for which you will be conscious, the other is a colonoscopy. I believe your body has stopped making albumen, but, even more serious, you have a form of hepatitis and to determine which form and to be on the safe side, we will do these tests and a test for albumen deficiency."

The tests were horrendous, especially the biopsy, but at the end of it, the specialist was right, I had hepatitis but it was not the serious one and I had stopped producing albumen. For this I was put on a drip. He was not too happy with the state of my liver either, but he said that if I was sensible, it would repair itself in time. This treatment would have to last for six months, twice weekly, but after ten days in his care, I was flown home to Cyprus and looking and feeling much better.

I was re-admitted into Nicosia Hospital for a further five days into a room with one other lady, who herself was very poorly indeed. In the Turkish culture the family do the primary care for the hospital patient and sit by the bedside. They even sleep in the room with the sick person. Her son, aged about twenty or so years old, used to come and sit with her for hours and bathe her lovingly with cologne. One day, he turned to me and said:

"I have not seen anyone come and bathe you, would you be offended if I did for you what I do for my mother and bathe your face, arms and legs with this Cyprus lemon cologne?"

I was very touched indeed and he, almost lovingly did the same for me as he had done for his own mother. What a lovely young man; and where in the Western world would a young twenty year old man care for another patient in a bed beside his mother in a general hospital? This kind of incident is what has always made Cyprus special to me and always will be.

Then I was released back into the outside world. Little by little, I began to feel a completely different person, I truly had not realised just how poorly I had been, I had had another 'brush' with the big "D". It was to take a full six months before I could really say I felt anywhere near fighting fit and truly looked it. Ron must have had an awful time again worrying and wondering if he was to lose me, but he always said so little in that way, and I could not seem to ask him if he had been saying prayers to this end, after all, he was, on his own admission when asked about religion, an R.C. and he would qualify that by saying "Retired Christian". I always believed that deep down he did have a genuine faith, though.

I did recover fully and I had gradually set about addressing the furnishings in the house and getting our new home to look stunning and fit for guests and for ourselves too. It was during this time that we were to meet two people who were to become maybe two of the closest friends that Ron and I were to have together, with the exception of our friends Jean and Don from Midsomer Norton.

We met them at Allan Cavinder's watering hole, a little restaurant in Kyrenia, which Allan turned into an ex-pat bar during the day. Instantly, we all took to each other. They were called Alan and Linda Aldridge and lived in a house where, years before, I had always done the outside catering for a dear old friend of ours, Molly Cooper for her many parties, so we knew their house well. Allan would have been 61 at the time and Linda about 58. They made a handsome couple, Linda being blonde and a very pretty

Our dear friends Alan and Linda – circa 2005.

lady, very neat in appearance. Allan was not much taller than Linda and was also a very neat and tidy sort of person, with a beautiful thick "shaving brush" type of greying hair and the most warm and wonderful broad smile. These two people were so much in love still after nearly forty years of marriage, and it always showed.

This was to be a friendship that was so special and deep that it is difficult for me to write about it. Alan had been a senior civil servant and Linda had been a senior nursing sister and they became the most incredible, wonderful people to Ron and me, it went beyond mere friendship, we all truly and deeply loved each other, and this friendship would last till the end of time.

Once truly on my feet and feeling better, Ron and I had a discussion about our finances. They were not good and I realised at the ripe old age of fifty eight, that I really needed to be looking at earning a living again, to help swell the non-existent coffers of the Smith family. I was offered another restaurant in Kyrenia Harbour, where once before I had done Sunday lunches every week and I played with the idea for a while. I even did menus and costings for it and started to look for staff. Then I suddenly realised that Ron and I were not youngsters any more and I did not really want to go down that road again, behind the grill again and be cooking late at night, so, with his much relieved agreement, I shelved that plan.

As all these things were going through my mind, I decided that with the little money we had left, I was feeling very unsafe for Ron and myself. This money was making nothing and Kyrenia was suddenly being noticed by more and more people. I decided to go, on my own, and talk to a friend of ours, Iain Fraser, who had opened an estate agency, about the prospect of buying an apartment as an investment. So I called in to see him and, quite tearfully, told Iain about my fears for our future, and mine if I should be ever left on my own, and the need to do something positive, moneywise, for myself, so that I knew that it had been done. We chatted for some time and he showed me details of an apartment that he thought would be very good for us to let out in the centre of Kyrenia. He also said that there was a new hotel being finished at the top of the High Street, and had I considered using my catering experience in this field instead of a business of my own?

I had to admit that I hadn't even thought about it, but this idea began to intrigue me. Of course I had no idea at that time just what might grow from this little seed of an idea and how much my life, and my emotions were soon to be so greatly changed. I also talked at depth, not only with Ron obviously, but with Alan and Linda about all of these problems too, and they proved to be the greatest friends as they were already, and helped me more than words can say, they insisted on lending me some money, to help me in whichever way I thought appropriate – no time limit, no conditions. I was reluctant, but so totally overcome, and I knew that we needed the help badly.

What I did know was that urgently we needed some more money; I needed a new job, and a new direction.

We got all three. And then some.

CHAPTER THIRTY NINE

Another Dictator from Austria? Friedrich Joseph Heiss

The new investment apartment, in Kyrenia town itself, was perfect.

It was a large apartment with three bedrooms, large lounge and kitchen/diner, bathroom and guest loo. It was ideal for renting out and we decided that I would go ahead and purchase it, which I did with the help of Linda and Alan's loan. When I say 'I', this meant that before and in case anything happened to Ron, everything would have to be all put in my name and I would not have all the legal complications of probate to deal with. I never considered things like that. It was Ron who suggested it all. Now we could bring in enough money to cover our own rent and the value of the new property would increase with the way things were moving forward in North Cyprus at that time.

On the very same day, I took a deep breath, and walked in to Kyrenia's swankiest new hotel, The Colony to see if I could get a job. The five star Colony stands at the top of the 'High Street', as it is known, in Kyrenia town centre and it is built on land that I remember well, where there had once been an old, but beautiful Colonial house standing majestically surrounded by tall palm trees. I presume that when the owners and shareholders got together to buy it, they would have imagined the Hotel carrying on some of the characteristics of the former building and, indeed, the era. I knew that it was a small, luxurious, high class hotel and the outside façade of the building, indeed the whole concept, is positively palatial.

I had never worked in a hotel before, and holding my head high and shoulders back, I confidently walked in. The sight that greeted me was not disappointing in any way. The place had a truly grand and almost 'Olde English' atmosphere; it all felt very 'gracious'. I went up to Reception and asked for an application form for a position with them. They gave me the form without question and I took it home and filled it in. I had to submit it with a passport photograph of myself and the only one I had was taken when I was so desperately ill with tuberculosis, and that illness does the face no favours I can tell you. However, I thought little of it and delivered the form the very next day, in the hopes of a quick response.

I was to be disappointed and annoyed. After having heard nothing for two weeks I set about finding out who was the boss. Using devious methods, I found out that the

With my beloved boss –
Friedrich Joseph Heiss, Christmas 2003 at The Colony.

boss was the Managing Director, a Mr. Friedrich Joseph Heiss, and a personal friend gave me his private mobile telephone number. I began telephoning Mr. Heiss on a daily basis until I became a real thorn in his side. I stuck to my guns and told him that I would continue to pester him until he agreed at least to see me. I had something special to offer him and I wanted and needed to see him. In the end he was screaming down the phone at me and told me that I was the most infuriatingly aggravating woman he had ever dealt with, but if I was not going to go away, he supposed he would have to see me just to get rid of me. He agreed to see me the following day in the afternoon. I thanked him politely and told him I would definitely be there.

I had been told nothing of this man, not his demeanour, his habits, his preferences, nothing. I thought it through very carefully and decided that my first impression on him would probably be my last, if I did not make the right impact on meeting him for the first time. I thought that I would be battling against my age here with a man that I had never met, and I had to steer him into believing that he needed me so badly at the Colony that he could not afford not to offer me a job. So I carefully selected my outfit and I dressed very smartly in co-ordinating shades of cream and brown, my best colours, and, with my usual neatly *coiffured* hair piled nicely on top of my head, my make up and jewellery just right, I arrived at the office of the Managing Director of The Colony.

Friedrich Joseph Heiss stood up to his full six feet three inch height behind his desk, and then came round and shook hands with me, a very firm and confidant handshake.

He was a very large man in stature, very well built, although not fat, dressed impeccably in suit with toning shirt and tie and with a very warm, broad smile. He possessed a strong and strangely attractive look about him.

He told me that he was Austrian – NOT German he pointed out very firmly, and that he had been born in Vienna on the 20th October 1947, so he was three years younger than I. Despite the harsh first approaches he had made on the telephone, he oozed self-confidence and power and gave you the immediate feeling that here stood a man who could see into your very soul, which gave you shivers down the spine. This was a man who, obviously knew people and his business completely, a truly professional gentleman. He also had a twinkle in his eyes that was somewhat beguiling, and of which I am sure he knew he possessed!

The interview began with him immediately pointing out that I bore absolutely no resemblance whatsoever to the 'hag' in the photograph that I had submitted, that it was one of the worst photographs he had ever seen, which was the reason why he hadn't wanted to see me at all. I immediately responded by telling him that I thought that was an extremely honest, forthright and to the point statement, and albeit in my opinion, exceedingly rude, but I promised that I would not take offence. He chuckled wickedly. I could see from that point that we were going to get on extremely well.

We then proceeded to have the most pleasurable one and a half hours' interview of my life and, I remember so clearly, we laughed a lot, about all sorts of things. He told me that he had done his homework, and he knew quite a good deal about me, which, somehow, came as no great surprise to me. He said that I was 'famous' in Kyrenia for having run Loch Manor and how highly my talents as a business woman, as a chef and my restaurant had been rated. He told me that he admired me for that, especially in view of the fact that I was a lady and how difficult it must have been for me to cope with getting things done back then. He seemed very impressed with my legal, secretarial, catering and artistic background and he told me just that, so much so, that despite the fact that he had no position to offer me, he wanted to see me again.

"I absolutely have to see you again tomorrow" he said, almost urging me not to say no. "There is so much that I still need to know about you and there are still lots of questions that remain unanswered for me". I readily agreed to come back the next day at the same time.

However, before we parted company, he gave me a personal guided tour of The Colony hotel and took me up to the Vista Terrace on the roof and we marvelled at the breathtakingly beautiful view together. I asked all the relevant questions about him, his attitude to the kind of reaction he wanted from people to The Colony and what he hoped that they expected of him and his Team. I then went on to 'tap' his intentions for the catering side of the hotel and he told me his views on the Heritage Lounge, the Premier Restaurant on the ground floor, the Misty Bar and snack area and the Vista Terrace Restaurant on the roof. With that the interview came to an end for that day and I left The Colony with a warm, glowing feeling inside. I liked Mr. Heiss, I knew that I wanted to work with him, but could I pull it off ? The thought foremost in my mind was that I am now fifty eight and am I really still employable? This man was most certainly no fool. He had affected me so much just at this first meeting, there was some kind of magic, some kind of spark, and to be truthful, I couldn't wait for the next day to come to be able to be in his company again. This was a man with that rare human quality, a genuine charisma. I felt like a child having been promised a day at the circus for my birthday! Whilst we had been talking, an idea was brewing in my mind that just might make Mr. Heiss forget my age and consider my talents, before letting Jacqui Smith slip through his fingers.

So, on my way home, I stopped off at the stationers shop

and bought some printing paper, some bottle green card – The Colony colour – and went to the haberdashers and bought some green strong embroidery thread. When I got home, I told Ron all about the interview, and he seemed very impressed, I told him the truth and about the sheer animal magnetism of this man Heiss, and he said that he would really like to meet him himself at some later date. I then went up into my office and I set about drawing up a complete set of menus for The Colony for all four outlets, quick 'up-market' light food for guests who wanted that something special in the bar, a full four page menu for winter for The Premier Restaurant, one for snacks for the Misty Bar and another four page summer menu for The Vista Terrace Restaurant. I made covers with the green card and put the large Colony 'C' emblem on the front of each – all done by hand, then I stitched the spines with the thread the way we used to do with the parchment documents in the Solicitors office and there they sat, four complete International menus. I went down and asked Ron what he thought.

"Darling, they're wonderful. I can't think that this Mr. Heiss of yours won't be anything but extremely impressed with them, I am proud of you". Ron knew me so well, he knew too that not only I, but we both, needed this job to survive.

The following day, armed with my surprises for Mr. Heiss, my menus and four new photographs taken on the way, I arrived for my second interview. How would this day go I wondered to myself, and would I go home with any kind of a job under my belt?

Mr. Heiss was standing in front of his desk this time, waiting for me to make my entrance, then gave me the Turkish welcome, a touch of a kiss on each cheek. I was moved.

"So nice to see you again" he said to me "I have to admit to having looked forward to this afternoon since I saw you yesterday".

"Me too", I admitted willingly, little butterflies jumping around in my tummy. "By the way, I have some little surprises for you", I said cheekily.

I then took out the menus, and the photographs I put at the ready, after all, he wouldn't need them if he didn't have a job for me, would he? I placed the menus in front of him on his desk and he beamed a wonderful warm smile. He went completely silent as he read each of the menus, one by one, very slowly and deliberately. After what seemed like an eternity, he folded up the last menu, looked up at me, and he just said:

"Wow".

After quite a long silence, and him looking straight into my eyes, he said:

"Jacqui, I am so impressed, I don't know what to say. You obviously went away yesterday and did these, I really mean it, I am so truly impressed. I have never met anyone quite like you. Now I am convinced, you and I must work together, I must have you with me, but I don't have a position to offer you at present. I can pay you a small salary till I can find you the right place and you can have an office in one of the little shops in the courtyard. I will work this all out. What do you say: please say yes?"

I was overwhelmed with happiness and joy. I knew that I wanted to work, not for, but with this extraordinary man too. Of course, I said "yes". What other answer was there?

I started to work at The Colony in September of 2002 and those menus, totally unchanged, became the first menus that we were to use. Mr. Heiss put them in his private desk drawer and said:

"I shall never forget what you did with these menus,

Jacqui, I shall keep them always". I simply glowed with pride. Step one, I had made my impression.

On my first day, I was issued with an ultra-smart grey suit with shortish skirt and three white blouses with long sleeves and turn back cuffs.

"You will wear high heels and nearly black tights with that outfit, Jacqui. I expect all my staff to be suited and booted to their best ability at all times, this is The Colony, but I do like my 'girls' to look that little bit extra". I appreciated the compliment.

Mr. Heiss told me that my temporary office would be in the first of the little shops in the Piazza Courtyard of The Colony where I found he had already had installed two desks and computers (I had never used one in my life). He then introduced me, one by one, to "The Team" and what a Team we all turned out to be too. We all worked strongly together with one exception, a man that I couldn't really take to and didn't ever really trust, the Director of Rooms Division. For some reason he didn't really quite fit in with the rest. Over time, I was to come to understand that Mr. Heiss had this complete and perfect knack of finding out the talents hidden within each of his chosen few, drawing the talents out of those people, and making them use those talents to the best of their best ability, for The Colony and for him, especially for him.

Mr. Heiss had made up his mind that he wanted to introduce a Butler Service into this Five Star Hotel, something which no other hotel has ever had in Northern Cyprus, and Peter Carl Neal had been a butler in real life and had retired to live in Famagusta. Mr. Heiss had come to hear about him from one of the more wealthy guests who had property in Famagusta, and who stayed regularly at The Jasmine Court when in Kyrenia, where Mr. Heiss lived before The Colony was finished. This all resulted in a meeting between Peter Neal and Mr. Heiss, who immediately invited him to join the Team on a Consultancy basis as Butler Trainer. Peter had readily agreed and I shared my office with him and a lovely young lady called Mevhibe; her title was the same as mine, 'Guest Services Manager', shared the other side.

At this point too, Peter and I were given the task of looking after the breakfast buffet in the mornings and especially the European guests and their needs, keeping the whole thing running professionally and looking professional, taking care of their personal requirements and enquiries and generally giving the feeling of firm management presence and control. This was the brief from Mr. Heiss, and again, he was using talents which he could not have found in the waiters and left the senior management able to do the more important aspects of their jobs.

Ultimately, the Director of Rooms Division left, and a Turkish gentleman by the name of Aybars Kutluba took over both positions as Director of Rooms Division and Sales

With Peter the butler at The Colony 2004

and Marketing and worked as Mr. Heiss's right hand man. He worked closely with Mr. Heiss and very soon became close to him as a key member of The Team. Another of the chosen few was Tunc Sirintuna, who Mr. Heiss spotted at The Jasmine Court Hotel. Mr. Heiss simply fell for Tunc's natural charm and warm American accent, acquired when he studied in the U.S.A. He was suave and exceedingly good looking and well presented and it was clear that Mr. Heiss had intentions to turn this young man into another Friedrich Joseph Heiss. So the training of this all important 'A' Team and the rest of the staff too went ahead all the time, with most of the staff not even realising how well they were all being groomed under his ever watchful eyes, which missed absolutely nothing, ever.

Six weeks after I started at the Colony, I had done very many different projects for Mr. Heiss which seemed to impress him, he would give me letters to answer and would simply tell me to 'handle them', no dictation, and he never returned one for alteration. The tasks were too many and varied to name them all, and one morning, he came into my office and pointed his finger at me. I wondered what was coming next, because he was looking extremely agitated, and then he boomed out, "You madam, in the office next to mine right now. As from today, you are my P.A.".

I didn't stop to ask how high he would like me to jump! He and his Turkish secretary had parted company, he told me, and so I merely stood up, looked him straight in the eye and said "Yes Sir" and down to his office I went and moved into the one next to him. He then called me in and he gave me my brief as to exactly what he expected from his P.A.

"You are now the Personal Assistant of Friedrich Joseph Heiss, my darling" he said in his lovely Austrian accent, "I know that you know exactly what I am expecting of you", which of course I well and truly did.

This was to prove to be singularly the most interesting, stormy, volatile, and deep, deep relationship that I have ever encountered with a man, with whom there was absolutely no sexual involvement at all. We had a relationship which Ron accepted readily and moreover, he understood it, encouraged me when I was under strain (which could happen frequently with the likes of Friedrich Joseph Heiss), and would prove to continue to do so, for which I was eternally grateful, more times than I can count.

I had managed to master my computer completely, with no tuition at all and very soon became what seemed like an extension of Mr. Heiss himself. When he asked me to do something for him, I knew instinctively what he was requiring. He was an arch delegator to those he trusted and never dictated anything to me, just explained the situation and then told me to deal with it, whether it be a letter of complaint to the air-conditioning firm in Turkey to dealing with the purchase of his apartment and finding the right people to furnish it for him. He even trusted me to do some of that myself. I came to know this man so well, and I was unquestionably, totally devoted to him and his well-being whilst I was at work. It was like being married to two men at the same time, but only one was requiring the services of a wife and the other demanded total devotion in the workplace, and yet somehow even far more beyond that sometimes.

Every day, I would not only do a personal letter to Mr. Heiss, covering any and every subject under the sun. He said that he loved my use of grammar and words but I realised that he was really using my expertise in English as a native tongue to make sure things went out "right" from the Colony. I have retained a few copies in my files and the following is a typical daily letter from me to Mr. Heiss:

Monday 5th May – 8.30am.

I have to begin this lesson with my utter dismay at my dismissal from your presence last evening. I have to stress, most strongly, that I hate playing second fiddle to sport of any nature, especially cricket and rugby and worse still football; but to be waved away in the mere twinkling of an eye by the gesture of the hand by your goodself was mortifying, especially so on thinking to myself, (quite naturally to my mind), that my chassis could ever be deemed less attractive than the four wheeled racing variety (they for their part, still endlessly pursuing each other's backsides, which has to be encouraging in some way, I suppose, though I still have not fathomed it out yet).

I have dealt with my two assignments on your behalf, the one I can vouch for successfully as far as dispatch is concerned, the other is in the lap of the Gods and the Florists' hands in Malaysia! I strongly emphasised, and asked that it be stressed to the person at the point of destination, that the delivery was to be more successful even than the last one, if that be possible. Now I pray that I haven't failed you in any way – yet again.

At 11.00am I escorted our Executive Chef to the Castle Court Apartments in Kyrenia, where we had an assignation to view a possible abode for him with an elderly, English, female Estate Agent of my acquaintance, of long time business standing here. She duly showed us round and our chef appeared to be delighted with the place. I have left the rest of the negotiations where they belong, with our Human Resources Director, but it does involve a formal lease as per your instructions, and this is accompanied by a full inventory.

12.15pm The Rees Saga beginneth –

Mr. David Rees came to the Hotel unannounced. I was completely taken aback, as he stood in the middle of the foyer and merely shouted out loud "And what about the rent?" Having assessed immediately that this was not going to be a pleasant interlude, I urged him to sit down. I told him that it had become a policy decision that our chef had not and would not be staying on at his apartment block and I handed him back the keys. He became quite aggressive and asked about the rent. I said that in view of the fact that the Chef had only spent two or three nights there, and that we still had a sizeable account outstanding for himself, that I felt that this was an unreasonable request. I went on to say that since his complaints to me, we had received on the morning after the incident, unsolicited information from another table in the restaurant concerning the behaviour of his table that morning, and that in view of the nature of this report, that you, yourself, were exceedingly disappointed with the outcome of the lunch which you had provided and also his attitude in particular.

He leapt up in temper, told me that there was definitely no-one else in the restaurant at the time, that we were all the same at the Colony and that I was "tarred with the same brush as Heiss – you work for him, you sound just like him". Fortunately, I had no need to restrain him further as, with that, he stormed out of the doors, hurling abuse as he went.

I feel bound to point out that, needless to say, his demeanour matched the hour of the clock, looking at it from a purely alcoholic point of view. The word inebriate comes easily to mind here. I repaired to my office in the hopes that the matter will now die a natural death and we will, hopefully, hear no more.

Well, dear boss, after reading this novel, I expect you feel exceedingly rejobulated in no uncertain terms! It is now 16.45pm and I have been to Lefkosa with Cem and the Chef on the trail of the ever-elusive ice cream glasses, almost to no avail I am sorry to say. However, my waistline is having a steam treatment all it's own – it must have been 40C plus in the car- I find myself in need of a shower and a spritzer before I return to the Colony at 7.30pm at my house guests' request to join them for dinner.

I do feel duty bound to add that the whole ambience of the Colony and the demeanour of your staff, one and all, will be much stimulated and enlightened with your return to work this morning.

Good morning Boss – Welcome to the Colony, and then some!

Your ever faithful P.A.

I took a copy home for Ron to read, and he chuckled.

"Does Mr. Heiss understand your use of the English Language" Ron asked quizzically, "because, I'm quite sure that if you got any more complicated than that letter, you would lose me completely", he mused, "but, you know, you really are a clever girl, I am never surprised at what you will come up with next". Of course, I always filled him in from day to day of my 'doings', because he went out so little when I was at work, and my tales always interested him and gave him pleasure, it was a bit like following a 'soap opera' for him I suppose, with something new always happening each day.

Mr. Heiss came to look forward to my correspondence and I also used to leave him a daily note telling him when it was my day off, just to say goodnight, whatever the reason I had a message for him, and they were done on small notelets headed 'A small note to the M.D. from your P.A. Once, knowing he was about to deal with a particularly difficult situation, I even left him one which read "To my mean, moody and magnificent Boss – you tell 'em", and I always ended them with 'deep down, your J', with a cross underneath (because he always maintained that 'deep down' I really loved him, no matter what he did to me). Sometimes he would put on the bottom, "I love you too!" and highlight it in yellow marker, but not on this occasion.

When I arrived the next morning and went past his office to get into mine, he let out this boom of a voice and called out for me to go into his office.

"What the hell do you mean by this"? he screamed at me, very red in the face and obviously angry and insulted, at the same time throwing the screwed up note into his bin, "I am not mean and I am certainly not moody, what do you mean".

I then had to explain to him that this was a complete *compliment* to his demeanour, it was a line from a film, and being an American film, I thought he would pick it up immediately. I explained that 'mean' meant that he was the big boss with the tough temperament to go with it, and moody, he was dark and mysterious with this overpowering air about him and, lastly of course, he truly was magnificent! He then gave a broad smile, positively glowed with pride, took the screwed up note out of the bin and lovingly flattened it out and put it in his drawer. "Thank you my darling" he said and motioned with his hand for me to go away, whilst he sat and gloated over this compliment.

Peter the Butler, was to share my office with me and over the next four years or so. Inevitably we became very close. We shared many personal intimacies although he did have a clear preference for male company when it came to friends and relationships. However we had something really special and we talked about almost everything. He came to

Ron and me at weekends sometimes, and I would cook gourmet food for him to take home, as I did lovingly for Mr. Heiss occasionally. Pate, pork pies, homemade horseradish and all sorts of goodies were the order of the day.

I got on exceptionally well with The Colony Team and, especially Aybars, and Cem, the Purchasing Director, who are both very special to me, Tunc, Mr. Heiss' protégé and Hasan, the Technical Director; but most especially I got on very well with the Executive chef Aydin and helped him to train himself and his team, in my own home, to cook the various continental and international dishes on the menu that they had never tackled before. We were subsequently to work together until his departure in 2007. Primarily, they were a Turkish team of chefs and they usually came as an entourage, so if you could help the top gun, the rest would soon follow on.

Mr. Heiss was married to a very beautiful Chinese lady called Belinda and she has a son called Nelson, of whom Mr. Heiss was particularly adoring – Nelson was his 'little Chinaman' and they used to have long telephone calls whilst they were apart. However, one day Nelson suddenly had a rift with his mother and it caused so much stress between the three of them that when Mr. Heiss went home, I wrote to Nelson personally. It was a very deep and moving letter, telling him of my rifts with my own sons. I showed Mr. Heiss the letter before I sent it, just in case I had mentioned anything that I shouldn't have done, but he really appreciated those kind of things that I went out of my way to do personally for him and an extremely strong bond had formed between us as boss and p.a., in my own way I loved him and I know he did me, as I said, he called me 'my darling' sometimes, but never in an intimate or a sexual way. It was a most remarkable partnership, the like of which I have never experienced before and know that I never will again. Friedrich Heiss was a very special man; a genuine Alpha male – and everybody at the Colony knew it!

Things didn't run smoothly all the time however. Alpha males don't take prisoners and can be harsh, even cruel. During the nearly six years that I worked for him at The Colony, I had several break-ups with Mr. Heiss. With a man like that you could not have a particularly volatile relationship and not have explosions from time to time, and when I say explosions, I mean that in the strictest sense of the word. He could actually blow up and you saw a side of him you did not want to see often, believe me!

I actually quit, just walked out, on no less than four separate occasions after he had done something unacceptable to me in my opinion, the first three of which were, in retrospect always extremely hurtful, but not huge *faux pas*. They were solved when I got home in a foul temper and just telling Ron all my troubles, as a sleek black limousine would pull up outside the gate and our *Concierge* Yacup would arrive with a beautiful gateaux or bouquet and a bottle of champagne on ice from 'The Man' himself, and I would simply melt and go running straight back.

The fourth time though was much more serious than that and by this time, I had been Mr. Heiss' P.A, and in a very close working relationship, for some three years. It was October 2005 and he had asked me to do something very secret and important for him, the details of which escape me now, which means that I must have blotted it out of my mind to deal with it. However, he told me that when I had achieved whatever my goal was for him, I was to find him *wherever he was*, and let him know the full details of the outcome. He stressed that I was to interrupt him with the news, whatever he was doing.

I did as instructed and found him eventually on the roof of the Colony with someone. I walked across to where they were and stopped a few yards away and stood quietly waiting for him to signal to me to approach. Instead, my beloved boss just glowered at me with a black and surly look, and with a contemptuous wave of the hand, gestured for me to go away and not bother him. I was absolutely mortified. So I did go away, and this time I stayed away. Despite numerous phone calls and messages from him on my mobile phone, I ignored them all and set about finding other small jobs to do to keep us solvent – anything from my outside catering, which was in a very healthy situation since we came back from England and much in demand, to helping friends in their own personal situations, business or otherwise. He had hurt me so very, very deeply this time, I felt as if I had lost complete face and I was not prepared to forgive that easily, if at all.

However, during all this time, I kept in touch with Peter the Butler and went to Kyrenia and met with him every week without fail. He would bring me up to date with what was happening at the Colony, and my first question would always be how Mr. Heiss was, how all The Team were, and did they and our regular guests miss me as much as I missed them. It was so incredibly hard, every inch of me ached to be able to go back, but I stuck to my guns this time, in retrospect, stubborn to the point of stupidity I suppose.

By now it was June 2006, eight months had gone by, and on the Friday 16th June I went to meet Peter on the car park next to The Colony and have coffee. He had come back from two weeks in England with his sister Jessie. When I met him I asked him if he was alright, he looked a ghastly grey colour with beads of sweat all over his forehead, not like Peter at all.

He said he was fine and in his broad North Country accent said "Ee, don't go on so ducky; I'm fine". We had a long chat and I got up to leave. I kissed him on both cheeks, as we always did and walked over to my car to leave. As I reached to open my car door he shouted over to me "Come back here 'Sweet' for a minute", a name he only used for me on very emotional moments.

When I got back to him, he grabbed me and pulled me close and gave me the biggest kiss, full on the lips and then looked me straight in the eyes and said so intently, squeezing both my arms so tightly, "You do know that I really do love you ducky, you do know that don't you?"

I said "Of course I do Peter, we mean a lot to each other. I love you too".

It was most moving and very out of character for Peter. I drove home feeling very deeply emotionally affected by this occurrence and told Ron the story. We couldn't really put any explanation to Peter's actions. He had never done anything like it before, but Ron knew that I was really upset.

At 9.30am on the morning of Tuesday the 19th June 2006, my mobile rang. The screen showed "HEISS". I told Ron that it was Mr. Heiss on the phone and he said:

"Given the time of the morning, Darling, I think maybe you had better answer it".

So I gingerly pressed the button and said "Good morning, Mr. Heiss".

Mr. Heiss said, with a touch of gravity in his voice:

"Are you sitting down Jacqui darling? I have got some bad news for you".

"Yes Mr. Heiss" I said and paused.

"Jacqui, Peter passed away this morning, getting ready to come into work, he just collapsed and died. We think it was a heart attack. He had not arrived in the Hotel by 8.00am and so, after telephoning the garage opposite Peter's apartment, we learnt that his car had not moved from the night before. We tried ringing his land line and mobile, but no reply and so I sent Yacup, the Concierge, and Cavit from

Security to Famagusta in my car, we called the Police on the way and his neighbour. They broke in and found him on the floor, he had been pressing his suit, the iron was still on". I was devastated. I had been with him just three days before.

"Thank you so very much for your kindness, in letting me know personally, Mr. Heiss" I said as I sobbed.

He told me that he would phone me the following day. As soon as I had pulled myself together, I telephoned the British Cemetery Committee in Famagusta and told the lady there of the occurrences and, to my surprise, she told me that Peter had already selected and paid for his plot recently in the cemetery there, and also, apparently, she knew his wishes. It seemed to me that Peter had actually known his fate, went home to say goodbye to his sister and then came down to say good-bye to me. I shall never be sure, but it all fitted so into place. Then, with great sadness, I telephoned his sister, she was inconsolable, but now the funeral arrangements were in place, we only needed the date from the police for the go ahead.

Mr. Heiss telephoned me the following day and asked me what he should do about a funeral. I told him it was all in hand and I would let him have the date, Jessie had asked me to handle everything.

"How did I know that that would be the answer you would give me? he said. "Jacqui darling, you will come to the funeral with me in my car. Please come in and have coffee with me this morning".

I said that I would and I closed the phone. Ron and I then had the inevitable conversation.

"You know what's coming next, don't you Darling" I said.

 "Of course" said Ron "and I know what you will do too; when will you start?" I told him to wait for the outcome of the coffee meeting and I would decide on the spur of the moment, but in my heart I had already accepted my obvious fate.

Peter Carl Neal was buried on the 28th June, 2006 and I duly went to the funeral with the "Team" and I travelled with Mr. Heiss, sitting with him in the back of his limousine. He held my hand tightly for the whole journey. The funeral was very brief, but moving, and I travelled back with Mr. Heiss.

On the 23rd June 2006 (my son Simon's 43rd birthday) I walked into the Colony to begin a new morning back in my office. It was a very humbling and emotive experience, I had been away a full eight months and Mr. Heiss was already in and in his office waiting for me. He came round his desk, kissed me, gave me a little squeeze and then told me that he had briefed all the staff and they were not to make me too emotional. He knew me so well. Every one of the staff came up to me and kissed me and welcomed me back, some of them were crying.

"Madame, how wonderful to have you back" they were all saying, "We have missed you". No more than I them, I can tell you.

It was wonderful to be sitting next to his office again and to have the long conversations we used to have, and just to take care of him again. I just slotted in as if I had never been gone.

It was getting close to Christmas, and Mr. Heiss asked me to take on the mammoth task that Peter and I used to share, of making all the Christmas trimmings for the hotel. This task took me about 60 hours in total but I did it with a lot of love and feeling and, I have to say, it really did look beautiful.

Christmas came and went and we were very busy in the Hotel. Mr. Heiss told me that his heart needed its regular check up back in Kuala Lumpur where his brother in law

My 60th birthday dinner at The Colony.

was his heart specialist. He had found a revolutionary new treatment for Mr. Heiss' condition and was anxious to start the treatment, so the date the 9th February 2007 was set for him to fly back to Malaysia.

On the Sunday 28th January was my birthday, but Mr. Heiss put off the celebrations until Monday. He arranged it all in the meeting room with the usual cake and candles, a bottle of bubbly that the whole Team shared and he made his usual very charming and warm speech to me. He gave me a kiss on each cheek and whispered "It is so good to have you back my darling".

Four days later, on the following Friday, after breakfast, and just before I left The Colony, Mr. Heiss came into my office and we had quite a long chat. I told him how well I thought he looked lately and he said he felt marvellous and was looking forward to going home.

I came in as usual and did my breakfast duty as always for the next two mornings and on the morning of Monday 5th February, at about 10.00am, I was sent for and asked to go directly into Aybars', Mr. Heiss's deputy's office. This I did and he quietly told me that my beloved boss, Friedrich Joseph Heiss, had passed away quietly at his desk, a few minutes before, aged 60 years.

I simply cannot find enough of the right words to express my feelings at that moment. If I am completely honest, now that I look back on the event, if you had told me that I had lost my Ron that morning, the feelings would have still been almost the same. The shock was total – I had lost someone who was genuinely precious to me and who for nearly five years, had made up one half of my daily waking hours. My husband made up the other half. I felt so completely at a loss, and I didn't know who to go to, to talk to about this loss. I hadn't seen Mr. Heiss that morning, I hadn't been able to say goodbye to him was all that kept going round and round in my head. Then I knew I had to talk to my beloved Ron, whom I phoned immediately. I was allowed to go home early and Ron helped me through this awful day.

Everything after that seemed to happen as if in a flash. There was a post mortem. Suddenly Mrs. Heiss was flying in and arriving to arrange everything to take him away and home to Malaysia. Before I knew what was happening it seemed, all the arrangements had been made and they took him away and I never, ever was able to be near to him to say 'good-bye'- one of the most powerful and significant men ever to have lured me into his life and we could not even have that brief moment to say that. There is not a day that has gone by that I have not missed him, I still do. I will always remember him almost as 'my impossible dream' the absolute professional and perfectionist. Whatever you did for him was almost always perfect, but to please him and feel fulfilled in your efforts to be one hundred per cent – impossible…..but that was him, that was my autocratic boss, Friedrich Joseph Heiss and that was always my dream. He was a great man.

This changed my life at The Colony considerably, but I stayed on and carried on doing all the things I had been doing, except my daily letter and notes to the M.D. When Mrs. Heiss came over to see everyone at the Hotel to say goodbye, she came to see me and pressed an envelope into my hand and gave it a squeeze. To my astonishment, it contained every little note to the M.D. from his P.A. including the crinkled one – he had kept every last one. He had also kept all my personal daily letters, they were all safely filed away at his apartment and she wanted to keep these herself she told me, because she knew how much he treasured each and every one. That meant such a great deal to me, and 'deep down' I knew there and then that he must have actually loved me in his own way. That relationship I shall treasure and remember always, and I shall and do, miss him like hell every day.

However, how can I say that the loss of Peter and Mr. Heiss were almost insignificant compared with what God had next in store for me? Certainly something for which I had never ever planned…

CHAPTER FORTY

Changes...

Life at The Colony lives on and Aybars was made the new General Manager, Tunc was made his Assistant for a few months until he was moved to Famagusta where another Hotel Called The Palm Beach had been brought into the Group fold. Mr. Alper Pinar took Tunc's place. There were other changes and replacements but without Mr Heiss' eagle eye and commanding presence though, it is no exaggeration to say that things would never be the same.

However life at the house in Alsancak was still the same as ever, except for two things. Firstly, each year we were informed that the rent would be increased despite our agreement and shaking of hands at £300 per year for life. We were now facing £350 for this year and an increase to £375 next January. Secondly, Ron was becoming very frail and I could see him for the first time, visibly getting old before my eyes. This was beginning to worry me and niggled at me day by day. He was having trouble using the stairs, hanging on for his life to the banister rail. I kept having nightmares that I would come home and find him at the bottom of the staircase, lying on the white marble floor with blood everywhere, not having been able to crawl to the telephone. I began to get agitated about this and my special friends were noticing.

Allan Cavinder had decided to return to England on the pretext that his wife Joan's leukaemia had got worse and he should be there. We threw him a tremendous goodbye party at Alan and Linda's house and I provided the food and Alan and Linda the drink. All his friends that were left were there. To Ron, Allan had always been a very close friend and I knew that he would miss this special friend of some twenty six years standing.

After he got to England, to our enormous shock, Ron and I received the following card:

"Dear Ron and Jacqui,

I rather think the jungle drums have pre-empted me on this but I would have preferred to give you the news myself, (and so it goes)." *

"I'd just like you to know a couple of things: first of all that I've not found it too difficult to come to terms with the verdict, (after all I've been able to enjoy a most rewarding life) and my only true concern now is for Joan, who doesn't deserve all this. We shall do as much to gain as much as possible from the rest of our lives together. Secondly, and the main purpose of this note – I want to thank you both very, very sincerely for the many years of true friendship you've given me. We've had some right good times together, haven't we?

Very much love to you,
Allan."
XX

The subsequent death of Allan, very soon after this card arrived, had affected Ron hugely. They really had been buddies and his card set Ron back to such a great extent,

---

*He was riddled with cancer and knew it. We had absolutely no idea.

that I am not sure that I was truly aware of the impact. By now he was having trouble getting up and down the stairs, his knee needed replacing but he would not hear of it. He could be very stubborn if he wanted to be and would fight me over things like that. Our relationship was changing with age, but none the less, it was still close and loving. He must have been looking at his own mortality and that of his closest friends and I wasn't really aware of it at the time. It's not really something you can hold a joyful conversation about, and at this time he needed joy.

I made a monumental decision all on my own, put the plan in motion and then went home and told Ron what I intended. I had become ruthless in my efforts to protect and preserve all that I had, mainly him, but I couldn't fathom out why.

I had put the apartment on the market for £60,000. When it sold, my plan was to purchase a ground floor apartment for Ron and myself with a little garden for him, if possible. That would be paid cash. As I said, Linda and Alan had given me a loan to help purchase the apartment and that would then be paid off, and the rest was to be put on deposit for our pension in our dotage. It all made sense, and if the apartment could be near to the Colony and not 45 minutes away as the house was, if there was any kind of emergency, I could get home in about four minutes flat. That made sense to me also.

Ron was not exactly of the same mind, though he could see what I was thinking and worrying about and he reluctantly agreed that it made sense – and best of all, no more wasted money on rent. In his mind, he had fought me all along really not to give up the lifestyle that went with living in a big detached house, with all the trimmings. In my mind, I was trying to make my Ron safe in our home and build a better future for our next years together. I needed for us to be secure, I couldn't properly describe what I was feeling inside to Ron himself or friends, despite trying, I needed to make Ron safe for me too, more than anything else in the world, hadn't I lost enough in personal relationships in the last few months? I could neither accept the possibility nor even give in to the thoughts that some day, before too many more years would pass, that I would have to prepare myself for losing my beloved Ron. After all, he had always promised me, when conversations turned around to providing for future events, such as life insurance and all those kind of things, that he had absolutely no intention of ever going anywhere and this would placate me for a while.

The apartment sold quickly, on the 23rd February 2007, and, after only viewing about two or three apartments, I walked into a ground floor apartment with small garden in the village of Dogankoy, and it fitted the bill perfectly. The lounge was exactly the same shape and size as the lounge we were leaving and so all Ron's beloved daytime furniture would all fit in and be familiar to him. Dogankoy directly adjoins Kyrenia and it is just four minutes from The Colony. The deal was done with Ron's approval in May 2007. It was just like it was all meant to be.

We moved in immediately. Ron seemed quite pleased with our new surroundings, even though he fought me a little when it came to down sizing and having to get rid of some treasured, but rather large items. However, we turned one of the bedrooms into a pretty little dining room, so we could still entertain.

We had some lovely new furnishings, courtesy of my outside catering business which was becoming very healthy and busier and busier. So much so that Graham, the ex-Abbey House chef and my dear friend, was now helping me put the functions together on the day, with me doing the preparation. It was working well, and right at the beginning of joining the Colony, I had told Mr. Heiss of my extra curricula activities and he had readily agreed to let off duty staff, waiters and barmen help me when I needed them. It was all going to work out really well and Ron and I were able to do extra things to the apartment, air conditioning, fencing, purchase a bright new shed for his tools, shutters at all the windows to make us secure, and Ron could now have the luxury of a gardener to help him with the heavy work. Finances were much improved all round, and I must say, it was nice to know that my talents were still appreciated in the catering field in the outside world, away from The Colony.

The icing on the cake was that we could still entertain our closest friends, Alan and Linda, who over the years had become so very, very dear and Ron was able to cook his shepherd's pies which were Alan's favourite and at which Ron became quite accomplished. Alan always used to tell him that his version was always better than mine, which always made Ron's day.

Alan had had a bad heart for some considerable time, having undergone a triple heart bypass when he was relatively young and retired at 51 years of age. That was why his home here and garden were precious to him also. However Linda and Alan were due to go back to England for Alan's check up just before his birthday on the 5th November 2007. I took them to the Airport as I always did and we waved goodbye.

On the evening of that day, Lyn and Brian, two friends of Alan and Linda telephoned me and asked us to join them the following night for dinner at the new chicken restaurant in Kyrenia. With Alan and Linda flying that day, they wanted our company for their last night in Cyprus, before they returned later on in the year. I told Ron and then we accepted, but as was becoming the custom more and more recently, Ron showed little enthusiasm when I told him. I knew he had little energy these days because the daily routine that he had normally followed was now very much falling by the wayside. It was as though he just could not be bothered to do little jobs that he once would have done automatically. I tried to make little of these situations, but on the night of the 6th he seemed reluctant to go and thought he would be better at home. He told me to go on my own and give them his apologies but I did say that we had accepted the invitation and that we should now get ready and go.

So off we set, with Lady in the back of the car as Ron drove us up to the new Ezic Chicken Restaurant above Kyrenia. He was fine once we got there and was all bright and chirpy again. We had a super table from where we could see the whole of Kyrenia laid out below us with all the twinkling lights. The magic of Cyprus nights even in November is something so special, something which we never ceased over the twenty eight years to wonder at and never tired of.

We all had a wonderful meal. Afterwards Ron rubbed his hands together and said, "Come on Brian, let's have some coffees, a nice brandy each and, for you and me, a nice big fat cigar."

So that was duly ordered and came. Ron sat there looking so self-satisfied and happy. He loved his life here in Cyprus so very much and nights out with dear friends only proved to him more and more over the years, that life here was so much better than anywhere else. For Ron, there was nowhere else like it in the world. There he sat, laughing away at the jokes and small talk, cigar in one hand, brandy in the other as we all sat remembering stories of our times together since we had all first met, and the wonderful times we had shared together as loving friends. We were discussing their next trip out to their Cyprus home and I felt so pleased that Ron had finally made the effort that evening to come out to dinner, because he was much more like his old self and he genuinely was really enjoying himself.

Suddenly, and as if in slow motion but in complete silence, with no warning of any kind, I sat and watched helplessly as I saw my beloved Ron quietly keel over sideways, still maintaining a firm hold on his brandy and cigar, and gently slide down to the floor.

I jumped to my feet, not really realising what was happening, and rushed round to him on the floor at the other side of the table. He was motionless as I came round to him and gently knelt at his side. He did not seem to be breathing, but his eyes were still open and he appeared to still be 'with me'.

My emotions completely took over at this point. I needed to tell him how I felt, because in my heart of hearts, I knew that this was going to be the end – the moment I had always dreaded for the whole of the time that he and I had spent together, loving and living. I took his hand in mine and as calmly as I could, I said:

"My love, if you can hear me, I beg you, then squeeze my hand." From somewhere in the back of my mind came his voice from the past saying to me, loud and clear, "Darling, don't ever beg Jacqui, you don't need to." That was my Ron. He squeezed my hand. My God, he was still with me, he had heard me, he was still alive. I then said:

"My darling, you do know that I love you more than anything else in the whole world, don't you?" He squeezed my hand again. At that point, somehow, I remembered something else he used to say to me: that you only know what you have had when you have lost it. I knew there and then as I sat looking at him helplessly, that I had lost my beloved Ron, he was slipping away and there was nothing, not a thing that I could do to stop it. I felt so at a loss and completely useless. The ambulance arrived within minutes and they placed him on board very quickly and left for the hospital, burning rubber as they sped away with all sirens blaring.

We quickly followed on after the ambulance, Brian driving me down in my car and Lyn driving theirs with Lady on board. Something inside me kept telling me that he would be gone by the time we got there, but I still felt ashamed to say that, at this point, I had not, and could not shed a tear, they simply did not come. Was it the shock of it all, or was it something inner that came from somewhere, maybe from Ron himself, that told me to pull myself together and act as he would have wanted me to? I shall never know. By the time we arrived at the hospital a few minutes later, I was taken to the room where they had examined him and they told me that he had slipped away. I went into the room alone and closed the door. He lay there so motionless and already so pale and colourless. I bent down and tenderly kissed him goodbye for one last time. "Goodbye my wonderful, wonderful love, goodbye".

I felt totally numb and empty inside, one complete half of me had gone, I just could not come to terms with it, but I still could not cry. I seemed to go into 'automatic' mode. I was doing things and telling others to do things, almost like a robot. At this point, I gave my phone to Bryan and asked him to phone Robbie in England and break the news to him. This he kindly did for me and told Rob I would phone him when I got home because I had asked the C.I.D. man how I could prevent them from cutting Ron up in a post mortem. I could not bear to think of that, and he would have been horrified. The C.I.D. man told me that we have to obtain a certificate of cause of death, signed by Ron's Doctor, to ensure that a post mortem would not be held and this we did there and then. I would not hear of them cutting Ron about, I couldn't bear for them to do this, his heart had just stopped, what would be the point? I wanted him to go to God intact, as my Bomber Command Navigator, he had risked his life for his country and just as he had returned from his bombing missions to Germany in his beloved Lancaster, whole and complete and with total dignity, so he would go to his final resting place.

This all meant that I could get the death certificate the next day so that all the paperwork could be done when Robbie arrived. Bryan and Lyn wanted me to go home and spend the night with them. I just wanted Lady and I to go to our little apartment and be there on our own, with the feeling of Ron all around us.

Once inside the apartment, I poured myself a stiff drink, and began the phone calls. Of course I called Robbie and he told me that he was arranging flights, he had spoken to Simon and insisted that he come out to Cyprus with him and attend the funeral. I was so taken aback that he had agreed, albeit reluctantly in the first instance, but we would all be reunited as a family for Ron in death, if not in life and he would be coming out too, my sons and I would be there for Ron as a total family, a family who had loved him and respected him for 27 years.

Then, I took a big deep breath and phoned Ron's brother Prior; they were always so close and we saw them every time that we had been back to England. He was so devastated that his 'little' brother had gone before him. Prior was 89 and Ron 83. We cried together for a little while and then he asked me if I had contacted Jan, Ron's daughter. I told him that that was the next call I would make. I didn't really want to make this call, why should I, she had had no contact with her father for some thirteen years now, but the Great Britishness in me came to the fore and I decided I had to 'do the right thing'.

I dialled the number and it rang a few times. Eventually a woman's voice answered and just said "hello". I asked her who I was speaking to.

"Well you phoned me, so you should know" she snapped back, "who are you anyway?"

I said "Jan, this is Jacqui in Cyprus".

"What do *you* want?" she again snapped. I was determined to be dignified and not retaliate.

"I am sorry to have to tell you Jan that your father passed away this evening at 10.30pm. It was all very peaceful and he was not in pain", I tried to say it as gently and kindly as I could.

"Oh *God*, and I've got to go to a funeral tomorrow" she said in a very irritated voice. Obviously her father's death was a great inconvenience to her; some daughter! I thought. I decided that discretion at this point would very much be the right thing and I just said goodbye and put the phone down. I was determined from that point on that I would not be calling her again. She didn't bother to turn up for the funeral, nor did her brother, despite calls from Robbie trying to help them with their arrangements, and ordering flowers for them and so on, and I was to hear later that they had not even bothered to put it in the local papers where Ron was born so that his peers would have known his fate. However, over one hundred people did turn up and they were all friends, I am proud to say.

Both my sons were there, standing by my side and Simon, at my request, read my favourite passage from the Bible, Ecclesiastes Chapter 3, verses 1 – 8 "To everything there is a season, and a time to every purpose under heaven". It was beautiful and he cried.

Robert gave a wonderful eulogy which he had written himself:

"To Ron – Ron has been a part of my life for over 25 years and throughout that time he has given me advice, support, direction, love and affection. To me he was my role model and a true father figure. From my early years to this day Ron has been there to give me the right advice, which I would point out I never listened to at the time, but now find myself teaching those same sentences to my children, "close your mouth and count to 3 before you speak", or my personal favourite, " always have the last word in your house ... Yes Dear", or the one when He and my Mum were first together and a customer came into her restaurant and asked if Ron could take a food order and he replied, "I have not taken an order since 1945 and I don't intend to take one now". Ron has always been there for me offering his wisdom when I needed it, something special that I really will miss, not quite sure who I will turn to in the future. But Ron left this world in the only way he would have wanted, surrounded by friends, a brandy in one hand a cigar in the other, laughing and joking. The way he would want to be remembered. Ron, I will miss you".

That was so beautiful and truly from his heart, and he just sobbed and sobbed. He truly had lost a Dad, the only one he had known.

Out of choice, despite the overwhelming sorrow of the occasion, I had said my goodbye to Ron in private, and I now wanted to say good bye to him in public. On the day, however, this was too much for me and so Robbie had to read it for me.

"To my Ron –
For all the love and adoration for the last twenty seven years,

for your unstilted love of your beloved Sarah and the continued pride in your family.

For your total support of me in my ventures, for the support for my children, for your unbelievable mischievousness and sense of fun.

For your love of all the dear friends past and present, for our way of life.

For your understated heroism for your country and your love of all in Cyprus.

Your love was unconditional – I thank you, as we all do, you now go to God with my blessing that he will take care of you until we are together again.

I LOVE YOU, RON SMITH – YOUR JACQUI.

A few weeks later our great and dear friend Alan passed away on the 16th April 2008 at his home. I used the following piece of prose for the eulogy at his funeral. It is borrowed from a piece someone gave to me once. I do not know the origins, and I changed it a little to make it fit all the circumstances that I wanted it to embrace and my apologies to the author for borrowing and changing parts of it for the eulogy. I volunteered to do it because I wanted it to come from Ron as well as me, as if he were still there, to do a eulogy using the theme of this piece, I think it is beautiful.

In it's original form I wanted to include this here in the book because, I feel it applies so much to everyone's lives …

"ARE YOU A REASON, A SEASON OR A LIFETIME?

People come into your life for a REASON….It is usually to meet a need you have expressed. They have come to assist you through a difficulty, to provide you with guidance and support, to aid you physically, emotionally or spiritually. They may seem like a godsend and they are! They are there for the reason you need them to be. Then, without any wrongdoing on your part, or at an inconvenient time, this person will say or do something to bring the relationship to an end –

Sometimes they die.
Sometimes they walk away.
Sometimes they act up and force you to take a stand.

What we must realise is that our need has been met, our desire fulfilled, their work is done. The prayer you sent up has been answered and now it is time to move on.

When people come into your life for a SEASON….It is because your turn has come to share, grow, or learn. They bring you an experience of peace, or make you laugh. They may teach you something you have never done. They usually give you an unbelievable amount of joy. Believe it! It is real!.... But only for a season.

LIFETIME relationships teach you lifetime lessons, things you must build upon in order to have a solid emotional foundation. Your job is to accept the lesson, love the person, and put what you have learned to use in all other relationships and areas of your life. It is said that love is blind but friendship is clairvoyant.
  Thank you for being a part of my life."

This prose belongs with all the people who I have known, all my life, it is appropriate to them all. Best of all was still to come though.

Mark, Alan and Linda's son told me at his Dad's funeral, that one day he and Ron were having lunch, his Mum and I out shopping, and Mark said to Ron:

"You know Ron, I will never know the pleasures of having had a wife". (Mark had been born with severe spina bifida and lived to tell the tale, but had to undergo terrifying surgical procedures over the years).

Ron said to Mark:

"Mark not many men have one good wife, ever. I have had two superb wives in my life, but this one, Jacqui, she really is something else". I will never forget that statement.

At the beginning of my book I made a statement "I want de moon".

Well, according to David Niven, "The moon's a balloon".

After years of struggle, I had finally managed to get my balloon.

Tragically, that balloon burst at 10.30pm on Tuesday the 6th November 2007.

EPILOGUE

Jacqui Smith on – Reflection

Now, in the stillness of the early evening, once the stinging rays of the sun have begun to quell and the moon makes itself ready for its nightly appearance, I walk up the little lane into the hills, taking my beloved Lady, my little dog, for her evening walk. I find myself recalling my first few months in North Cyprus and subsequently trying to make some sense of myself and my life.

Walking past the village houses with the bougainvillea lolloping over the garden walls, falling into cascades of gorgeous colour, the cooler evening air is filled with the scent of the pine trees, and as I continue to walk up the lane, either side is filled with lovely Cypress trees, with their little round green cones carrying the precious, soothing oil to refresh the tired and aching joints, wild garlic, so wonderful in salads, wild rosemary for all those culinary and medicinal uses, baby tangerines on a tiny tree trying to survive in the heartless heat, prickly pears ripe for the picking, sitting in rows on the top of each cactus lobe, like soldiers on parade, waiting patiently – pick me, if you dare!, full, fat green figs ready for the ripening, olive bushes waiting to flourish and give forth their own special fruit that is so much Cyprus.

All these sights force me to accept that I have gone full circle; the moon has taken me on its own special journeys over the years and here I am, still wondering at everything around me that simply has not changed over these last twenty eight years. With all these many thoughts racing through my mind, I am feeling now compelled to look inwards at myself and wonder what was all this about, what have these journeys accomplished and just how have they affected 'the me' that was then, and is now.

However I may come to look at myself, my loss of Ron and the other people that I have loved and lost in my life, I can't get away from the fact that I have ended up where I wanted to be, as I now believe that I would have come out to Cyprus with or without Ron. I was meant to be here. It would have had a very different outcome had Ron not been with me but what that would have been, I shall never know. I believe I am at peace with myself, or at least almost; there may be a few demons I still yet have to face. Demons like facing my own and possibly other people's questions about the Jacqui that remains and the Jacqui that was. Was it possible that through all these years, I could have been naïve and gullible on a lot of issues, but especially with those who have had the greatest impact on me, the men in my life? Recently this question was asked of me and I am now forced to face it and answer.

Over time, it seems to me that it has been the men who have usually made the rules, set down the standards and generally led the way. Equally, it is usually the women who have been the ones to respond to these standards. Does that, therefore, make the woman, in this instance myself, so naïve and gullible for reacting to the actions of the men in my life. I have given this a lot of thought since the question was asked and I came to some conclusions.

I can most certainly admit to being naïve and gullible with three men in my life other than my husbands. In all three circumstances, which were all very different, I was most certainly at my most vulnerable at the time when they occurred, and that was my only mitigating circumstance. All three left me feeling ashamed for responding the ways that I did, or even for responding at all. That is all that I am prepared to say about these instances, and they are now in their right place, just memories.

Naïve – no, generally, I do not believe that I have ever been this; gullible – possibly a little, but no, to my mind, I was in fact somewhat selfish, if that is the appropriate word.

With my parents, I was selfish because I wanted the childhood and treatment that my peers all seemed to have and which was denied to me by my upbringing. My parents, but particularly my Father, did it that way because that was the way they thought was best. After all, he was born in 1906 and had been brought up by Victorian parents. I was being selfish for what I wanted, but now that I am forced to look back, there is nothing in my growing up that really hurt me. In fact it gave me the backbone that I have always had, and I do not believe that I have ever not given everything my very best effort before conceding defeat or coming out a victor.

With Chris I was selfish. I was young and greedy for life and love. I so desperately wanted him to be the husband and father that I thought he should be – in fact the perfect husband and father, 'picture book perfect'. Chris could be none of that because of his mother and because of the awesome and destructive illness from which he suffered. I always thought and believed that *he* was the selfish one. But in truth he was merely being what he was, and there was nothing that he could do, mentally or physically to change that. Perhaps more importantly, I could do even less. He was who he was. Everything he touched: relationships, feelings, family, and even those most dear to him, were damaged by some deep psychopathic desire to destroy everything around him. From the time that I met him, even probably before that, no matter what anyone tried to do for him, he would die as he had lived, still a very confused and sad, sad person, and never to know that this lady never let him down and loved him 'till death did us part'.

Selfish with Peter because I conveniently let him persuade me into a life that I knew I would absolutely hate with a man for whom I had little feeling, because he made so little effort. I should have known that I would tire of that attitude very quickly and saved myself, but more importantly others, the effort and the hurt. I never really wanted to marry him and share his life. I was weak.

Selfish with Ron, because I let him envelop me in a cocoon of safety and security so that the big bad world out there could not get at me and make me unhappy. If I was unhappy, he was unhappy, so I let him do all the things to make me feel secure, financially and otherwise, which left him completely holding a hot bag of cinders, robbing Peter to pay Paul and shuffling non existent £.S.D. from here to there to give us the lifestyle that we both loved so and to which we had become accustomed. This gave me twenty eight years of perfect bliss. Ron and Cyprus was wonderful, and worth every moment.

Now, looking deep into the photographs of Ron and me together, it's all there on Ron's face. Our love story really was far more intense than the one I had with Chris and it has taken me all these years, and this 'tome' to make me take a good hard long look and see it for the first time.

Ron was always there for me; he didn't go away till the day he died and there I was, so wrapped up and hanging on to memories that haunted me so, the men who had hurt me greatly and let me down. Ron understood it all, he never criticised me or chastised me for not being able to get the past out of my present, and he remained always my quiet

Airman. It's only now that I see it clearly for the first time.

I really did have 'de moon' so much – and then some – in Ron and I missed it. I knew that he loved me but I still just didn't realise or see it properly, at the time. Then I was gullible and naïve. For all those twenty eight years, I loved Ron intensely, I never stopped telling him so, but added to that, I never quite realised that I had at last found the love that I had always looked for in Chris. There was no-one else from day one for Ron but me, and he adored me. I never took those two steps back to look at Ron and what he had created in me. I am truly ashamed of the fact that Ron finally removed the dreadful but haunting memory of Chris, my first love, for ever. He absolutely loved, adored and admired me – I was everything to him. My only saving grace, and one of the things that used to infuriate me about him is that he never said these things to me at the time; only about me to other people, like the conversation with Mark which I had after Ron died and because he didn't tell me often enough, I merely took it for granted.

Ron rescued me from a loveless union with Peter, not knowingly or with premeditation. He rescued me from the ghost I had been living with for all those long years; he gave me such an uncomplicated love in return. I am now left wondering if my balloon did burst or whether I let my balloon escape from me. I had 'de moon' and never really realised just how lucky I was – or we were.

Ron had the 'emu syndrome' also though, and over those years I could never get him to see that paying rent was like standing in the street and waving money into the wind, which would result in a financial situation that would all but cripple us in the end and subsequently take me months to sort out. I was also selfish in moving him into a little apartment when he really wanted to stay in the big house. Did my actions actually result in Ron not being able to cope with life because he did not have to shuffle the £.S.D. any more, and moving him from the opulence he was used to and loved, to the lifestyle that we could actually afford? Maybe I broke his heart, for he lived and fought for this image for so long and now we were reduced to what we actually had. Was it all a façade? Did he just give up at the end? We never got to talk about it properly, and so I shall never know. The only way in which I was unselfish with Ron was my eternal and unbounded love for, and devotion to this lovely man of mine. God, I miss him more than words can ever express, and I still love him so very deeply.

I am now, more than ever, aware of the fact that the kind of love that Ron gave me was like a blanket; a blanket of warmth and security, of feeling totally safe and of a love that was always, unconditionally, there. Now that that blanket has gone, I feel so totally vulnerable, useless and so dreadfully alone. Sometimes it is almost all too much to bear.

Amongst all these reflections too, through all of my time since being a small child, I could not look back without wondering at this glorious gift that God has given me – the gift of being a natural chef. It has helped me in so many ways over the years and, sometimes, when a new idea for a recipe comes into my mind, I do still marvel at where all this has come from. I still do cocktail parties and dinner parties for friends and acquaintances, and I now think back to the 'Sundowner' parties in Kenya and remember preparing the food with Mum; this thought comes to my mind with every canapé that I make. That whole scenario has certainly gone the full circle of the moon.

Do I have any regrets in this respect? Only one, despite being able to make countless people happy with their parties and functions, I have never made any serious money from it, just a little here and there. Despite Loch Manor, this grocer's daughter remains just that. Looking back, I realise now that I did have 'de moon' on several occasions, only to lose it again; but nothing can take away the happiness that I have had over all these years. I have received intense love and passion but I have also lost it, all with the same intensity of life itself.

Now in the twilight of my life – and reading this, what a life! – I face my uncertain future alone. At least I have the knowledge that I have and always will 'give it my best shot', and that I am, more than ever, now very much in God's hands and those of my good friend – fate.

What next, I wonder?